Reflections of a Successful Wallflower

Reflections of a Successful Wallflower

Lessons in Business
Lessons in Life

ANDREA MICHAELS

Outskirts Press, Inc.
Denver, Colorado

The opinions expressed in this manuscript are solely the opinions of the author and do not represent the opinions or thoughts of the publisher. The author has represented and warranted full ownership and/or legal right to publish all the materials in this book.

Reflections of a Successful Wallflower
Lessons in Business; Lessons in Life
All Rights Reserved.
Copyright © 2010 Andrea Michaels
v3.0

This book may not be reproduced, transmitted, or stored in whole or in part by any means, including graphic, electronic, or mechanical without the express written consent of the publisher except in the case of brief quotations embodied in critical articles and reviews.

Outskirts Press, Inc.
http://www.outskirtspress.com

ISBN: 978-1-4327-4909-5

Outskirts Press and the "OP" logo are trademarks belonging to Outskirts Press, Inc.

PRINTED IN THE UNITED STATES OF AMERICA

Praise for Andrea Michaels

When people think of the special event industry, they think of Andrea Michaels. She was the guiding light for the development of the special event industry as we know it today. She is a leader, mentor and educator to virtually the entire industry. I will never forget the first time I met her at an industry educational conference. She literally took me under her wing, and to this day, I continue to learn from this remarkable individual. Andrea Michaels has set the extraordinary standard against which all special event professionals strive to be measured!

–Steve Kemble, America's Sassiest Lifestyle Guru

Many people espouse a life philosophy of positive thinking, or "whatever it takes" determination. Andrea Michaels leverages intellect, humor and humanity by actually living out her philosophy, instead of just talking about it. Finally, someone got her to sit still long enough to document details, events and thoughts of an amazingly successful, interesting and funny life.

To call Andrea a friend is a privilege. To call her a teacher is a fair assessment. To call her a model for entrepreneurs, leaders and people who just love what they do for a living is the most accurate, telling and reliable description of someone whose entire life is an event.

This book is a life lesson, a success road map and a laugh-out-loud look into one of the great business and creative minds working today.

- John Klymshyn, Author of <u>How To Sell Without Being A JERK!</u>
and <u>The Ultimate Sales Managers' Guide</u>

Andrea Michaels is the quintessential talent that includes an aesthetic vision that continuously evolves; incredible people skills that allow everyone to love her from the minute they meet her and the unique sense of trust knowing you are in the best of hands with her. If Andrea Michaels could clone herself, she could eliminate global warming and world hunger with style, grace and great speed!

-Susan Allan, Leading Marriage and Divorce Coach

I first saw Andrea Michaels at The Special Event Show in 1996 when I was new to the United States from the UK and clearly recall her being an awesome force and inspiration that I could only dream of emulating.

Over the years, we have become colleagues and friends, and she remains an inspiration with her vision, drive and comprehension of market trends. She is a motivated speaker who continually encourages her audiences to be better event professionals.

Her work is truly outstanding and whilst she is imitated by many, she is equaled by few. Andrea has an extraordinary intellect, a passion for excellence and a kind nature. I am proud to have her as a mentor and friend.

-Sally Webb, Managing Director, The Special Event Company, London, England and North Carolina.

I am continually impressed by how generous Andrea is. She could easily sit back and care for her own company and clients. But she doesn't. She repeatedly speaks at industry functions and shares the practices that make her the ongoing success she is. She has opened many doors for *Special Events* Magazine and has challenged us to do and be more. I respect her greatly.

–Lisa Hurley, Editor, *Special Events* Magazine

Andrea has such fascinating stories to tell ... I think this will be essential reading for anyone who is in the business and can relate to all her experiences and how she lived and laughed through them.

-James D. Murphy, Vice President, Asia Pacific Operations,
George P. Johnson

Congrats, Mazel Tov! I, personally, can't wait to read your war stories, as they are not only amusing but highly educational, and I certainly can use some light moments every now and again that I can personally relate to!

–Mona Meretsky, President, Comcor Events

I think it is fantastic that after mentoring so many in the industry Andrea has embarked on this new venture ... it will be a great read, and I'd like to be first in line at the book signing.

-Jonathon Cripple, Wackos, Inc.

There's something inside Andrea that only she has that probably has most to do with [her] success. It's not just hard work and dedication. It's [her] intellect, moral fiber, values, God-given talent, personal and business integrity, personal need for fulfillment, connection with people and innate understanding of what makes them feel good. There's much more to the success story when you really analyze what's behind Extraordinary Events and Andrea's success. That's what really draws me to [her] as a supplier and friend. Anything but superficial, she is complex with a multifaceted intellect and intriguing on so many levels.

–Robert Abbott, Director - Corporate Marketing
Communication, Mueller Company

When we speak of Andrea, it is always in the tone of perfection. Her style of process is one of clarity, serious commitment and perfection. The great part of our Aruba project was the total trust part ... how wonderful to put that in the mix. Aside from the Event role, it's the way she cares, the way she holds eye contact and the way she uses words. Andrea is a woman with many interesting layers. She never doubts or spends too much time pondering on the negatives. We all have a blue moment from time to time, but she will remember, close her eyes and look for the blue sky, always.
    –Richard Carbotti, Perfect Surroundings Event Design

    I first met Andrea 22 years ago when I was the launching publisher of *Special Events* magazine and had been tasked with creating a convention for the yet-to-be recognized industry. I was on my fourth show when Andrea came into my life. After producing The Special Event in San Diego, then Palm Beach and then Dallas, we put together an organizing committee for Los Angeles. She was an integral part of that group. And, she truly opened my eyes. I remember her sitting me down at the Bonaventure Hotel. She didn't say anything for a minute but just stared at me with those piercing eyes that look right into your soul. Then, she dropped the bomb. "You've done a good job of pulling the industry together and convincing people to share with each other. But, if you want to make this show the 'must-see' event that you keep talking about, you need to start wowing people."
    Wowing them? I thought I had. I'd created Gala Awards and a celebration. I'd put on some great education. My promotions were spectacular, weren't they? The show was growing. Needless to say, she just smiled at me with that knowing look and leaned forward. "You have accomplished a lot, but you need to start relying on the professionals who can pull off miracles for you, particularly with the opening night reception and the Gala Night. There's too much detail that's overlooked and not enough creativity. Let me help you. Let me help teach you."
    And she did. That was the beginning of a friendship that has

remained constant through the years. She stayed on top of me, always reminding me of when I was letting the details fall through the cracks, and regularly calling to give me new ideas to spice up and improve the show. The following year, she produced a complete awards "production" in New Orleans. In the years to follow, she gave me choreographed dancing waiters in a convention center of all places! The Gala that evening was so full of delightful surprises at every turn. I think in part because of her unswerving efforts to help the convention grow, other professionals followed suit to do the same. Like she has for so many of us, she has been my mentor and friend. She told me not to make this a testimonial or an endorsement, but how can I help from doing that? Every memory of her is such an example of how to do it correctly.

–Carol McKibben, McKibben Consulting

Andrea, you have been my mentor, my boss, my friend and my family. There are so many defining moments in our relationship. Each time you explained your thought process to me; each time you were inspired by a thought and that inspiration touched us all; each time you stood up for your team and we saw that you truly supported us; each time you were able to turn a difficult situation around to your advantage; each time we observed you listening to someone and we recognized that you really heard what they were saying and what was unspoken … you are truly an inspiration, and I am so lucky to have you in my life.

–Megan Reynolds, Extraordinary Events

To Friendship

And

A Special Thanks

To my friend, Carol McKibben, who is also my editor. A big thank you for prodding me, encouraging me, praising me and understanding me. Without you, I would not have my book. And I love you for all of it.

A Personal Foreword

It finally hit me after a flight to Orlando in 1992. As I anxiously waited for an airport van to take me to a downtown hotel, a middle-aged woman sitting to my right asked me what brought me to the Sunshine State.

"I'm here for an awards show," I replied.

The well-dressed, friendly woman asked me if it was for the special events industry. I told her it was, and she introduced herself.

When I told her my name, a strange expression overtook her pretty smile.

"Are you related to Andrea Michaels?" the woman asked.

I was taken back. I wondered if this was an old acquaintance of my mother's.

"That's my mother; are you a friend of hers?" I questioned.

"No, but everyone knows Andrea; she's the queen of the industry!" I was told.

For the first 16 years of my life, I thought I knew my mother. I knew how hard she worked, how many long hours she put in and the endless weekends that she would vanish to travel the country on new work adventures.

But I never knew how much the hard work had paid off until that rainy day 3,000 miles from home. *The queen of the industry,*

I remember thinking. It was the first time I had run into a perfect stranger who let me know how wonderful and talented my mother is. It was the first time in my life that I had looked in at her life from the outside and thought about how much she had accomplished.

I was so proud of my mom, the so-called queen of the industry. I looked at her differently that entire weekend. I had a new respect for her and how much she had given to her chosen profession. I was one of the few who knew how much she had gone through. One of the ones who knew how much she had given up in her personal life to devote to the industry and how proud she was to see it grow.

I took time that weekend to discover how lucky I was. I was a child of the special events industry, because from the time I was six, the two of us would head to Palm Springs for Meeting Planners International meetings and to all of the wonderful productions of which she allowed me to be a part and the travelling that ensued. I loved it and was allowed to do a lot of things that any child would be lucky to experience.

My mother is not a greedy woman. I learned long ago that she would rather see a large group of people succeed, even if it meant making less of a profit, or no profit at all. She instilled in me the proper way to do business and to treat people. She made me realize that sometimes being a good parent didn't mean being there for every meal or for every sporting event, but rather building a future for herself, her family and an industry she loved.

Now, in Orlando, we were putting on another show in front of the entire industry. Most people might be afraid to attempt this. The production did not have any monetary value. This was just another of her gifts back to her colleagues. And, as usual, it went off without a hitch. Sure, there were minor setbacks, but nothing the audience ever witnessed. And that's what makes a great event. She knew it, and I was starting to get it. Pretty soon, she thought, the entire industry would get it.

Later that weekend, they started to get it as she spent an impressive night collecting numerous awards for a variety of spectacular events. Then a few years later, she became to the industry what she had always been to me, and strangely, a worldly woman I had met on my trip - the true queen of special events. In 1997, she became the first inductee into the special events industry Hall of Fame, awarded by *Event Solutions* Magazine.

She is still winning awards (50 major ones as of January 2009 and counting), but it's quite obvious that she is equally proud of an industry she helped build, helped nurture and helped mature into a major career path.

As a son, and now a co-worker, I couldn't be prouder.

–Jon Michaels, Executive Vice President, Operations,
Extraordinary Events

Professional Forewords

It would be an understatement to say that Andrea Michaels is a leader in the Special Event industry. Indeed, Andrea is one of the pioneers who has shaped the business of Special Events into the multi-billion dollar industry it is today. But, she is so much more.

In this book, her experiences are shared with such candor that I could not help but find myself flipping the pages as quickly as possible to see the outcome of the scenes that she so vividly describes. The event stories are fun, but more importantly the insights and lessons that they teach are invaluable. The cost of this book will be realized in the first event tackled after reading it. We all believe that we know how to dot the "i"s and cross the "t"s, but this read gives the perfect road map to success in not only business but in life lessons as well.

We are all the sum of all our life experiences, and thankfully Andrea has used every life lesson as a spring board toward a higher elevation in her world. Lessons learned are not always pleasant to experience, but somehow her grace and style shine through in this compelling book that reveals every stone in her road of life. This most kind and loving person is blunt and direct in every way throughout this book. The epitome of "if you don't want an answer don't ask a question," Andrea has written a book that reveals the essence of a true entrepreneur. I am proud to call her my dearest friend.

-John J. Daly, Jr., John Daly Inc., The Guru of Event Design

Many people ask me ... who IS Andrea Michaels? And I often respond with, she's a human being just like you and me. They gasp and exclaim, "But I'm so intimidated by her and by all she knows." Well people, there's no need to wonder or be intimidated anymore. In this "insideful" book Andrea shares the pieces of herself about which you are so often curious. She writes about her experiences, her successes, failings, heartaches, triumphs and her fascinating life story, all twisted into a fun read that will make you laugh and cry with her - sometimes simultaneously.

With her uncanny ability to paint a picture with words and making one feel extravagant emotion, she draws you in, telling the story, laying out the lesson while you never really realize that you are learning at all. It's just the way she does things. She is never one to beat you over the head with a lesson, but rather she'll leave you with a thought to ponder or a question to answer which inevitably draws you to the correct solution. You'll love this subtle, empowering way of learning and management style. And now it's all at your fingertips.

Whether you are a newbie or one of Andrea's fellow pioneers, you'll find this book a valuable tool to have at hand. Whether it's inspiration to start a business, successfully resolving a challenge in life or how to handle a difficult client, it's all in this book. There is something for everyone.

I promise you'll walk away entertained, educated and understanding what it is that makes this extraordinary woman tick. Her energy and passion clearly shine through as she shares the intimate details of how she views life, business and the lessons she's learned on a lifelong walk as a pioneer in the events industry.

–Ruth E. Moyte, Vice President Production, Extraordinary Events

Author's Note

Why This Title?

People are afraid of me. That's what I keep hearing. And it amazes me. Lurking inside this "fearsome" persona is a shy wallflower who has to force herself to talk to a stranger, enter a cocktail party and of course never EVER be present where there's dancing. After all, no one will ever ask ME to dance. Slack-jawed wonderment or disbelief has been the reaction whenever I've shared this with anyone. They see aloof. I see and feel frightened and intimidated.

Why?

Oh, there are SO many reasons that you will discover as you read this book. I was "abandoned" by my mother in my early childhood, or at least that was my perception of what happened to me. Well, that creates a feeling of worthlessness. Then a few years later my family moved to Burbank, California, a cultural desert in the 1950s where I was the outcast ... more worthlessness. And then there was a family environment where I was very secondary and was to be neither seen nor heard except when appropriate ... again, my perception. Being one of the only Jewish kids in Burbank, there was no one to date, so school dances were horrid for me ... no one asked. I matured early (tall and buxom and dressed like a European countess by my mother) and thus was not one of the poodle-skirted popular ones.

I learned to be an overachiever … anything to get noticed. I was the good and quiet one. But what I wanted was to be popular. I wanted a full dance card, not to sit out every dance feeling desolate and unwanted.

And so, introverted to the max, I retreated a lot into myself. Yes, I excelled in class. Yes, I had a lot of great friends. And I put on a great front. But inside I was the eternal reject. Who would want me?

That brings me to now and the title. I've overcome, but inside, the wallflower is very much a part of my psyche. So when you see me, don't be afraid. I'm the shy girl who really wants to get to know you.

Preface

If you're like me, you're going to read the end of this book first to see where it's going. That's what I do. Once I know the end, I enjoy what precedes it, appreciating the writing style, reveling in the turn of the phrase, reading a paragraph several times because I am not driven by my curiosity to find out how it all ends. So feel free, because what you'll see is that this is all a personal journey. My career has been part of a very personal trip through life and its experiences; it doesn't end at the last page. Actually, I look at the last page as the beginning of what comes next, and I just can't wait to get there.

One of the questions I'm often asked is, "When are you going to retire?"

If I'm flippant I'll say, "I plan on dropping dead at an event I'm producing." But if I'm serious, I have to confess I cannot think of a single reason why I should ever retire. I love my life, the experiences I am offered, the people I meet and with whom I become friends, the travels and new worlds that are constantly inspiring me, and I look forward to being able to write a sequel to this book because I'll have more stories to tell you. So get ready for the memoirs of the 100-year-old event planner … life, here I come!

I am writing this book not only for personal satisfaction, but because I hope that, in addition to being a fun read, it will inspire young people and women - two distinct populations I am dedicated to educating. Youngsters need to understand that their own power and internal drive can lead them to think creatively and decisively on more levels than tapping the keys on their computer for solutions. And women need to know that there is no "glass ceiling" if they can figure out a way to work around it. They have to believe that they can do anything, including raise a child, enjoy a marriage, run a business (do I sound like a Helen Reddy song?) and do it all successfully and happily without sacrificing any one of these relationships.

My stories are about survival, business survival, and about approaches to challenges and how to overcome them. Business is no more than one element of life, and surviving in business is the same as surviving in life. It's all about approach and attitude. People tell me I'm strong, but I don't believe that I'm stronger than anyone else I know ... I just believe that when we have the will to overcome adversity, and the drive to keep getting on, we can (as my good friend John Klymshyn says) keep moving it forward.

I have a favorite story about my stepfather's father who survived life in Nazi Germany, a concentration camp, the ghetto in Shanghai and new beginnings even when over 70. He used to tell us (albeit every other sentence) that "When you walk like a millionaire, everyone will look at you as if you are a millionaire." And he looked happy, prosperous and successful, natty and engaging, and people treated him like a million bucks. He was always about attitude and found good even in living in that camp because he made the best of it and motivated everyone around him. He found positive in the most negative of situations. Though I giggled when I was young because he repeated his stories so many times, I never forgot that what I learned was real wisdom.

In business, we constantly win and lose. Obviously we all like winning, but it's how we handle the successes and failures that matters. After I pissed and moaned about losing a big account, another friend of mine (John Wood, without a doubt the best salesperson I've ever met) told me, "Get over it and move on. It's negative energy if you focus on the one that got away." He was right.

So I try to incorporate life's lessons from everyone around me, and pay it forward anytime I can. I truly believe that the mind is a wondrous thing and that maintaining a very positive focus keeps us young and happy. I look at every person I meet as a new and thrilling experience with which I'm gifted; every new city or country or continent that I visit as a beautiful exploration from which I can learn and every new client or project as the possibility of meeting new people and having new adventures. Obstacles are just challenges to be overcome. Challenges are just tests. Life is to be lived to its fullest, and I'm thrilled that the events world has provided me with a life of opportunity and fulfillment.

To all of you who have contributed to this amazing journey, my sincerest thanks. I treasure all you have brought me and will continue to bring me in the years to come.

Introduction

"You eat too fast," my good friend Jose said to me as we were having dinner in Palma de Mallorca, Spain, not too long ago.

I thought, yeah, Jose, I do *everything* fast. *Absolutely everything.*

That defines how I approach life and, of course, then that means it's the way I approach events. There simply isn't enough time to do everything I want to do. So, if I don't do everything quickly, I'll miss out on something. And I don't want to miss out on anything ... ever.

Where did *that* start? Actually, I remember my mother telling me from a very young age that I didn't have "sitzfleisch," which in German/Jewish means I couldn't stay in one place for very long doing one thing ... I had to move and do a lot of things at once. Yes, I'm one of those people who watches TV, reads a book, talks on the phone and makes dinner at the same time. Or at the office, does my email, writes a proposal and talks to clients simultaneously. Now this might be wrong if I did any of those things badly, but I don't. It is my way. I know no other.

You might call me an opportunist. Is that a bad thing? I don't think so. I just see possibilities in everything that I encounter or experience. You'll see as you read on that I am a storyteller (that started at the age of five or six), so let me share a story to show you what I mean.

A couple of years ago I traveled to Milan prior to a business trip to Torino. It was holiday time; it was snowing but I wanted to see the city anyway. Most of all I wanted to go to La Scala. My parents raised me to love opera, and I have always dreamed of La Scala. As luck would have it, La Scala was closed, but its museum was open. Better than nothing, right? So I wandered through the museum, and, in one corner behind an exhibit, I saw a door. Well, what would you do if you saw a door? I opened it and discovered a stairway leading downward. So down I went into a dimly lit stairwell. Down and down some more, and finally I reached another door. So I opened that one too. And what was on the other side ... the orchestra pit where the La Scala orchestra was about to begin dress rehearsal for opening night's *Elixir of Love*. I approached one of the musicians and told him of my love for the opera, and he invited me to sit in the pit and enjoy the entire rehearsal. The point? There are opportunities everywhere. I believe in seizing them quickly, or they might be missed.

In events, this same philosophy began in 1973, with a part-time job for Ron Rubin, a Southern California band leader, a job I needed while I was completing my college degree at U.C.L.A. That evolved into my working with him for a decade (five or six of those years as his partner.) And how did that evolve into what I do now? In the 1970s, there was no real event industry, and I was sure there should be. It was an opportunity to create an industry where none existed. I couldn't stand to lose an opportunity! Just wasn't possible. Still isn't.

Some associates and clients have called me a visionary. But that's not how I see it. My philosophy has always been, if it's out there, grab it. If it isn't, create it and then grab it!

This book is my opportunity to share stories that relate to not just my life but my life in events. How did it all begin for me? Where has it gone? What does the future hold? How did I keep it together with all of the personal and business challenges that are a part of everyone's life? The events in this book will define that process. They all go back to the questions that people have been posing to me for years: How do you deal with the stress? How did you venture out globally? How did you manage to raise a child with a career that took up so much of your time and energy? How do you work effectively with different cultures and values? What do you do when nothing goes right? Unions? Missteps? What about the weather? How do you deal with inexperienced and difficult clients? Develop trust? What do you do about new and current trends like "Going Green" and "Sustainability" and "Social Responsibility"?

I've included all of that and much more. So curl up with a glass of wine, snuggle next to your favorite person, cat, dog or pillow and get ready to be entertained. Didn't someone say life and its events are really just another form of entertainment?

1

Dealing with Stress

United Space Alliance (NASA Parent Company) Event

I'm often asked how I deal with the stress of my business. Let me begin with a story about an event that would have driven anyone else to commit suicide, close their business and run away to hide in some remote place. The event itself was a ten plus, but wait for the behind-the-scenes story! To prepare you for it, let me set the stage with some of the event details.

The first of its kind, the Space Shuttle three-day conference and tradeshow was sponsored by the United Space Alliance (USA), a prime contractor of NASA's Space Shuttle. Its purpose was to explore new and emerging space shuttle technology, specifically its applications in the private sector. My company, Extraordinary Events, coordinated a full schedule of high-caliber speakers including NASA and USA dignitaries, astronauts and politicians. Additionally, we handled a tradeshow, coordinating technical demonstrations and tours of NASA's Ames Research Facility and produced ancillary events, such as an opening reception and ceremony, breakfast and lunch throughout and a VIP dinner. We also helped the client achieve its goal of promoting the future of Space Shuttle technology to the masses by publicizing and producing a public educational event the day after the conference for 10,000. The highlight of the conference was a new film premiered at the opening event which was developed for USA to use as a tool to "sell" the space shuttle to the children of America. It would be distributed to every school in the U.S. and was also to be the "new" NASA, used for tradeshows, promotions and possibly commercials.

Oh, by the way, the events took place in a huge airport hangar (the size of three football fields, eight acres contained within its walls) at Moffet Field in Northern California.

The opening night reception featured an elaborate buffet, a preview of the 141 tradeshow exhibits (occupying 154,000-square-feet of exhibit space) and a formal opening ceremony in a custom-designed multi-tiered amphitheater, all within the hangar. To create an amphitheater, we rigged three 60-by-65 Transformit fabric sculptures around platform seating. Additionally, the amphitheater was illuminated with landing lights, and the Transformit structures were lighted for the dramatic effect that was achieved as daylight turned to twilight, then evening. Huge as they were, they were dwarfed in this immense space, but they added needed color and detracted from the dinginess of the bland aircraft hangar with its years of dust and oil-spotted floors.

Host Miles O'Brien, CNN anchor and correspondent, welcomed guests and introduced dignitaries from NASA and USA, including NASA's Dr. Henry McDonald and Russell Turner, CEO of USA, who spoke about the emerging Space Shuttle technology and its applications within the private sector. After their speeches, the film produced by Extraordinary Events (EE) was shown on giant video screens. Film crews had attended shuttle launches, buried themselves in NASA archives and weeks later created an MTV-styled work aimed at today's generation. The objective was to shake up the tried and true. It did.

The two-day conference and tradeshow began the following day, with a general session in the same amphitheater area as the previous night's ceremony. Speakers the first day included shuttle commanders Andrew Allen, director of space shuttle development for USA, and William Ready, deputy associate administrator for space flight, NASA. Throughout the day, attendees could elect to participate in the conference, explore the tradeshow, which featured elaborate booths by companies such as Lockheed and Boeing and technical demonstrations on the show floor, or take tours of the NASA Ames Research Center, which EE also coordinated. A four-course, sit-down VIP dinner at the host hotel ended the day.

The conference continued for another day and concluded with a closing session and a final reception hosted by Lockheed Martin. On Saturday, the tradeshow was opened to the public for Ames Research Center's Space and Education Day and featured 90-minutes worth of speakers, including astronauts and politicians. Videos from the opening ceremony were shown, and attendees were invited to explore the tradeshow.

Our audience was techies. So the AV had to be perfect. Our bosses were Space Shuttle commanders. Timing and execution were everything. Precision was expected. A professional stage manager and first-class crew orchestrated everything to an extended countdown. Caterers wheeled in and out, timed to set up and tear out on a set schedule.

When Andy Allen turned to us (he had commanded five missions and had walked on the moon) and said, "You guys pulled off a miracle," we were awed and humbled.

But the true success of this event can be found behind the scenes when the producer quit without warning on the day of load-in. So we were required to learn the event specifics from the ground up - in five days. And in spite of all these challenges, our event team was able to pull off an extremely successful event. This was a government (red-tape) project on a government base with government personnel. The visibility was incredible – *Time, Newsweek, US New & World Report* – no failure could even be considered. It wasn't about aesthetics. It was about perfection. Gather around, and I'll give you the inside scoop.

"Houston, We Have A Problem"

The planning of The Space Shuttle Development Conference started in a very ordinary fashion. Our Texas Account Executive was introduced to the meeting and event planning team from USA.

He had a face-to-face meeting, and we were asked to submit a bid for their upcoming conference to be held in Houston. We did so and won the bid.

Then, USA moved the conference to California and set up a site inspection. Our Account Executive was on another job site. I was, too. So, as I caught a red eye, I asked EE's Las Vegas Director of Sales (hence known as DOS) to cover the first day of the unmovable site inspection. I would join her the following day. When I arrived, after 36 hours without sleep, the client and DOS were best of friends. Perfect connection. The site inspection went flawlessly as "they" explained what "they" were planning.

The Account Executive (AE) and I continued to fine-tune the bid with all the new specs. DOS wanted to remain involved as she was a former Air Forcer and wished to stay connected in a project that was this exciting. Okay.

Another site inspection was planned. Again, everyone was busy the first day. DOS offered to go until the AE could join up with her and the client. The site inspection was fine. I lay back, knowing it was all in good hands. We asked the client; he was very, very happy.

DOS began to communicate directly with the client regarding concept and production issues, all with our approval since they had developed such a close relationship. We asked for a paper trail. None appeared, but "it's coming." Client continued to sing the praises of DOS.

Another site visit was planned, this time with technical crew and all Ames (the site) people present as well as many, many upper echelon VIPs from USA. DOS publicly proclaimed herself as "executive producer" of the event and demanded that every item regarding the event had to run through only her. Our Texas rep was the account executive, but SHE was the point person. Several unpleasant conversations later about this issue, we decided to leave it alone, since it would only be troublesome to the client to undermine her authority.

Weeks and weeks of work. Constant checking with the client. Was he happy?

Yes, everything was fine. DOS was great! She gave him tickets to Aerosmith; his seats were in front of the Texas governor and most celebrities in attendance. DOS was terrific! SO creative!

The AE and I asked to see what this creativity was all about. "It's coming." We demanded to see the budget. "It's coming." The client began to ask for paperwork. "I sent it!" she said. "Where is it?" we asked. "It's coming!"

I finally flew to Las Vegas and demanded to see "the book" with all notes in it. "It's at home." I was able to get handwritten notes for the budget. I went over it line item by line item. To keep from being excessively tedious, there was a lot of paper shuffling, next to no backup, and we had to carefully readjust the figures. The concept she seemed not to "get" was that the budget was THE BUDGET. We were assured that everything was handled. We again checked with the client who was very happy.

The dates of the event approached. According to DOS, technical elements were being donated because of the high visibility of this event. Wasn't it terrific that so much was being given to us? A Jumbotron; a high-resolution video truck to film and memorialize the entire conference; food and beverage. Wow! Lucky us!

Days before the event our Line Producer, the AE and I asked to see all creative, plus a sign-off from the client on all budgeted elements. Finally a very loose creative treatment came in the middle of the night with no budget. We were all uncomfortable, but it was time to get on our planes and start "producing." After all, with years and years of experience in the industry, this person had to know what she was doing. And the client was happy.

The day before DOS was to fly to San Jose for the first day of load-in, I left a message that I didn't have all contracts in hand to execute payments for items being delivered the next day.

On Thursday, Load-in day, I checked voice mail at my office at 4:00 a.m. "Hi, this is (well, name-dropping isn't polite, so I'll be good and not name names), and I just want to tell you that I'm disassociating myself from this project and Extraordinary Events."

We did not have the master production book. We did not have contracts. We did not have agreements. We called our Las Vegas office and were told that she had instructed them to forward all calls to our Los Angeles office. We called her home, her cell. Only voice mail. She had gone underground.

Our first call was to the Line Producer. Get on the next flight. The next was to the client. The truth. Yes, you heard me, the truth. This is the situation. Tell me every last thing you are expecting, and we will deliver it. Let's not discuss the whys or wherefores. Let's just get it done. With excellence.

Our Line Producer arrived in San Jose to be met with a barrage of people and their questions. Every sentence started with "She promised" or "She said she'd taken care of that." Seventy tour guides showed up to walk the route of the tours. WHAT TOURS??

Boeing showed up with a jet propulsion engine from a shuttle. Where's the fork lift? WHAT FORK LIFT?!

Again, I'll shorten the story. No equipment had been ordered. No labor had been ordered. No food had been ordered. The conference was woven around the introduction of this amazing video that we produced. No AV had been ordered. There was no sound.

We had a dirigible hangar, the size of three football fields, where we were producing a meeting and tradeshow, with five Space Shuttle commanders as our bosses. We had to make it happen.

On Friday, the Line Producer was in San Jose, and the AE was on his way. I remained in Los Angeles. My first job was to preview the video. Excellent. What do we show it on? Oh, yes, the donated Jumbotron. Wrong! It didn't exist. Broadcast from the donated high-resolution truck. Donated?

"Who told you that? It's $98,000, and 'she' confirmed it with me. By the way, it's 58-feet long, and we need to park it in the hangar. It's on its way now. Have the check ready."

In the midst of this, the Line Producer called. "The FAA is calling. There are jets circling the field and they want to land." WHAT JETS? Oh yes, "she" had promised five astronauts that they could fly their private planes into the field and she'd provide clearance. Keep circling, boys, we'll take care of it … somehow.

I begged, borrowed favors and stole from my accumulated years of professionalism to get everything in place. We secured sound and audio visual equipment and the best professionals in the business. Then the bombshell hit. The meetings were during broad daylight, and this dirigible hangar (remember the size, folks?) had 360-degree windows bringing in the beautiful July sunshine. And "she" had promised the client that all their AV, all their PowerPoint, would show up beautifully. How? "She" told them that Navy Seals would rappel down the hangar with velon to cover all the windows. Guess who got to break the news that it wouldn't and couldn't happen this way?

With more intense brainstorming we found some solutions, like building an expensive tunnel to shelter the equipment, but it wasn't easy.

I arrived on Monday morning to find both the Line Producer and AE in remarkably good spirits, considering.

I was approached by one of the shuttle commanders. "When do we see our speeches?" SPEECHES?

"Yes, 'she' promised she'd write our scripts, cues ...." FOR SPACE SHUTTLE COMMANDERS. By that night? Two hours worth? No problem!

"Who's directing the show?" SHOW? WHAT SHOW? "Why, 'she' said we'd have a professional director, stage manager, producer and emcee."

Now, as if this wasn't enough, add one more tiny component. That very same weekend after one scrub, the Space Shuttle was launched, but had a hydraulic leak. Our client had a lot more to think about than the problems associated with this meeting.

I could go on. But I think this might give you a good picture. Unfortunately, not the financial one. I can't even bear to talk about that. From Thursday night load-in day one, I never asked how much. I just said, "Do it." I had to stand behind the company, keep my own troupes from slashing their wrists, diffuse the tension with the vendors and communicate with the client like this was just one more daily challenge.

So, that's the story. After reading it, you might label this event stressful, but was it? Yes, but not worth hyperventilating about ... not for me anyway. Why not?

The Lesson

My life is filled with would-be stressful events like my NASA event.

For example, several years ago I gave one of many seminars for the International Special Events Society (ISES). Exactly as I mounted the podium and started thanking everyone for attending, my phone rang. As usual, it was a client demanding I do something immediately, a dire emergency, with no time to waste. As I was explaining where I was and what I was doing, my pager went off with a 911, while a bellman simultaneously ran in with a message about an emergency in some part of the globe and that my staff needed me immediately. Everyone needed something that second.

In the midst of it all, I simply looked up at my audience and said, "I was born in a concentration camp. When I was three weeks old my mother, my grandparents and I escaped on a fishing boat across the Adriatic and went into hiding in Italy for the next three years. The other boats with the rest of my family were shot out of the water, and they all went to Auschwitz. None survived. In Italy, my mother met and later married an American pilot, moved to the United States and left me with my grandparents. The next time I saw her, four years later, I had no idea who she was.

"Do I get stressed out because one rose in a centerpiece is a little wilted or a drummer is 15 minutes late or the client demands unplanned elements at the last minute or the producer quits and I have to build the event from zero up on load-in day? If no one dies on the job or I don't read about it in the *New York Times*, it simply isn't that important and not worth stressing over. And when you really look at it, what do you accomplish by getting stressed? Absolutely nothing."

2
Lelja
(1925-2009)

The Making of a Wallflower

To understand me, you must get to know my mother. And, you need to learn about the three major relationships I've had with the men in my life. Then feel free to analyze the rest. Let me tell you first about my mother, and a bit later about "them."

When I first started writing this book, I went on and on about my mother, unloading all the hurts and disappointments I had accumulated over time. I admit that it was a purge. But it was bitter and resentful, and though those feelings are legitimate, I don't want to be a bitter person. I truly do believe that every happening in my life got me to where I am today, and where I am is good, and happy. So, why dwell on so much pain? (This is just another way of saying that you'll get some of the story, but not all of it.)

With all of that said, I can honestly tell you that everything that formed and forms me is really all about my mother.

Her name was Lelja. My second ex-husband (Mark) referred to her as "the ultimate chick," and he was right. When I was growing up, she was the totally dominant presence in every environment she entered. Lelja was beautiful, sensual, flirtatious and totally Type A.

She always believed that the world revolved around her, and as far as I could see for most of my life, it did. Though I am sure that there were unplumbed depths in her, she liked to keep things "shallow," if you know what I mean. I'm not one for small talk, but that's what she liked. As a result, we didn't have much to discuss.

While there is little we had in common, she did take me shopping a lot, and to this day I still love it. She also made sure that everything I wore was the ultimate in good taste, and I'm sure this has influenced me in business as well. My event life is all about how things look, and I have very discriminating tastes. For that I thank her.

I spent the first third of my life trying to be just like her – clothes, hair, boyfriends. I never managed to be as seemingly irresistible. But I always kept trying. I also kept striving to win her approval. Maybe it was there, but it was not easily voiced. My friends tell me she was proud of me, but there was no real pride associated with this, just something that she could brag about to her friends when they were still alive.

She died as a little old lady. She was quiet and confused most of the last five years. Amazingly, though she was no longer the model of immaculate grooming, she still managed to attract the attention of every man who crossed her path. Wheel her into a room, and if there was a man present, she came alive, flirting and captivating. Many an older gent (married or not) tried to woo her into dinner dates even in her last years. It never ceased to confound me.

You might be asking at this point what this has to do with my life and my business. A lot. When I think about my success in business, it's all about recognition. The recognition I felt I didn't get from my mother and later the other various relationships I chose. There's not an award I have ever received that she acknowledged. She always wondered why anyone wanted to hire me ("What do you do that is so special?") or take me to far away places ("Aren't there people there who do what you do? Why do they need you?") Instead of letting this "get to me," I became an over-achiever and worked harder to achieve more success and recognition.

We all have different paths on our personal journeys ... and this book will tell you about mine, filled with that search for approval, for recognition, for admiration and for self-esteem.

3

Communicating with a Client
Who Doesn't Speak Your language,
Even Though You Both Speak English!

Holiday Event in Manhattan

Often, a client causes stressful situations with last-minute requests only because he or she doesn't understand what is being demanded. In this case, the client doesn't speak my language, and it's up to me to provide the education. A large technology-based company that shall remain nameless comes to mine as an illustration.

Close your eyes so I can set the scene. Well, since this isn't Books on Tape, that won't work. Shut ONE eye.

It was a December Friday night in Manhattan at one of the piers. It was sleeting and snowing – imagine traffic – and we were in the final countdown for a holiday event for our client's CEO and his 1,000 employees. All the elements and the meal were planned for a wonderful event to begin with cocktails at 6:00 p.m.

The rather young, powerful CEO would be giving a speech and holiday salutations.

"Does he need support for his speech?" I had questioned the corporate planner.

That's a "No," confirmed in writing. "He's just reading off his PowerPoint."

At 5:30 p.m., the CEO, looking like a football tackle in a business suit, loomed above me asking, "Where are the screens?"

I shuffled through my binder, so beautifully tabbed, and advised him that he didn't need them per my written confirmation with his planner.

"Get them now!" he said with no "please."

"Get them NOW," he repeated.

I looked up at him and calmly responded, "Okay, sir, I'll do my best."

"Get them now!" he ordered yet again.

I made calls, and, as luck would have it, one of the AV companies I utilize had what I needed and could "probably" get it to me (across town) in time. Good thing I had everyone's cell phone and home numbers and that they liked me well enough to take my calls.

We were now into the cocktail hour, but with a bit of a scramble and no time to test the equipment, we set up the screens. Then, I asked the question of doom. "May I have your PowerPoint presentation?"

"I don't have one; YOU were supposed to have it!" He spouted.

Again confirming with my handy dandy tabulated binder I said, "I don't have your notes, sir, but we'll do the best we can if you can tell me what you plan to say."

"I have to greet my guests," he snorted and stomped off.

Enter the corporate planner, who, shaking and scared, started feeding info to one of our techs.

Minutes passed, and the CEO approached me and pinched my arm jovially. "Wait till you hear what I want to do," he announced, quite pleased with himself.

I couldn't wait to hear what was coming now. But I kept smiling and showing great interest.

"My main guys and I are called 'the three matadors.' Get me three matador outfits," he chortled.

I dared to ask, "What sizes are the three of you?"

"They are mediums; I'm a large."

He was an extra large if I've ever seen one, and I hadn't seen the other two, so it was anybody's guess.

Again as luck had it, I got them. Imagine. An entertainment company I've worked with was open after hours on a sleeting Friday night, and they could messenger them to me just because they liked me. (And I've always paid them on time.)

Still in the cocktail hour, our charming CEO walked up to me and said, "The weather is lousy and we need to get our people home before it gets worse, so serve dinner NOW."

Most people would have argued with him. I simply smiled and said, "Absolutely. Let me tell you what we are serving: A warm lovely pumpkin soup, which we will now serve chilled - which is fashionable nowadays, though not in the dead of winter; a lovely filet mignon, which we'll make into Carpaccio ... that's very trendy ... and the Chocolate Soufflés will just be served as chocolate pudding. Guests will love pudding, don't you think? This is what you'll get if we serve it now, or, *if we serve it when we are supposed to,* they can have a wonderful hot soup, a perfectly cooked filet and a magnificent soufflé. Either way, I'm happy to do whatever you wish. It's your choice."

He stared at me and simply said, "Keep it the way you planned."

The Lesson

What made him think that we could get costumes and screens and serve dinner early? It was obvious. Here's a man who sits behind his desk and clicks for whatever he wants and gets it, immediately, with no repercussions. But the timing of an event was beyond his scope of experience. So, by not arguing with him, creating a clear picture for him and making it his choice, the situation turned out well. Otherwise it would have dissolved into a totally adversarial confrontation. It didn't, and we continued to do the event for years.

Growing up in a multi-lingual house made me understand the power of words. I love them and learned at a young age that telling stories creates a clear communication for others. I adore telling stories; my life is about telling them and providing clear communication, because everything has a point to it. Doing so has helped me work with others, such as the CEO at this event, more successfully.

Oh, and by the way, the Matador outfits were a bit snug but served their purpose well!

4

When It Ain't Finished ... Punt

The Opening of the Venetian Hotel, Las Vegas

Sometimes we're faced with situations over which we have no control. This story begins in December of 1998. Extraordinary Events was invited to bid on the Grand Opening of the Venetian Hotel, a Las Vegas property of unparalleled beauty, splendor and epic proportions.

In order to understand my preparation for even this most preliminary of meetings, you also need to understand me and what gets me excited. I am a dreamer. I dream of producing one-of-a-kind events for one-of-a-kind venues. And the prestige of a hotel such as this made this event worthy of Technicolor dreams. In a lifetime, how many people get to be a part of history in the making? This, and more, was what this opening meant to me. With all my heart I wanted to be a part of it. Why? In addition to "coordinating" the opening, I knew that I was also being called upon to act as the entertainment producer for a very high-profile event.

I met with the Venetian team and listened to their dreams for the opening. Though budget was a consideration, it wasn't the primary focus. The focus was that owner Sheldon Adelson built the hotel to fulfill his personal visions, and the opening needed to reflect grandeur, romance, loveliness, excellence and tradition. It was not only a replica of Venice, it was Venice. Every element had to capture that fact.

So, along with several other premier event companies (I was in "big time" company here), we prepared a bid. The Internet became my best friend. I researched every fact on Venice I could find. Festivals. Holidays. I watched every movie, from *Summertime* to *Dangerous Beauty*, to get a feel for the culture. I had spent a week in Venice not long before and fell in love with it, so my memories were clear.

I spent hours at the library, and my office is filled with books about Venetian palaces. It was divine research, fulfilling in every way as I steeped myself in Italian lore and learned about the ruling classes, the masks, the glassworks, the canals, the history. Marco Polo, the Doge - they all became "friends" as this exploration continued.

I prepared the presentation which developed a full promotional campaign for the hotel. Events were based around Venetian holidays, and Streetmosphere characters would work the hotel 24 hours a day and be an ongoing cast of characters threaded in and out of every event. I carefully researched Venetian entertainment to see what we could bring to Las Vegas. The Academy of San Rocco Ensemble, Massimo Cacciari, the Mayor of Venice and even an exhibition of Vivaldi's Original Instruments ... all these were considered.

The hotel had sketchy plans that could be shared at this point. We knew there would be canals. We knew there would be gondolas. We knew there would be a shopping arcade, a pool deck and the world's biggest ballroom, but we didn't know how anything would look. Our first hard hat tour was dampened by Building and Safety curtailing our preview because of safety, or lack thereof.

We prepared the proposal blind.

January, 1999, we were invited back to make a formal presentation to the executives of The Venetian. One of the most major requests passed on to me by my contacts was that we develop a fashion show, and we did. I knew that though they said "fashion show" what they really meant was a pull-out-all-the-stops extravaganza presented unusually. No standard runway show, this, but a spectacular entertainment piece that would be the jewel of the weekend.

After several meetings and many proposals, we won the bid and the honor of producing the opening events. We combined forces with the hotel and Fireworks by Grucci to create a memorable theatrical show for 5,000 high rollers that combined an exquisitely choreographed fashion show, opera, costumed talent, celebrity appearances and a dazzling fireworks display that lit up the skies of Las Vegas in an unparalleled demonstration of pyrotechnics. All this was accomplished in a space that four days prior had not been completed or approved by Las Vegas codes.

The Best Laid Plans

Logistics was a very important part of the event. For most of our planning stages all we ever saw were steel beams, concrete and hard hats. Most of the time we would fly a team to Vegas only to be told that the area we most needed to see was "off limits." We designed by guesswork. In all fairness, the hotel had more to worry about than a fashion show; they had rooms to get ready and conventions for which to prepare.

Logistics in Pre-Production

The pool deck became our main focus. Originally, we tried to plan the fashion show for the canals. It's a good thing we eliminated that location because it wasn't open on time! However, even had it been, we could not be sure how many people could physically fit around the canals. The plans were elusive, and whenever we looked at a piece of concrete and asked, "What goes here?" we were alerted by the darting glances between the engineers that they weren't sure. It might be a restaurant. Maybe a shop? Much time went into researching how long it took the gondola to move from one end of the canal to the other. Finally, we realized that any such consideration would be impractical. We all agreed on the pool deck, which wasn't available to survey until four days before the event.

The wind blew constantly every day leading up to the actual

event. The pool deck was on the fifth floor, and, since it had never been used for an event, was not rated for the weight of either the equipment or the guests. We had to partially drain the pool to lose enough weight to keep the entire deck from falling into the hotel. There was not enough equipment or labor in Las Vegas with all the other shows happening in town, so air freighting and trucking tons of equipment became necessary, and only one-third of the requested labor showed up when scheduled.

Because the hotel wanted their VIP guests to use the pool during the day, we couldn't work during daylight, so 200 moving lights plus all other equipment, including a very elaborate stage, were moved in during the night, all night, three nights prior to the event. After the first night, we were told that working at night disturbed hotel guests, so a tired, cranky crew went back to working during the day. Since the hotel was not willing to secure the pool deck from the guests, watching adorable, unsupervised children spinning our $6,000 per piece moving lights around like toy tops was not something we found entertaining.

Construction work continued on the upper stories of the building throughout load-in. Falling tools and glass made walking the deck interesting. Falling asleep on the job became a moot point!

Equipment didn't fit in the loading elevators, so at the last minute we needed to secure a 200-foot crane and load in all equipment from the street, five stories up.

Then, the day of the event dress rehearsal became a challenge because the clothes were a problem. Fashion show coordinator and choreographer Carin Holmenas had worked with the hotel and its outlets to preview and order all the clothing. Unfortunately, Building and Safety didn't approve the opening of all the stores, so when they didn't open, the managers and owners were reluctant to display their wares. In essence, they were pouting and uncooperative. With a great amount of cajoling and pulling many strings from her years of experience, Carin secured the fashions. But it wasn't without effort.

The set was in place. The lighting was designed. Models had been fitted with captivating fashions from the Venetian outlets. Our contacts specified that the hotel wanted an up-tempo and entertaining show. We spent hours picking the music that supported the trendy, modern fashions. Then the Adelsons showed up for dress rehearsal and frowned. "This hotel is about opera," they quietly said and walked away. Up-tempo and opera? Hmmmmm. Back to Tower Records. (I toyed with the idea of the duet between Bono and Pavarotti but didn't think they'd get the gag. Little did I know that years later this would become a reality ... I was again ahead of my time.)

With new music, we now had the models with which to contend. Beautiful, but lifeless, with no sense of playfulness. Try dancing, we suggested. How about smiling? Have a good time. It's not a traditional runway show. They assured me that when it was "showtime" I'd see some life. Add "crossed fingers" to the production schedule!

With everyone's full cooperation and enthusiasm - models in full makeup and hair styles looking glorious, guys pumped up and shining, teeth white, eyes twinkling - we were ready for one final run-through. And then the swans arrived. SWANS?

"Wait," I yelled. "What are THEY doing here?"

"Why, ma'am," said the swan wrangler politely, "They're going to swim in the pool." This was said as he released two squawking beauties into the water.

They flapped and screamed and squirted water onto the lighting and onto the stage, drenching everything in sight so that rehearsal was no longer possible. The wranglers took off into the pool to try to capture them, realizing this wasn't a great idea.

Forty minutes later as we mopped and cursed the swans were returned to their dog crates and driven off to parts unknown.

Finally, at 10:00 p.m., we were ready to begin. The night was perfect with ideal temperature and only a soft breeze.

Farrington Productions, the in-house entertainment agency, provided us with eight costumed opera singers in addition to characters such as Casanova and Marco Polo. One-hundred hotel personnel, dressed in vintage costumes brought to the Venetian from Venice specifically for this event, greeted our guests. In both areas, the eight opera singers roamed, mingled and sang Italian arias (concentrating on The Adelsons' favorites) to the guests as they arrived from the dinner and casino areas.

At 10:30 p.m., attention was directed at the stage, as patio lighting dimmed. We had constructed a stage to look like an Italian villa with windows and porticos overlooking Italian gardens. Interesting stairways had been built directly onto the pool into the set. From this main set a large runway extended over the pool (Note: to accommodate guests, it was constructed so that guests could swim around and under it safely). Dressing rooms were built into the stage set as part of the design so that models could quick change efficiently. Created from steel instead of fabric, everything was designed to withstand possible winds.

We began with Marco Polo and the eight opera singers serenading The Adelsons with their favorite aria, *Santa Lucia*, followed by Marco Polo introducing emcee Robin Leach who in turn introduced The Adelsons. After they greeted their guests, Robin introduced the fashion show set to an exemplary combination of pop tunes and opera, all enhanced with the hotel's costumed personnel to decorate the stage as living décor.

Twenty gorgeous models. Exquisite clothing. All presented beautifully. All available for purchase by those present. The last "model" (actually a pyro technician costumed as the spirit of Venice) walked forth carrying a huge torch and extended it into the water. It exploded into fireworks, which carried across the pool and onto the building, forming a "V" that extended up the 34 stories and onto the roof, where a four-minute pyrotechnic display became one more choreographed element of the evening.

Now, lots of people do fireworks. But Phil Grucci and his team took the show beyond any previous definition. Most people think of fireworks as putting on The 1812 Overture, sending up some shells and hearing "kabooms" a lot. But Grucci is a true master.

To prepare for this event, Phil made numerous trips to the property and reviewed multiple drawings of the high-rise and low-rise before he had the opportunity to custom manufacture the first item. It is important to realize that pyrotechnics designed and manufactured for any rooftop performance is of high precision and far from the "standard" aerial shells or fireworks you might see on the fourth of July in the park. Grucci fired from both the low-rise (800 devices) and the high-rise (2,000 devices) that had a polyvinyl (very, very WHITE vinyl) membrane as the roof surface. No room to use South of the Border projections and leave black spots or burn marks.

After the selection of music from the Grucci library, Phil was off to the scripting/design studio. He used the digital precision of a computer for the split-second timing and characteristics of each device designed into the production. After the scripting and casting, Phil produced the devices needed for the design in his 100-acre manufacturing facility.

On location, Phil had 10 pyrotechnicians (licensed Federally, as well as by the State of Nevada and Clark County) to load in the program for four days. A semi-tractor trailer of equipment, coupled with a 24-foot straight truck from his Nevada distribution facility, was essential to transport the fireworks and equipment necessary for the event.

From the choreography of the devices to complement the music and the "model" lighting the torch, to the progress of the "V" (standing for "Venetian") up the sides of the hotel and the musical presentation and performance of the devices, this was a magnificently integrated finale.

This show not only entertained its Venetian guests but everyone in Las Vegas who had only to look to the skies and experience this marvel. By the way, the Grucci Family designed and produced the incredible pyrotechnics for the Beijing Olympics.

The End of This Dream

After the event, I stood in the halls of the hotel, gazing at the frescoes and realizing that I had been an integral part of one of the most magnificent events in my career lifetime. I was full of pride and a sense of accomplishment. I had watched the construction of magnificence and then added to it in my own little way. All of the difficult logistical challenges were overcome with patience, hard work and persistence. I'll never forget it, or the honor involved.

The Lesson

Life constantly throws you curve balls, and "openings" are their own special animal. With them, you won't know what a space is going to look like until it's actually completed and you first see it, and sometimes that means you see it when you start your installation! "Punt" is the first lesson here.

Next, creative problem solving needs to be the mainstay in everything you do. It is for me. This event included a variety of additional ongoing challenges. For instance, the Venetian was a non-union hotel. The hotel was picketed as our 3,000 VIP guests and the press arrived. The answer: quickly come up with an alternate entrance to bypass the pickets.

The stores and restaurants were not permitted. How do you showcase them? Voila! The fashion show ... take product that will soon be in the stores and showcase it. Build kiosks throughout the hotel (in permitted space, of course) to show the product. Move the food and beverage portion of the event to the ballroom and have the restaurants cater to the 3,000 instead of doing the planned dine-a-round in the not-yet-permitted restaurants. Spa not open? Put spa technicians throughout the hotel to give massages and facials and talk about product. Improvisation. The key to all event planning. Actually, the key to life planning, right?

And the biggest improv of all...Treasure Island (across the street) found out about our pyro extravaganza and decided to move its fireworks show to go off at the same time as ours. When we discovered it (through an employee at the competing hotel) at the last minute, we put a few test blasts into the air so that Treasure Island would start its show! As soon as theirs was over, we did our full show for real. Necessity is the mother of invention, along with some sheer chutzpah. If it hadn't been so last-minute I would have gone to Treasure Island in advance, explained what we were doing and asked them nicely for their cooperation. However, then it would have been in their hands, and potentially the outcome would have been the same. It's always better to aim for the higher ground when it's possible.

Life lesson: think on your feet, every waking moment.

I learned to think on my feet and punt a lot before I was eight years old, because I was either sick with tonsillitis or alone. Lelja had to work, and for the ultimate Jewish princess born with a silver spoon, this was not her idea of how she should live. So much of my time was spent with her friends (who took me after school) or with paid babysitters. I started writing and using my imagination. We lived in Hollywood off of Canyon Drive after my mother married Peter, her last husband, and writing was a natural progression for me as a way to express myself. And it was something I could do while alone.

I was crazy for David Niven in TV's Four Star Theatre and wrote a screenplay for him and sent it off to the producers, and Four Star offered to buy it! My parents got the letter and were in shock. When the producers arrived to meet with the woman who had written a script in long hand for Mr. Niven, they were just as shocked to learn that an eight-year-old girl was the author. Of course, my parents wouldn't let me sell my script to them. A child simply didn't do those things.

I also became quite the entrepreneur. I made money selling flowers from other people's yards door-to-door! I even responded to an ad in a magazine for selling dresses door-to-door. I sent away for them, not telling them my age of course, and, since my parents were never home, I received the dresses and went out selling and doing quite well. Unfortunately, my parents discovered my business activity and, once again, put that career path to a drastic and abrupt end. Walking the streets with clothing samples was not seemly. Since my parents both worked and I was alone, they felt I should stay at home. It was a different time, and "latch key" children were not perceived to be endangered, but my parents didn't think my actions were age-appropriate. Actually, they really didn't know what to make of me.

They were greatly absent from my childhood and not (in the 1950s) what was considered to be Ozzie and Harriet type parents. They weren't very interested in my school work, friends or really anything that I did. The most interest they did show was in the clothes I wore and how I looked. So, I filled my alone time with creative outlets. I collected the cardboard from my Dad's shirts from the Chinese laundry (my mother refused to wash and iron shirts) and designed dresses and houses. I spent entire afternoons making mud pies and decorating them with ferns, leaves and flowers. I spent a lot of time writing and reading everything from comic books to *War and Peace*, which I had read twice by the time I was eight. I went to the library every day to check out or return more books.

My single most creative influence came from Sharron and Louis Zaboy, a very bohemian couple. They loved me and taught me that there were no boundaries to the imagination. Sharron was the aunt of Lelja's pilot husband (her first husband met in Italy during the liberation). Sharron was certifiably nuts but talented with imagination and art, and, between Louis and her, there was nothing they didn't know and couldn't do. With hearts of gold and no children of their own, they were a constant inspiration to me. They lived off the Valley side of Laurel Canyon, and Louis had reel-to-reel tape recorders into which we would perform readings.

One night we even did *Bell, Book and Candle* with me reading out the Kim Novak role. It made me feel very grown up.

My senior year in high school, I was given an assignment to memorize and read aloud a poem. I picked one by Goethe and delivered a reading of it both in German and then in translation. Louis decided I needed to give it a "kick," so he took parchment and scribed it into Old English letters and Sharron illustrated it. It was about 100 feet long and magnificent. I unrolled it as I recited the reading in class, and it was beyond what my Burbank classmates could imagine. So they made fun of it.

I had to really learn to punt and make the best of it when my parents moved us from Hollywood to Burbank. I was like a fish out of water there. I had loved Hollywood – I was popular in elementary school there and had a great circle of friends. When we moved I really stood out. I was a big kid. By the time I was 10, I was five-feet-six-inches tall, weighed 128 pounds and had boobs, having already gone through puberty! I began to struggle with my weight after I had a tonsillectomy. My mother didn't make it any easier. She was European and everything was about sweets and desserts. Exercise was the devil, and, because she was thin, it didn't affect her. But because my weight reflected upon her, it became important to her. I had to look good and was on a constant diet. As a result, I became very self-conscious and disappointed in myself that I couldn't conquer my addiction to food. I always perceived that when people saw Andrea, they saw "fat."

So all of these experiences have molded me into what I am now.

My young life was spent fending for myself, thinking on my feet and finding creative solutions to my problems. My work has simply been part of the process to fine-tune those abilities and to overachieve so that others would see more than just my weight.

5

Hurricanes, Unions and a LOT of People...

SAP International Annual Users Conference - Streets of Philadelphia

Producing events can often be compared to running an obstacle course. Such was the case with a 1999 event in Philadelphia. For SAP's annual users conference, Extraordinary Events was asked to produce Streets of Philadelphia in a city with no available indoor venue large enough to hold the 10,000 that would participate. Working with all the various city departments, the event was executed on the Terrace of the Philadelphia Museum of Art (the City's most recognizable landmark) and adjoining Eakins Oval Parkway with 1,200,000-square feet of land and approximately 50,000-square feet of concrete. Street closures, city permits, traffic control and security were the beginnings of the logistical challenges. Careful planning of each and every bus route to transfer 10,000 guests from 50 hotels throughout Pennsylvania and New Jersey was complicated by traffic to a Bruce Springsteen concert at the same time during midweek rush-hour traffic. We needed to transform an ordinary-looking park into a festive and attractive party venue. We planned exemplary food and beverage that featured the best of Philadelphia's varied ethnic cuisine so that our thousands of guests could eat and drink without standing in line. Now that alone sounds daunting, doesn't it?

Event Objectives

Entertainment was the cornerstone of this event, and, by the way, it was being compared to the previous year's that had five times the budget and a performance by Rod Stewart! This event would feature simultaneous rock and roll in four locations. Guests would be greeted by a local marching band playing *Streets of Philadelphia*. This would be followed by a traditional Mummer's Parade. In a tent, a Philadelphia favorite, The Nerds, would alternate with an interactive DJ who would move between the main tent and the Terrace Stage at the Museum to provide ongoing entertainment. Though not technically a festival, a street fair atmosphere was being created within this corporate event. The entertainment was complex and unique and spoke of "Philadelphia." The timing of the entertainers, combined with a fireworks production, was to be executed split second so that there was never a moment where something wasn't going on. Sound had to be perfect so that one stage did not interfere with any of the others.

On one of the main stages, World Class Rockers would do a one-hour performance.

On another stage, Earth, Wind and Fire was destined to thrill the audience.

On the third stage, representing SAP Latin America, Gilberto Santa Rosa from Puerto Rico would leave people jumping to the rhythm.

A spectacular fireworks display was another featured entertainment element. We conferred with Grucci Fireworks who was given the directive, "Take what you did for the 4th of July in New York and do more for this show ... all in no more than five minutes." It was planned as a rock and roll fireworks show that could be seen everywhere in Philadelphia. The music was customized and intertwined with tunes about the City. Beginning with Louie Armstrong's *Wonderful World*, it was programmed so that, for example, when guests heard, "I see fields of green," the pyro was green. When "and red roses too" was sung, the pyro roses in red burst into the sky. The sound system was designed to be heard over the extensive acreage of the area we were using. Not an easy achievement considering the vastness of the space.

Branding was key as SAP was establishing global presence for its U.S. Headquarters in Philly and needed us to introduce its new ad campaign. The purpose of creatively branding this event was to cement that SAP is THE cutting edge of technology in the attendees' minds and to say to the home town in general, "SAP is a presence, a force with which to be reckoned." New slogans and branding had to be done in an area that allowed no signage, and it had to be everywhere and creative. So, we accomplished this significantly through all the décor elements.

With our goals clearly outlined – entertainment, food and beverage and branding - we knew almost immediately that the focus should be placed on the Museum. The park alone, though tree-lined and scenic, didn't make a statement for an industry leader in the tech sector. Structures and decor could be built, but this event was for 10,000 people, with time and budget restrictions. The Museum stood at the apex of the event area and became a monumental task.

The structure of the museum on its own didn't fulfill the goal of a high-tech, cutting-edge visual statement. So how could lighting transform this historic site into a contemporary work of high-tech art in under three days?

The designers quickly formulated a plan: Let's paint it ... with LIGHT, a lighting design utilizing almost 275 automated fixtures and miles of electrical distribution cable.

The lighting units would highlight and accentuate the existing architectural elements: columns, frescos, stone setbacks and a large Calder sculpture in the courtyard. These fixtures would create a kinetic mural of vivid color, fluidly brushing over the architecture in an intricately programmed pallet of movement and composition. The intense color washes would form a backdrop to frame the client's message. Projected over the colorful background on the two "sides" of the Museum was a 150-feet-wide-by-five-stories-high visual display of SAP's logo and its catchphrases. The "branding, images and hooks" that SAP wanted guests to see were produced from a separate lighting system. Video-like roll-ins, sweeps, complex reveals and one-by-one word fade-ups for entire sentences created the client's logos and messages. Due to the fact that the designer chose to utilize one of the brightest intelligent light fixtures at that time, the corporate branding became visible for blocks, all the way down the parkway and into the downtown area. When the kinetic color washes and the graphics were combined, it created a stunning visual mural. The Museum was now the subject in a live painting of light for one dramatic evening. It made such a statement that camera crews from the local news channels taped it for broadcast.

Creative use of graphics and the above-described lighting as well as use of new products, such as the huge AirStar projection inflatable, displayed all current ad campaigns through slides in this unique object. Immense backdrops on the stages previewed the new ad campaign, CityofE. Even the fireworks spelled out SAP in the sky. Guests saw "SAP"everywhere - on cocktail napkins, on signage where possible, in lighting, in the fireworks, on the stage, in the inflatable and in street banners.

Under the very best of circumstances, a job of such magnitude would have been a challenge. But, it gets even more complicated!

Philadelphia is a union town, and the union was not happy that we were in a non-union facility and threatened to picket our event if we did not bow to their demands. All of that paled when Hurricane Floyd (yes, that's right, a hurricane) unleashed its fury during the event. Logistically, it just doesn't get more complicated than this. We had to: create a location where none existed and execute bus pick ups and drop offs in impossible situations; close major city thoroughfares during rush-hour traffic; coordinate with every city department individually to get our event approved and re-approved when one department would countermand the agreements of another; pave roads that were torn up in order to get our guests across the street to access the event; fight teamsters and IATSE (the International Alliance of Theatrical Stage Employees) in order to get our crew working and productive; seed and re-seed an entire park both before and after the event; re-grade acres of land after the event and fulfill a multitude of insurance claims resulting from weather-related incidents.

Promises were broken by every entity ... the venue, the city, the city officials, the parks department, water and power, safety, police and the streets department. There was salvation only once the Mayor intervened. So, I repeat, this was just about as hard as it gets.

So how did we do it all? Grab your galoshes, and read on ... you won't believe how creative we got just getting this event delivered with all the obstacles standing in our way.

Venue Challenge

Let's look at our venue challenges. Remember, we had 10,000 guests to accommodate. The entire convention center was being used for the client's own tradeshow, and Bruce Springsteen was performing at the new arena. Translation: any location anywhere near this arena could not be considered because of street traffic. Several locations were considered but eliminated because they were in seedy and unsafe neighborhoods and, therefore, not appropriate or safe. And SAP was conscious of image.

So, we focused on the Philadelphia Museum of Art, a non-union venue, a definite plus, or so we thought. (As everyone who has ever worked in Philadelphia knows, the union has an extremely strong presence.) We then met with the city and Eakins Oval Parkway officials to describe the event. Headline entertainment. Huge amounts of food. Fireworks. No problem. (Oh, do I rue the day I ever hear "no problem" again.) Just follow city regulations. What are "city regulations?" I was handed a 500-page handbook. Hmmmm. We read it.

Before our selection, we performed several site inspections. In order to use the Museum, SAP had to become a member, which entitled them to such a privilege. They joined. For this membership we were told that we could use both the inside and the outside of the Museum. We agreed that we intended to use the outside on the terrace for one of our stage areas and food stations and the inside for backup in case of bad weather. We asked for a contract with all details spelled out.

Between the Museum and Eakins Oval Parkway was Philadelphia's main thoroughfare, which would have to be closed so that 10,000 guests could cross back and forth between the two areas. A simple matter of permits, we were assured, even though our event would be held during rush hour. The city agreed that they would divert traffic. We filed the applications for these permits. Seemed simple, right? Nope. It doesn't end there.

Prior to the event, we arrived days early and paid a visit to the Museum. They knew nothing about the event! With their signed contracts in hand, I informed them about what we were doing. Our production schedules had been delivered; we had proof of it on our fax print outs. Our FedEx packages had been received. We showed them the signatures. They knew nothing about the fireworks and decided they would not allow them. They said that we had to use their caterer if we were on their premises, and yet we had a signed agreement that we could bring in our own catering. Many hours of meetings later, we settled the matters by paying an additional $20,000. Additionally, if we wanted to use the interior at all, we would need to pay for security guards, ushers and bathroom attendants for another several thousands of dollars. Additionally, they would close at 11:00 p.m. and not 12:30 p.m. when the event was scheduled to end, and to this there was no explanation and no compromise.

That was the easy part. I'm not sure how to describe the following, so after you read this paragraph, I ask you to close your eyes and try to visualize what we saw. Recall the multi-lane thoroughfare, one of the city's most traveled routes, between the Oval Parkway and the Museum. Then visualize the large sidewalk area which leads to the Museum steps, the only pathway to the Terrace where we were holding a large part of our event. When we arrived, there was NO sidewalk, only shards of concrete. It was all under construction, never before mentioned during our extensive meetings. When I approached the city officials and the Parks Department, I was told they were getting ready for the Republican Convention (strange … this was 1999, and I thought that was late in 2000). I asked when this would become a sidewalk again, and they said, "Later this year."

"I need it fixed."

"You'll have to fix it yourself."

So I paved the sidewalk and street the day before our event in order that our guests could walk on concrete and access the very venue I had rented.

And what about the lighting you ask? The real challenges surfaced about an hour after the first on-site inspection meeting began. Suddenly, the city that was quite accustomed to hosting events in the park (complete with large stages, name talent and full productions) said that lighting the front of the Museum was another story.

"It can't be done! You'll need to talk to this agency, no - that other city agency." And this preceded a host of bureaucratic red tape. After meetings and more meetings, we received the necessary permission and accessed the required permits. As they say, money talks. Museums usually need money. This one certainly did.

The Park. Imagine our surprise when on the day before the event, crews came in and started seeding the grounds, mulching the soil and creating mud where there had previously been either hard earth or lawn. Would they stop? No, they had their orders. By the time we could reach the appropriate city official, the work had been completed. Aargh! Later, you will know how much this affected our event.

Of course, we needed everything for the park. We ordered power, toilets, tables, chairs and all that accompanies such a food and beverage event, as well as stages for the talent and on-site dressing rooms for the entertainers with all of their hospitality needs. The limos. The suites. The first-class air arrangements. The roadies. The runners. Phone lines and RVs for offices. Loads of details. And, we determined we needed a tent in case of inclement weather so that those who couldn't get into the museum could be sheltered in case of rain. We logistically planned the placement of the 600 linear feet of food tents.

Containing the area also became important, so the entire perimeter of our event space, 600-feet-wide-by-2,000-feet-long, was contained within fencing.

The Union

Still not as bad as it's going to get. As soon as we started set up, our technical director said that we had a problem. A bad problem. The city had assured us that we did not need to use union labor. However, the unions had called on the TD to inform him that because we were not using union labor they were going to stop all local labor from working on our event. He was told that if we proceeded to hold the event they would form a picket line around the entire affair and prevent guests from entering. I tried reasoning. No luck. I was told that if I hired union crews it would be an additional $30,000 to $50,000.

I'd had it. I called the Mayor's office. God bless Philadelphia's mayor. Within hours he had his deputy meet with the union officials and me, and we resolved the matter amicably. Amicably for me. Not for the Union. The official had in hand (literally) representatives of each of the threatening unions (who had told us there would be bodily harm ... yes, really!) and told them to apologize to me, and sincerely. He then said that the union crews would be happy to pitch in and help and would work for non-union fees, including any needed overtime. So we agreed to use union personnel on our job. All was well. Or so they pretended. Union guys just love being ordered around by a woman, don't they?

The day before the event, we had everything set up and tested. Everything was a "go" with the police and fire departments and city officials. However, city plumbers would not turn on water to the cook tents or bathrooms until 4:00 p.m. on the day of the event as they cited a water shortage! The fountains at the museum (another of those no problem requests) were never turned on. Water shortage. Little did they know that shortly there would be no shortage of water.

The Hurricane

Prior to the event, we had calculated all the possibilities, provided weather contingencies and accommodated every anticipated need. (Note: the *Farmer's Almanac* indicated it had not rained in Philadelphia during that week in 40 years!) Hurricane Floyd was all the way down south in the Caribbean when the install first began in

Philadelphia. But with all the options that the weather front could have taken, of course it headed straight for our site. As the production team began programming numerous lighting fixtures, it quickly became apparent that the event could be in trouble. Fortunately, when the hurricane hit, we had taken care of all the event details and were prepared to handle it because everything else had already been coordinated. This prevented our attention from being diffused.

Dozens of cases of trash bags were purchased and distributed to each of the 275 fixtures, as temporary raincoats. Just as programming finished the night before the event, the first raindrops began to fall. The four key technical staff, still working at 3:00 a.m., began scrambling to cover and protect the equipment. When you consider that each fixture has the electronics and processing similar to a laptop computer, and costs upwards of $7,000 each to purchase, the team was running. Would you leave your laptop open and in the rain?

The crew quickly jogged around the enormous site, turning over fixtures, and watching pots of water pour out from the electronics and the delicate control motors.

At this point, we were glad that we had a huge tent (30,000-square feet) installed. Just in case. And the Museum as back up ... sort of.

To be safe prior to the rain, we found a supplier of 10,000 ponchos which we handed out as guests got off their motor coaches. Our salvation. And then we just pretended it was "Woodstock 1999." What else could we do? We had a significant amount of shelter so that people could gather in the tent to eat and drink. The main stages were sheltered by trees and with their ponchos on, guests plodded through the mud to see the main stage acts. The acts performed, albeit reluctantly. We did say to Earth, Wind & Fire, "Hey, guys, with a name like yours, you can't refuse to play in the elements." With a forced laugh, they did.

The only real hiccough was the fireworks. With the fire marshal at my side, he at first said, "No, absolutely not," because the winds were too high. We negotiated. I did not want to be the one to tell my client that his $100,000 fireworks show was not going to happen when everything else was so slushy. He finally agreed that we could test the air by sending up an occasional pyro burst, and, if it looked okay, we could "go" but only when he said "go." By doing this, we ultimately found a window of opportunity and the resultant show was truly magnificent. "SAP" was written in the sky in pyro, and the clients agreed that it was the most magnificent fireworks display they had ever seen or imagined. Phew!

Guests loved it and said it was the best event they had ever attended. Great food. Great entertainment. Fun. They hoarded the ponchos. They loved the rain and the environment it created. At one a.m. it was over, or was it?

The morning after the event the first call came at 5:30 a.m. Hurricane Floyd had landed in full fury, and our tents were all blowing over. Our kitchen equipment was on its way to the next county; the stages were sinking into the mud and our semis were stuck in the middle of the park and unable to move. Debris was flying everywhere. Ah, the life of an event producer. Off we went in over 100-miles-per-hour winds and pouring rain to manage the load-out. The union? Oh, no, they were not allowed to work under such conditions. So they abdicated all responsibility for load-out.

The final challenge was racing millions of dollars of valuable fixtures, controllers, and miles of cable into the waiting semi trucks, before the full force of "Floyd" shut down the entire city. Let's just say we were very wet and tired.

However, the guests never experienced this part of the event production. In the world of "memorable" events, this one is at the top.

Could there be any more challenges? Of course. For instance, the aftermath.

There was a great deal of damage. We had ample insurance, and that was a good thing, because we were blamed for the damage to the park though it was indeed caused by an act of God. However, in lieu of all that had preceded the event, we chose to cheerfully accept our responsibility and replant the park that had been reseeded the day before the event. We fulfilled all insurance claims (tents that hit cars) and insisted that our vendors also act responsibly.

Overall, the event went a bit damp, but without a hitch. The dedicated crews were left with the satisfaction of a spectacular design, overcoming obstacles and the gratifying statement, "We're sorry, but that flight has been cancelled; the airport just closed due to weather."

The Lesson

Everything in life is about persistence ... the dogged pursuit of what you want to achieve. When the going gets tough, the tough get going. What the heck does that mean? In my case, it means I will do anything and everything relentlessly to meet the needs of my client. It's all about creative solutions. I may start to sound like a broken record, but, please, soak this in. Creativity is not confined to making a pretty centerpiece; it is also in conflict resolution and innovative communication ... like with the union with the help of the mayor, and that meant not being afraid to go to the top and cry "help." Hurricanes? Unions? Forgetful city officials and museum personnel? Obstacles only, obstacles to overcome ... creatively. The lesson? Don't give up!

6

Persistence

My Blessing and My Curse

Persistence has been and will always be my blessing and my curse. I am absolutely incapable of giving up. I always believed with all my heart that someday my mother would thank me for a gift that I had brought her from somewhere in the world or that I would find out who my father was. Or, she would recognize or appreciate anything I have accomplished. It never happened, but I always still hoped with all my heart that it would. I believe that the simple truth was that she didn't care because it wasn't about her. As an example, let me reflect back to my 60th birthday party. It was a beautiful affair in my home. My industry friends had constructed a tent in my backyard and provided catering, décor and entertainment. More than 100 of my close friends gathered that evening to celebrate with me, and I was reveling in the love and recognition I was receiving. My best friend John Daly (dubbed by *Special Events* magazine as the "guru of design") gave a heartfelt, beautiful speech in my honor, and, afterward, my mother turned to me and said, "I don't understand why that man had to talk so much about you; it was boring!"

So, I can't think of anything, including Lelja and my terrible marriages, in which I don't persist. I have turned things so often.

To me, no doesn't mean no. It's not rejection but an opportunity to make things happen. I have always believed that if I want a relationship to go a certain way that I can make it so. Unfortunately lucky in cards but unlucky in love lends itself to me because things that were personally lacking gave me more impetus to succeed in business. I believe you can have it all even with the misery and even if you make bad choices along the way.

My relationship problems stemmed from the personalities that attracted me. I am always drawn to the unattainable. The more difficult it is, the more I want it. Great for business; not so good for my love life.

I've had three prime relationships. By describing those relationships through the gifts that each of the three gave me, you might get a picture of the type of men I chose. Why did I not see BIG RED FLAGS? I guess I chose not to see.

The first relationship was with Bob, Jon's father, and began when we were 17. Bob started telling me about a gift that was going to be extremely special. He talked about it for weeks before I received it. He played it up, building my expectations. It turned out to be a bowling pin that he had hand-painted to look like a bowling pin, and I just accepted it as wretched as it was. To this day (almost 50 years later), I still don't know why he gave me this. I married him anyway.

Jimmy, my next long-standing relationship, honored me with my first birthday gift after we met and fell madly in love. It was an old, leather-bound LP record player that he brought out from his garage. At that point, technology had moved on but you would have thought I was receiving the latest innovation. On the record player was Roberta Flack's LP of The First Time Ever I Saw Your Face. I would have been happy with just that but accepted the junk with the LP as if it were a piece of jewelry.

Years later, I met Mark, a musician playing with Ron Rubin's band in 1978. When we met, he told me he was getting a divorce. Naturally, I perked up. Jewish, divorced, good-looking, good conversationalist. What he didn't tell me was that he was getting divorced while living with another woman. So, not knowing, I started seeing him (all the while he thought that I did know his circumstances.)

By the time I discovered his situation, I was hopelessly involved. And, at that point, he was going to marry his girlfriend and insisted I come to their wedding! Like an idiot, I did. After the wedding, his Christmas gift to me was a picture of the two of us *at his wedding to another woman.* Years later after they were divorced, I married him, too.

Why did I put up with those things? They should have been clues of insensitivity I could never overcome, but my need for recognition and love blinded sensibility. I just always wanted to make things better. I wanted to be fair and honorable and giving. Eventually, I modeled myself to be the opposite of what they were. I did take these lessons to heart in business, and when someone gives me clues that it isn't going to be a good relationship, I back away.

My personal relationships with Bob, Jimmy and Mark could fill an entire book, but the details throughout will reflect my persistence to succeed and will reveal how these personal failures actually strengthened and molded my overall character.

Bob

I met Bob in summer school at junior college between high school and Berkeley. He was quite tall, Jewish, handsome, very witty, extremely self-assured, self-centered and loads and loads of fun. We studied together and then went our separate ways. We bonded even more the few times I was home from Berkeley for vacation. After my freshman year I came home with every intention of going back to school, but he had broken up with his girlfriend and I with a current boyfriend. We started dating, and I fell in love. Even then he was a player and liked to pit girls against each other. Did I take note? No, I wanted to do everything for him, partly because his parents were terrible to him. He found a great connection with my parents who were good to him and who were also outgoing and happy and very self-centered. Obviously they all got along famously. He was very ambitious and was studying to be a CPA at California State University at Northridge. All I could see was that he was handsome and Jewish and that his ambition would make him a good provider. I liked that he proclaimed to love kids.

We were 19 or 20, too young to get married. I don't think he wanted to get married, especially to me, but he was pressured into it by family, friends and me. His parents were devoted to each other, so he did have a model of a strong marriage though not strong parenting as their devotion did not extend to their children. Almost from the day we got married our relationship disintegrated. He would pick fights so he could storm out of the house and go out with somebody. But I was oblivious, because in the 1960s people got married and were together for life. That wasn't Bob's way of thinking. Blindly, I supported him through college, giving up my own scholastic efforts to work full-time.

Soon, he got a draft notice for the Vietnam War, but because of his education, he was able to enlist and enroll in Officers Training School. I ended up following him around to places like Hopewell, Virginia, and Lawton, Oklahoma, (a horrible place). All the while he kept reverting to form and picking fights so he could go out. He started an intense affair with an Army wife whose husband was in Vietnam. Phone calls in the middle of the night with the lies and excuses that go with it ensued. There was lots of crying and running home on my part. One day, while I was back home in Los Angeles having run away from his deceit and horrid behavior, he called and told me he was being sent to Vietnam. I went back to Oklahoma to try and patch things up, which I thought had been successfully accomplished, and off he went to war.

We exchanged lots of letters, but I didn't know he was also writing my dad and sending him photos of his Vietnamese girlfriends! He received leave after six months, and I excitedly met him in Hawaii. Unfortunately, all he could talk about was how big I looked compared to Vietnamese women, and he really wanted nothing to do with me.

Finally he came back after a year, and I found an apartment for us. All I can say is that we got along. We eventually bought a house in Canoga Park in a new tract, and I got pregnant. I was ecstatic because he had been told he could never have kids. When I called him to tell him I was pregnant, so excited I could barely contain myself, his response was, "Who's the father?" The entire time I was pregnant, he was running around. I accepted it, too embarrassed to do anything about it.

Jon was born and, to me, he was a miracle - beautiful and perfect.

Even then Bob made it hard for me to enjoy these special times. He turned it into a contest. The minute Jon needed something, Bob would demand my attention, and I gave it to him. When Jon was less than a year, we separated for the first time. Ultimately, we got together for a short period of time and then, when Jon was less than two, we separated and divorced after being together for a decade.

For all his proclamations that he loved children, Bob was a crappy father.

In essence, I married my mother, because, for Bob, it was all about him 100 percent. When he left us, he took all the money from our accounts, but this was the kick in the butt I needed to begin my journey to a business career.

Jimmy

I met Jimmy at a racial encounter group weekend. He was short, stocky and dark black. He frightened me at first. He was the leader of the encounter group and was a very powerful communicator. We honed in on each other from the beginning, and he made me feel absolutely precious. In his eyes, I was beautiful and wonderful. Everything I did was perfect. And we were in love from minute one, which was the impetus for getting out of the marriage with Bob. If Jimmy could make me feel like this, why should I stay with Bob who made me feel horrible?

Jimmy was kind and doted on Jon, who was very little at the time. The fact that he was married with a small child should have been a problem for me out of the gate. It wasn't because I was so desperate to be loved.

For the first few years of it, he was such an enabler. I felt like I could accomplish anything. And it is probably what pushed me into re-joining Ron Rubin, which was the start of my career in events. Then, suddenly, he wasn't so nice anymore. As it turns out, he was a compulsive liar, and nothing he had ever told me was true. He also had a wandering eye, about which I didn't know. I think I wanted too much of him, and that of course was difficult. Finally, one night his wife landed on my doorstep, and the two of us started talking very openly. As it happens, he was off with someone else. We put it together and both went to the airport to pick him up from his assignation! Even after all this, any sane person would have ended it, but I stayed with him. I was in love.

Ultimately he and his wife split, and he got an apartment by himself. As a compulsive liar, he knew how to use his lies, so I thought I was the one who was crazy. He would make a date to see me and wouldn't show up. Then he'd say he was there and I wasn't home. This made me doubt myself. Had I gone somewhere briefly?

Unfortunately, all this was very hard on Jon. Jimmy would promise to do things with Jon and then not show up, even forgetting to pick him up after school. On those days when Jimmy had promised to be there for Jon after school, I would worry myself sick. The pattern that developed was that Jon would be left with a teacher, and, hours later, I'd get a phone call asking why I hadn't picked up my son. Guilt. And more guilt. And still I didn't do anything.

Finally, we moved into a place in Malibu together with both of our kids, and this ultimately showed me that he wasn't who I wanted. As I was putting away his laundry one day, I found an envelope sitting on top of his shirts and discovered he had children about whom he had never told me. I called his wife (not yet divorced), and she didn't know about them either. That was the ultimate lie for me. So while he was working, I packed up my stuff and left.

Why did I do those things? I still don't understand it. But I went from a man who rejected me to one who made me feel like I was the most desirable woman alive. In the beginning, I was absolutely obsessed with him. I was with him for seven years, and I have to give him credit. He made me feel as if I could accomplish anything in my career. For a long time I felt treasured. After all, he had a wife and daughter and still he wanted me. Funny what tricks you let your mind play on you, isn't it?

Oddly enough, there was hardly a day between moving out from Bob to being with Jimmy, and the day I left Jimmy I re-met Mark.

Mark

So had I learned from my first two mistakes? Apparently not. I thought

Mark was the most beautiful man I'd ever seen. He was thin, and for someone who was worried about weight my entire life, that was appealing. Intelligent, quick, very verbal, very bohemian and talented, Mark knew things about which I had no knowledge – weather, earth, water, nature, animals, music. Real, real things. Also he was very boyish and made no effort to hide it. He told me upfront that he didn't want children because he was too much of a child himself and wanted to stay that way! At first, he and Jon got along well. He had a way of ingratiating himself at the onset of a relationship (also according to his other ex-wives), and then the dark side would take over. Of course, I didn't see the dark side ... at first.

When I met him, he had a small horse ranch in Chatsworth. After buying four horses, he invited Jon and me to come see them. When we arrived, he was off in the distance on a beautiful black horse. The moment he saw us, he took off galloping, jumped over a fence, stopped next to us and bent over and kissed me. For the person who devours romance novels, this was right out of my fantasies. I fell instantly in love. He could also be extremely charming. He was making *The Rose* with Bette Midler, and he invited Jon and me to watch some of the shoots. He also invited me to a late night rehearsal at 20th Century Fox and just going onto that lot was exciting. In the midst of rehearsing, he brought Bette over and said, "Bette, I'd like you to meet my friend, Andrea." He didn't do the reverse. How important do you think that made me feel?

Because I never got over that 12-year-old's love of horses, I thought Mark's idea to establish a horse business was a great one, so we formed a business partnership, for which I ultimately paid. Raising horses is comparable to pushing Rolls Royces off of cliffs. They eat; they get sick; they eat more. But buying horses, and buying more horses (the goal was to breed and sell) made him happy, and my life was all about making someone else happy. The result – 52 horses.

Obviously, I had serious self-esteem problems, but I loved him. Remember that I was invited to and attended his wedding to someone else? They were married two years, and then he moved out of her house into mine. We were married after that. Ultimately, he needed someone to take care of him.

For awhile we had a fairly good relationship in all our dealings, whether it was with the horses, music, our friendship or our love, particularly when we first were living together. He was very mellow when we were doing drugs, but, when we stopped, the dark Mark (that had appeared intermittently and that I had ignored) came out full-time. Suddenly, my blinders came off.

We had a lot of verbal violence at the end. I could never predict what he would do or say but knew that it would be horrible. Our marriage ended because I discovered I was being deceived and totally disrespected. Despite his claims of loyalty to me, I learned he was having an affair with our kennel help. (I forgot to mention that we went from the exercise of raising horses, none of which he ever sold, to raising German Shepherds.) The affair had been going on for years, and she pretended to be my friend. He had me pay her substantial amounts of money while she lived with him in my house whenever I was traveling, which was a large amount of the time. There wasn't a moment of the 20 years we were together that he wasn't sabotaging what I needed to do while wanting the benefits of it.

The Lesson

Even though these three relationships were riddled with flaws, the experiences helped mold me into the person I am today. They made me stronger, better and taught me the importance of my own self-worth. Had I not persisted through the misery, I might not have finally recognized how to give up on something gone wrong, and I might not be the independent person today that my friends know and respect.

I allowed it to happen to me. Though bad moods, bad treatment, poor ethics, disloyalty are acts another person committed, I allowed them to continue. So in essence I have no one else to blame that I lived with my own bad choices. The lesson in it all? You never have to embrace someone else's bad treatment of you whether they be a lover, a friend or a client. You are worth more than that.

7

Working with Clashing Cultures

Hong Kong/China Tourism Promotion in the U.S. - The China Travel & Folklore Festival

Making history is every event producer's dream. For me, that dream came true when Extraordinary Events was called upon to create and produce a history-making event for China - the first joint tourism promotion (after the turnover) between Hong Kong and mainland China - and the largest public festival ever held at Minneapolis' Mall of the Americas. The event was designed to bolster American tourism throughout China and had two components. An exclusive, black-tie VIP opening reception, followed by an 11-day festival called the China Travel & Folklore Festival, were both to be held at the Mall of the Americas, the country's largest enclosed retail and family entertainment complex.

Though we had a wonderful relationship with our client, the Hong Kong Tourist Association, we had never worked directly with China before. And, given the shaky political climate between the two, we knew we were in for an unusual event experience. Imagine working with two clients whose relationship makes the Hatfields and the McCoys look like bosom buddies! Add to that vast cultural differences and a language barrier that makes basic communication almost impossible, and you'll have a good idea of what it was like trying to produce an event with communist China and the formerly British-ruled Hong Kong—two entities that on paper are one country, but in theory, are two.

Pre-Production Challenges

The first indication of the challenges to come took place in our initial meeting with dignitaries from the two countries. Five minutes into the conversation, neither group was speaking to the other. They would speak only through us. The meeting concluded with the Minister of Tourism for China directing the following comment at his Hong Kong counterpart, "I wish for you to remember that I am the father, and you are the daughter." With that, the meeting ended, and our challenge of bringing two clashing cultures together for one big happy event was about to begin.

Weeks of pre-planning were exercises in cross-cultural communication. The design team was in Hong Kong and Beijing. The Mall wanted to approve the plans. Hong Kong sent pages of stunning renderings and detailed architectural drawings. Beijing submitted ink sketches with notes in Chinese characters.

We sent detailed outlines of shipping information for packing and customs. They were virtually ignored.

Seven days before the event we received three containers of props from Beijing. Since there is no ocean in Minnesota, the containers had to be shipped first to Los Angeles to clear customs, then onto Minneapolis. While Hong Kong hired a designer to create sets here in America, Beijing coordinators assured us that they could do a better job at a cheaper cost and would design and manufacture their props in China and ship them to us. Fine. When the props arrived in Los Angeles, however, most were broken or damaged. What's more, all assembly directions were in Chinese. And of course, the translator they had promised was nowhere to be found. Without a clue as to what the finished products were supposed to look like, we had only the hope that our scenic company in Minnesota could help piece them together. So, we shipped the damaged props to Minnesota. They arrived four days before the event, and our scenic company was able to fix them—at a cost of $13,000. So much for China saving money.

The next shipping problem occurred three days before the event. We knew that the 400 elaborate costumes coming from Hong Kong could not be shipped directly to Minnesota, as the state's customs agency could not accommodate such a large shipment. We were pretty sure that Hong Kong knew this too. Well, apparently, they did not. Hong Kong shipped the costumes to Minnesota anyway, and, of course, they would not clear customs. All the performers were in town, ready for a dress rehearsal, only no costumes. We contacted the Mayor of Minneapolis and the Governor, and we still couldn't get clearance. So, the costumes were shipped to Los Angeles, where they cleared the next morning and arrived in Minnesota the day before the event.

Loading in the event presented its own series of logistical challenges, among them the fact that, since it was a public place, we could do load-in only between the hours of 9:30 p.m. and 7.a.m. Since it was a mall, there was no central loading area. Additionally, we had to load in everything from the underground catacombs. The catacombs were not only dark, but every corridor looked exactly the same and contained no signage to let us know under what part of the mall we were. So, we were constantly getting lost as we tried to find the four corners of the mall where the exhibits—two for Hong Kong and two for China—would be set up. Once inside the mall, we had to continually walk from one corner to the next for 16-18 hours a day.

Members of our production team walked an average of six to seven miles a day, which prompted us to hire a foot massager for the duration of the event! An electric foot massager because this was long before "foot messages" (with human beings) became so well-known.

Once the festival was set up, the Chinese entertainers presented another issue that needed to be handled delicately. They spoke no English, and, through no fault of their own, were completely unaware of American protocol. Littering was not a big deal to them, nor was changing their costumes in the middle of the mall during business hours! Representatives from the mall, of course, were perpetually horrified by their behavior and told us so on many an occasion. So, it became our responsibility to play "bad cop" to the Chinese entertainers. This had to be done delicately without offending them— not an easy task when you don't speak their language and they have no idea what you are trying to tell them. And unfortunately, there were never enough interpreters on hand. Between the mall and its rules and regulations and the Chinese and their customs, we had many different protocols to bear in mind at all times. There we were, right in the middle. It was an educational experience to say the least.

The Event

The festival itself began at the airport. In an effort to promote the event, we had decorated carts in the most traveled areas of the airport. The fully-staffed carts remained there for the duration of the festival. Strolling musicians and costumed characters were added on the concourse for even more impact.

With all of its challenges, the China Travel & Folklore Festival was a truly fantastic event. The opening night event, a black-tie benefit gala for more than 300 guests of the Metropolitan Public Airport Foundation, took place in the mall's rotunda in the heart of Camp Snoopy, the mall's amusement park. (Don't laugh! Oh, and did we mention that during set up someone fell out of the roller coaster at Camp Snoopy and died? That made for a festive set-up time.) Back to the dinner ... it began with a ceremony featuring dignitaries from Hong Kong, China and Minnesota. Dignitaries gathered at the rotunda on a beautifully contrived oval-shaped, all-white stage backed by a video wall showing a custom-created presentation of all the attractions of China. This played as guests were seated. Over the video wall, a massive 4,000-pound dragon head (created from carved foam) was suspended with a 40-foot banner declaring the theme of the festival that rose over the entire four-story elevator bank. The dragon, whose golden scaled tail fully encompassed the perimeter of the rotunda, was created to fulfill a marketing challenge. What would get the press there? The solution: The world's largest (and by the way, heaviest) dragon, head all of 4,000 pounds. Every promo piece talked about the Dragon, called Mou-Ling by our staff.

Once the ceremony began, it was a logistical challenge to determine the order of dignitaries. China first? Hong Kong first? Minneapolis dignitaries and officials? To solve the potential protocol dysfunction, they were paraded in together by costumed folk dancers from Beijing. After many speeches, all three entities joined together on stage to push a big button that was hooked into the dragon's mouth. When activated, the mouth appeared to open to spew forth flutter fetti "fire" onto the audience, all accompanied by dramatic music and lighting effects. This was followed by the traditional Chinese lion dance and the dotting of the eye (ceremonial blessing), signifying the beginning of the festival. The lion dancers paraded the guests into dinner in the interior of Camp Snoopy. Guests sat around "the fountain" (of which event planners' nightmares are created - Snoopy, Linus and a fountain that looked like it dribbled - but enough criticism. It had one glorious feature that more than made up for its ugliness - it was HUUUUUUGE).

But, wait! That was our next challenge! Since this fountain virtually blocked the view of almost every guest (imagine that it is the hole of the doughnut, and guests are seated in the body of the doughnut), how could they see the highlight of the gala, a fashion show? We solved this by building four mini-stages and sending out the models four at a time, one to each stage. We then choreographed their movements so they would rotate stages, enabling all of the guests to see them. When the first group of four exited, the next group of four entered. The fashion show featured the designs of exclusive Hong Kong designer, Blanc de Chine.

The fashion show continued throughout the 11-day festival, which began the next day. Chinese and Hong Kong vignettes were created in each of the mall's four corners. The rotunda was outfitted with kiosks for Hong Kong and China, as well. A main stage featured on-going daily entertainment, which included Chinese acrobats, martial arts demonstrations, singers and ballet and folk dancers. The area was punctuated by stands featuring various Chinese artisans and practitioners demonstrating such crafts and practices as Chinese painting, flour doll-making, grasshopper weaving, rainbow calligraphy, tai chi, Feng Shui, paper-folding and tea ceremonies. Celebrity Chinese chef Martin Yan appeared intermittently throughout the festival to do cooking demonstrations. Also, my team distributed brochures to all four courts, supplying them with posters as well as giveaways, and supervised the entertainment schedule, making sure the video was playing. We even worked to schedule what music the stores could play and when they could play it, since their in-house musak directly conflicted with the performances in the rotunda.

Describing the intricacy of the décor and the scheduling of the entertainment would fill a book. It filled seven 30-pound notebooks for us. Simply put, we created a Hong Kong/China experience. A miniaturized tram, a sized-down clock tower, the Great Wall, Hong Kong street scenes and Terra Cotta warriors were only some of what we displayed in the mall, along with giveaways and prizes, all packaged to entice the visitor to explore.

The event was a tremendous success. Hong Kong was happy. China was happy. And, hopefully, Americans were sufficiently "wowed" enough to travel to China one day. I am hopeful that those who were wowed attended the 2008 Beijing Olympics! As for us, we were happy too. We made history.

From shipping problems pre-event to language barriers and cultural differences during the event, not a day went by that did not require special handling on our part. The logistics involved learning all the aspects of a new culture. Though Hong Kong was an old client of ours, China was not. And we had no guidance, since it was a new situation for Hong Kong as well. Add to that the complexity of the enormity of the site (often taking 30 minutes to walk from one problem to the next all day long) and what it took to fill it for eleven days, the logistics were quite challenging at best. Additionally, we worked for six months long-distance with Hong Kong and China. Someone was always awake during normal sleep time …usually us. When a page with 46 numbers on the pager would go off in the middle of the night, we knew we had to call overseas—and right away. But we produced the largest public event ever held at the Mall of the Americas for a continuing repeat client. We paid attention to the clients' needs and respected their requirements and their way of doing business, even when it differed from our own and made the job all the more difficult. We become an extension of another entity, in this case, two foreign entities, in representing them to an American concern (the Mall) and to our country. We became a mini-United Nations and had to delicately handle these two cultures, keeping peace between them while producing the event. We had to act on their behalf as well as on behalf of the Mall at all times. We succeeded and created a history-making festival that brought three cultures together.

We were producers. We were politicians. We were interpreters. We were shrinks. Twenty-four hours a day. We're now ready to negotiate peace treaties in the Middle East!

The Lesson

We learned a lot about patience, and a lot more patience. Speaking slowly and carefully was key as communication was far different. Each word expressed a different meaning to a culture with which we were not too familiar. When dining at one of our many pre-event meetings, I ate things that I still can't identify (and may not want to) as my client looked on watchfully to see if I would eat them. The lesson is the client rules, so respect his needs and wishes and his mode of communication at all times. The key word here is respect. It may not be our way, but so what?

Whether on a business or personal level, respect is so important to me because I crave it. It goes hand-in-hand with recognition. I hoped that someday my mother would tell me she was proud of me. Oddly enough, I think she probably did respect me but just wouldn't say it. I want to get and give respect. I've come to realize that with the three male relationships in my life I loved intensely but respected not at all. How very critical that ultimately was to the relationships. It is so important to me that I have dispensed with all the relationships in my life where I don't have respect for the friend, lover, husband or business associate. Without respect you've got nothing.

8

Venturing Out Globally

Chubby Checker - A "Twist" on Working Internationally

A few of my stories are very old, but I'm trying to save YOU the trouble of learning things the hard way, as I had to do.

I had never before worked internationally when I was asked to book Chubby Checker and his band for a date in Cancun. I tried to think of all the things I needed to know and handle them. I was too young and stupid to realize how different it was to plan an event in an international destination with which I was unfamiliar. I thought that if I added airfare and hotel room that was going to do it. Mexico? How hard could it be? I learned quickly and painfully when I lost money because of that stupidity and lack of preparedness.

First on my list were visas. Didn't need any. Did the band have passports? They did. Work permits? I called the Mexican Consulate in Los Angeles and was told no, they didn't need them since they were an American band and would be paid IN the U.S. IN American dollars. I didn't believe them, so I called the Mexican Consulate in San Francisco and was told the same thing. I still didn't believe it, and since Chubby resides in Philadelphia, I had a friend of mine go to the consulate there. Same answer. Well, I figured that if three consulates told me the same thing, it must be true.

I arrived in Cancun a day earlier than the band, checked out their room, confirmed the pick up at the airport with our destination management company and went to the airport to meet Chubby and his band the next day. I waited, knowing that sometimes it takes time to get their luggage and equipment and clear immigration. I waited and waited some more. Hours later they still hadn't appeared. I was getting intermittent reports from our DMC who said they had been held up in customs. Finally, after a few hours (and imagining what a good mood they were in by this time), I asked if I could go back and speak to immigration and customs. I couldn't, but they sent out an officer.

The problem was … wait for it … that they had no work permits. A flurry of Spanish between various airport employees started flying around, and because I can understand Spanish fairly well, I knew I had a problem. I explained, through our bi-lingual DMC, my diligence and why I didn't have work permits. A book was brought out (in Spanish of course), and the official told me quite adamantly that it was "the law" that no one could enter to work without a work permit. He didn't care what anyone else had told me. This was THE LAW. Of course, it was in small print in a book I couldn't read, because it was all in technical terms.

Now what? I asked if I could pay for work permits right there and then as I had cash on me. If I had negotiated them in the U.S., they would have been less than $100 each. But now they were $250 each, and they needed them in cash or the band could not enter the country.

The band was upset. Can you blame them? And, it was now evening, and banks were closed. Unfortunately, the next day was a Mexican holiday, and banks were closed then, too.

After much negotiating (and trying not to cry), they agreed to let the band into the country as long as immigration held onto the passports. The band was now even unhappier. They were in a foreign country without passports if I agreed to this. And, the officials added, until I paid for work permits they could enter the country, but they would not be allowed to play.

So, passports were turned over; we drove to their hotel, and my next day was entirely spent in finding money. No banks open. The hotel didn't know me from Adam and couldn't help. I finally went to the client and explained what had happened. Fortunately, he gave me the cash. I drove back to the airport, paid, got the passports and returned to the hotel. I had called ahead to my production manager to tell him that the show could indeed go on.

By the time I arrived back at the venue, the show was over and everyone told me it had gone well. My first international show and I had missed it!

The Lesson

It's a lesson I'll keep repeating. Get it in writing. It might not have made a difference, but it could have. Prepare for the worst. Bring along extra money ... a lot of it ... especially when working out of the country. And wherever you go, get all the permits, no matter what anyone tells you.

Additionally, be completely well-versed in the customs and laws of the country being visited and be sure to put all the rules in writing and insist that musicians and entertainers adhere to them. A manifest of equipment (including laptop computers and miscellaneous instruments) and costumes is imperative. Talent as well as technicians need to be educated that this detail is crucial.

Some related advice — if you don't figure in VAT or local musicians' union fees, you could easily get caught with your drawers down, and this can be a loss of thousands of dollars you didn't account for in your budget.

One of the scarier aspects of doing business abroad is not having the security of working with vendors with which you are comfortable. Again, seeking the expertise of other professionals in the industry will save time and money. Ask friends or colleagues if they can recommend vendors in a particular area.

Finally, never forget, when you travel abroad, build in a substantial phone and fax and cyber café budget in order to correspond with the home office and clients.

9

Clarity of Communication

American Society of Travel Agents Gala
- Glasgow, Scotland

A Prologue to Andrea's Scottish Tale

In January of 1997, the day after The Special Event, I had won three Gala Awards and was I ever pumped up. I could do anything. I sashayed into a meeting with the Los Angeles Convention and Visitors Bureau (LACVB) filled with confidence, waiting to hear just what challenge the Bureau could throw my way. Little did I know.

In September of that year the Bureau wanted to host a dinner for 3,000 guests of the American Society of Travel Agents (ASTA). The meeting was to be held in Glasgow, Scotland, and the event would be in the brand new Scottish Exhibition Hall. "A piece of cake," I thought. "One convention center is like another convention center." Then they added the twist. The evening would end in a concert to be held in the new theatre, yet uncompleted, but promised to be ready in time. Was I interested?

Was I interested? I'd never been to Scotland, and my heart lives in the annals of English history since I'm a long-time devotee of Queen Elizabeth (the first), Mary Queen of Scots and all the romantic history of Elizabethan times. This job was the project of my dreams. (Side note: Be careful what you dream; dreams are known to come true.)

So as not to bore you with the in-between negotiations, I will skip to the part where I was awarded the business in conjunction with Avalon Entertainment Group (later to become TBA) that was selected to produce the show in the yet uncompleted theatre. "Well," I thought. "They have the hard part."

The Logistics

We planned a site inspection for March and flew to Glasgow. Did I mention that I don't sleep on planes and am easily jet lagged? Not that it's an important part of this event, but let me just describe my trip there. It's so typical of my adventurous travels! We flew to London and changed planes. Terminals at Heathrow are so far apart that you have to take a taxi between them. We did. Just as I was trying to exit the cab, it took off, while I had one foot in and one foot out! When I jumped clear of the screeching cab to save myself from amputation, I left behind my four-carat diamond bracelet purchased in Las Vegas on my memorable award-winning night. As you can imagine I was now NOT in a great mood.

We flew to Glasgow, and I had my first lesson about how Scots and Yanks don't speak the same language. "What?" "Huh?" "Could you say that again?" were my mainstays.

We arrived, checked in and immediately went to the Conference Center. The problems began as we sat in a room with the Center staff, the in-house caterer and the LACVB staff. The hall allocated for us, the only one large enough to accommodate 3,000, was going to be part of the tradeshow. Booths were in our space. No, they couldn't come out in time.

"Is there any other available space?" I inquired.

"No."

I asked the Bureau representatives to show me other possible space. The caterer, who was contracted to the Center and was seeing the revenue from 3,000 meals disappear, pouted.

Before we took a tour of Glasgow to see other space, we took a hard hat inspection of the theatre. Impossible to even visualize with only steel beams and lots of "We think this is where the stage is going to be" conversations. Oh, well, that was Avalon's problem. I now had one of my own.

For two days we did walking tours of potential venues, none of them able to accommodate more than 1,200. Since jet lag and sore feet dominated, I asked to be driven around. As we drove, I noticed a magnificent building in the distance. The Kelgingrove Museum. I asked to be taken there. Perfect! As soon as I walked in, I themed the event. We would do scenes from Hollywood movies like *Braveheart and Mary, Queen of Scots*. Clever? The curator was skeptical that it could hold more than 1,500. If I could show her that it would hold all 3,000 (no seating), would she allow it? The answer was "yes," and I was in heaven. Time to start planning. I took lots of photos.

Our visit at an end, we returned to the airport. Flight Adventure Number Two. As soon as the plane lifted off from Glasgow, the man sitting in the center seat next to me started screaming at the man in the window seat. He then started to choke him as the steward came by and said politely, "I say, chaps, is there a problem here?"

Is there a problem? My seatmates were trying to kill each other, and we had barely lifted off! Luckily, I was just tilting back as window person tried to stab center seat person with a pocket knife, which was aimed dangerously close to my face. And the screaming and cursing were deafening. (The issue was over who got the armrest, by the way.) At this point, my client from the Bureau and the producer from Avalon were telling me that we'd have to take separate planes in the future!

Adventures aside, once we returned, I designed. I rendered. I planned. I created. The curator put me in touch with the Museum's caterer, the City Catering firm that serves her majesty, Queen Elizabeth. Oh, boy ... my dreams were coming true. The caterer George Aitkin was wonderful. Gentlemanly, punctual, fair ... and I could understand him. I drafted budgets.

It sounds too good to be true, doesn't it? It was. A mandate came down. This had to be a sit-down dinner for 3,000, and we had to try to finesse it at the Convention Center. Now, to all of you who plan events, let me ask a question. What happens to you when a facility knows that you have no choices? Do they give you a break?

They did concede to giving us the space ... not with enough time to set up, but we had one area for one day, another area for eight hours and a final area for four hours. The prices they presented were twice the budget with which we had to work. The client didn't want to pay what they were asking. But they also didn't want to go to the Museum since there'd be no sit-down dinner possible.

In the months that followed, we did cost comparisons between Kelgingrove and the Center hoping to show that we had no alternative. Wasted work. A sit-down dinner it had to be.

They also didn't want to transfer people across the city to dinner and then bring them back to where they started for a show. Did I mention that by now Natalie Cole had been confirmed as the entertainer for the still uncompleted theatre? It was coming along, though. It had a roof!

More weeks passed, and I insisted on going back to look around yet again. This time there was no adventure. (Without an audience I guess there's no drama ... it seemed almost anti-climactic.) Previously we had stayed in the Moat House, next to the Center. This time I was in the same place, only in another room overlooking the Clyde River. Facing the Clyde, I looked across the River. A vacant piece of land. Hmmmm ... empty space. A canvas upon which I could paint?

I called the Bureau to see who owned the land and was given the name of the management company. I called. Everyone was "on holiday." I left my name and number in the U.S. I constructed a very convincing letter. I then started calling tenting companies, though in all truth it took me a while to find them, since they are not called tents; they are called "marquees." No one had, or had even heard of, a marquee big enough.

I called George Aitkin, who was proving to be heroic in responding to my many needs. No luck. No one knew of such a tent, sorry, marquee. I called event companies. No luck. I called a lighting company. No luck. I called the LACVB to tell them I had failed. My client announced that she had just received a brochure from an English company that had an interesting looking tent ... why didn't I call them while I was there? And I did. Success! They had a tent the size of a football field. It was bright blue, blocked out light, had a high ceiling, and it sounded like manna from heaven. Could I see it? No, sorry. It was packed up and wouldn't be used for a while. Were there pictures? On their way!

As soon as I returned to Los Angeles, Kayam (the tent/marquee company) called me. The marquee would be up for a festival in Galway, Ireland, in a couple of weeks. I had to go see it. I flew to London, then to Dublin and then took a train across Ireland to Galway. I slept for six hours, saw the tent/marquee (which was perfect) then took the train back to Dublin, flew to London and home. Is this what they call commuting?

Still no word on the land. I called George. May I now just refer to him as "George"? He's an integral part of everything that follows. He did some leg work and was able to contact the land management company. They were going to be building condos soon, but they thought they could lease us the land for a week if we needed it. We just had to fill out a few forms.

Those few forms turned out to be about 100 sheets of paper consisting of English legal terms I couldn't figure out ... did you see Charles Laughton in *Witness for the Prosecution*? I filled them out.

Now we get into the real challenges. Trying to analyze what this would cost.

Our dollar is their pound, and the exchange rate fluctuated every day. I tried to persuade all vendors to quote me in dollars, but they wouldn't. I tried to persuade the Bureau to be flexible, but they couldn't. What's that expression ... between a rock and a hard place? Why don't people understand the word "estimate?"

I returned once again, this time with my production manager and my technical director, Greg Christy of Brite Ideas. We set up appointments with the marquee people, various production companies, florists, designers, rental companies and anyone we could think of that would move this event forward. The theatre was coming along, but 45 days out, it did not look close to completion. I called Avalon and tried to sound hopeful, but, when he asked me if the seats were in, I had to tell him that the walls were not even all complete yet.

The budget was limited. We had to plan carefully.

So, let's recap. We have a piece of land larger than a football field. I'd tell you the number of feet, but I only know the number of meters. The land was slanted, rocky, ungraded and dilapidated. It was surrounded by barbed wire fence. There was only one point of access ... across a l o o o o o o n g bridge known as the Bells Bridge. No problem, unless it rained. And, as I discovered, it rained 360 days a year in Glasgow.

Never mind. More later. Let's talk about the marquee. If we could grade the land and if we could secure the tent and if we could find flooring and if we could get all the appropriate permits ... how could we brand "Los Angeles" when our entire budget was being blown on grading, permits, land use and marquee-ing, not to mention porta-potties, called mo-bile loos?

Greg Christy and I developed a perfect solution. The marquee would literally be filled with tables and chairs. Other space would be needed for upright lighting trusses serving as the poles to hold up the marquee. We decided to build a panorama of the entire city of Los Angeles in lights that was geographically correct. Let me be specific. On the south wall we started in Long Beach with the Queen Mary, traveled to Santa Monica Pier and Pacific Park, with palm trees and ocean waves in-between. Moving north we passed the hills of the San Fernando Valley with Universal Studios and Magic Mountain. Way behind all that, the Space Shuttle represented Edwards Air Force Base. Moving west, we passed Beverly Hills and Rodeo Drive, onto the Sunset Strip toward Hollywood, moving past the freeways of Los Angeles ranging from Mann's Chinese Theatre to the Capital Records Building and on toward the skyline of downtown Los Angeles, south on the east wall. Guests sitting in the middle of the marquee would be surrounded by Los Angeles and all of its most famous sights recreated in spectacularly innovative custom lighting gobos.

We interviewed everyone we could think of from production companies to flooring people to linen purveyors. What we found was that most people could not fathom what we were trying to achieve. When we asked about floor-length tablecloths, they all looked at us askance. I finally worked up the nerve to ask the caterer why no one had floor-length linen. His reply: "Why would you have a table linen that came to the floor? What would people do with their feet?"

The Plan

Finally, this was the plan. Guests would arrive by motor coach and walk across the Bells Bridge. From the bridge, a walkway with carpeted flooring would lead them to the main marquee. Here they'd enter an elegant dining environment where tables would be covered in black floor-length linen (and they'd just have to figure out what to do with their feet), black napkins and stunning red rose centerpieces. Chairs were red velvet (all brand new, promised the caterer). Around the walls the magnificent lighting gobos, and all over the tent, special lighting accented the beautiful blue. Background music only. No speeches. A fabulous dinner created by our special chef (seasonal salad with grilled shrimp and goat cheese croutons, Scottish beef with Scotch glaze and carved vegetables and sumptuous berry compote with mousse. Yum!) Then, our guests would exit the tent, and while crossing the Bells Bridge, be treated to a spectacular fireworks display. From there they would walk to the brand-spanking-new theatre (lovingly known as the Armadillo) to experience the magic of Natalie Cole and a few speeches, of course.

Challenges and Solutions for the Best Laid Plans

Another personal note: my production manager and I decided to go to London for a couple of days prior to arriving in Scotland. Remember ... castles! Our excuse was that we just had to pick up our linens in person.

First, he forgot his passport and had to call home to get his son (175 miles away) to drive it to the airport. It was literally "run" to him at the gate, and he got on the plane just as they were closing the doors.

Upon arrival, our taxi driver asked us, "Have you heard the news?" The news was that Princess Diana had died that morning. We were staying across the street from Kensington Palace. Castles were closed.

The uneventful train trip to Glasgow was beautiful, and then it was time for set-up.

We began to grade the land, cut holes in the barbed wire

(which we would have to replace) and get ready to drill holes for the marquee poles. And then, our first on-site problem greeted us. Beneath the red clay dirt laid the wreckage of an old shipyard... meters of cement that were virtually impenetrable. Glasgow is one of the shipbuilding capitals of the world, and the shoreline of the Clyde is almost solid cement. Special drills. Mission accomplished!

The crew laid the marquee out on the red clay and then, over the course of a few days, raised it to become its own magnificent structure. Looking at it from my hotel room, it was very blue and very clay red. At closer inspection, the inside was red clay and filthy. I told them to clean it. Blank stares. We ordered various forms of washing equipment, but the mud was so deeply ingrained that the inner tent was terminally dirty.

"GREG!!!!!!!!!!!!!!!!!" The entire lighting of the inner tent was redesigned to hide the dirt and make the inner tent look like clouds.

Next came the flooring, meters and meters of flooring. The floor did not fit the tent when it was set in place, so all the tent poles had to be moved to fit the floor, which was filthy. I asked George, the floor man, if he intended to clean it. Blank stare. I asked again.

"Ye only said you wanted a floor, mon," he replied. "Ye didna say ye wanted it clean."

So George was told to hire a floor sweeper, and we prayed that the dirt would be covered by tables.

"GREG!!!!!!!!!!!!!!!!!!!" The lighting was redesigned again to cover up the dirty floor by turning it lavender and blue.

The rentals, tables and chairs followed. Not all the chairs were new, but we let that pass. We soon discovered that there were many pits in the floor, as tables tilted dangerously. We found cork to fill the holes. George, the floor man, spent much time on his hands and knees.

The walkway marquee arrived. It was flimsy, made of skimpy wood and was yellow and white striped. I asked the tent man if he had an all white one. "No."

I then asked why he never told me that it was yellow and white striped (just gorgeous with bright blue), and he gave me a blank stare.

The client did a walk through. The president of the Bureau wanted us to cover the billboard in front. He also wanted us to cover the fence. There were no local materials which would take care of this. However, our logistics coordinator, with all his ingenuity, went across to the exhibit hall and, as they were dismantling the tradeshow, had them bring carpeting across the bridge to cover the fence. Hundreds of meters of fence. To connect it we needed zip strips also known as zip ties, but no one in Scotland had ever heard of them. Once we gave an in-depth description, it was decided that what we were looking for were "cables." We drove to a local hardware store, where they were sold by the piece as opposed to being sold in packages of 100 in the U.S.

We took the one piece of extra tent we had and covered the billboard. Then, back to the tent for a final walkthrough. The doors were still not completed and were being painted. None had knobs. We asked why. Blank stares.

"Ye didna ask for doorknobs, mon."

Bungee cords were installed to open the doors. Necessity is the mother of invention.

The Bridge. Ah yes, the bridge. Filled with graffiti. Salvador Coordinator to the rescue. We repainted the bridge. The city wouldn't do it. Then, the sound of a ship's horn, and we realized that we had overlooked one detail. If a ship had to pass under the bridge, it would have to be opened. Could this possibly take place when our guests arrived? A quick call to the Harbormaster and all of the river boats were informed that during a specified time there would be no travel on the Clyde. Except one. If one of the ships belonging to the Royal Family passed through, the bridge HAD to open. And just as all guests arrived, one of the Queen's yachts did as well. The bridge was opening as we scurried to get our arriving guests back onto shore.

All the kitchen equipment arrived. Then the centerpieces, which were placed on the sides of the tables. Funny, I could have sworn that the definition of "center" piece meant that it went in the center. Moving 300 centerpieces an hour before the event is exhausting, especially considering that every table was pinspotted. If we hadn't done so, we would have had a pinspot in the center and the centerpiece on the side! When I asked the florist why she did that, she replied, "We can always move the creamer and sugarer into the middle."

Did I mention days of gale force winds? Constant rain? The marquee did not blow over, and there were no leaks. So far so good. The night of the event, as buses pulled up, the rainstorm started. The umbrella brigade was ready. Just that day my client had purchased huge umbrellas and from the time guests disembarked the coaches until they reached the bridge overhang, they were under Hugo Boss umbrellas ... only the best for our ASTA guests.

Doors. All was ready. Hundreds of waiters stood by holding silver trays laden with glasses of champagne. And then ... quite unexpectedly ... one waiter decided to go crazy. Yep, crazy. He began to rave that the L.A. Bureau president was a political assassin who was trying to kill him. Security picked him up, and four guards (each holding a limb) carried him off thrashing and screaming. Then, the first waiter dropped his tray, and like dominoes, waiters behind him began to drop theirs. Our first arrivals were greeted by the tinkling sounds of hundreds of breaking glasses.

Our caterer and his staff scurried to clean up, and I resisted saying, "I'm not paying for the wine or the glasses." He looked pained.

Almost simultaneously, the roof sprang a leak. Right at the front entrance. We put a bucket directly in front of that entrance, but it was the first thing guests saw.

We had worked on the guarantee for days. ASTA had promised that no more than 2,200 would show up; 3,000 arrived. We were on the banks of the Clyde in a driving rainstorm; we have maxed out on tables and chairs (and there were no more onsite), so we walked several hundred guests back across the Bridge to the Moat House and fed them in the dining room.

Dinner was served, and it was splendid. Salad arrived with a police escort. Since it had to go slow through rush hour traffic and it was on tray stands, the caterer protected it with a sirened escort. Glasgow has a code on how long food can be pre-set on a table, so it had to arrive at almost the last minute.

Dinner completed, we were ready to cue the fireworks. The

rain had stopped. The theatre was lit wondrously. Guests began to emerge from the tent. As I'm ready to say "go," the safety inspector appeared and asked me to usher guests four at a time to one side of the bridge or the other. He explained that he was afraid the bridge would collapse if we didn't distribute the weight properly.

Finally, everyone crossed. The fireworks were spectacular. The concert was magnificent. The evening was a resounding success.

Then came the billing and VAT. But that's another story.

The Lesson

First, just because you and your crew in Scotland use English to communicate, don't assume you speak the same language. Don't presume that you can understand each other, either by what you are saying or by the accent in which you are hearing it. Everyone in Glasgow sounded like Scotty from *Star Trek* or Mike Myers caricaturing Scottish! Listening carefully was the key. Providing clear details was also important.

Would you think you'd have to ask for a floor to be clean or for doors to have knobs or for centerpieces to be placed in the middle of a table? Well, details matter, especially if you are collaborating with new people.

As I indicated earlier, clear communication became important to me because I was brought up in a multi-lingual house. My mother and stepfather Peter spoke German. My grandfather and mother spoke Croatian. As a result of listening to other languages, I learned that intonation makes a difference. I listen differently than I speak. Because of this, I can go to almost any country, even if English is the second language, speak slowly and give the correct emphasis, and it is understood and much appreciated.

And there's one more important lesson from this story. Never fly with me.

10
Truth and Trust

Chicago Event Spectacular

Extraordinary Events was hired by the George P. Johnson Company to produce an event spectacular at Chicago's Field Museum and adjoining Grant Park in October of 2001. Our goal was to create not only a memorable evening event but an important and effective marketing tool for the two end clients, Siebel Systems and Avaya. The theme of the night was *Innovation*, which had to be apparent in everything we did. These challenges took on greater meaning following the tragic events of September 11th because this project for 3,000 people was scheduled a mere three weeks after disaster struck the U.S. The biggest question of all became, "Will this event be cancelled?"

As our fellow event professionals were facing similar challenges and cancellations all over the globe, we felt helpless wondering what the fate of months of hard work would be. We began discussions with the clients almost immediately. At first we were at the mercy of the FAA, waiting for them to re-open the skies to air travel. The majority of our attendees (many international) would have to fly to the destination. Once we knew we "could" fly, the question became, "Would" we? We analyzed cancellation fees and estimated rescheduling fees on behalf of the clients. In the end, our clients made a brave and distinctly patriotic decision; the show would indeed go on. Now we just had to hope that the attendees would be as brave and still come. We watched the online registration daily for signs as it slowly sputtered and came to life. There were some nervous moments, but, by show date, any drop-off experienced in online registration was replaced onsite.

This level of support by both clients and guests created a unique atmosphere of prevailing patriotism and solidarity. Everyone present felt they had a purpose, and everyone was thankful to be there.

The Event

We were challenged to create a suitably elegant dinner experience in The Field Museum while encouraging networking and not being overly stuffy. We enhanced the already stunning central hall of the museum with theatrical lighting, accenting the architecture and paying particular attention to "Sue," the Tyrannosaurus Rex exhibit. We strategically projected gobos of the clients' logos on prominent wall positions to ensure proper branding.

Wolfgang Puck Catering created an appropriate menu that reflected innovation in presentation and recipes. Marble and granite slabs were used as platters for display while wait staff tray-passed hors d'oeuvres on beautiful textured "rock" serving trays. The Chinois Chicken Salad was served in miniature Oriental containers with chopsticks while the butternut squash soup (a special request from the client) was served in miniature soup ladles. We strongly felt that there had to be playful elements to the evening.

So far a lovely event ... but what made it truly special? What made it innovative? Let's start with the entrance. It is often said that the first impression is the most important. We wanted to make it BIG. Literally. Using a patented technology called "MAX," we projected giant moving images across the entire façade of the museum. Huge sunflowers, butterflies, trees, patriotic Stars and Stripes ... even cityscapes. Hundreds of feet wide and three-stories tall, this flowing visual was the first impression as buses pulled up. The façade of the museum was a breathtaking showstopper. Contrary to the usual "get in and get to the bar as fast as possible," guests stood outside to watch the panorama.

Two groups of musicians inside the museum played jazz-fusion. Based on the underlying theme, we invited local musicians to play traditional and non-traditional instruments in innovative ways. Downstairs next to Sue, unique instruments like the Chapman Stick and the Upright Electric Stick Bass, as well as an EWI (electric horn), were used by a five-piece technology ensemble.

However, that was just dinner music. The big entertainment of the night was yet to come. Towards the end of the delicious feast, a spectacle of costumed characters appeared to entice guests to follow them outside to the front of the museum. The costumes were based on the designs of Julie Taymor (of *Lion King* Broadway fame), who was currently exhibiting at the museum. Taking our cue from her wildly fantastic jungle creatures, our "King" and "Queen" of the Jungle paraded through the guests. A Shaman drumming atop the grand staircase announced their arrival. Accompanied by several "gazelles," the guests followed the talent and were reloaded onto coaches and transported a few blocks away to Grant Park.

Little did the guests know what planning and logistics had transpired to create the second half of their evening experience. A virtual city had to be created in the park to facilitate this two-hour concert. A 132-foot-by-344-foot ClearSpan tent was erected complete with flooring, staging, lighting, sound, video, décor and theatre-style seating.

Intelligent lighting that created a constantly changing design covered the outside of the tent. Colors and patterns continuously moved and danced across the canvas. Inside, a prehistoric rain forest (remember Sue?) was created using hundreds and hundreds of plants along the perimeter as well as hanging spheres of Spanish moss, curly willow and orchids. Intelligent lighting enhanced the entire effect. Ah, another lesson. Our plant man was almost (well, actually MORE than) parental in his feelings about his precious plants. He agonized at crew even looking at a tree or moving it without proper respect for every perfect leaf. Why is this important? Well, it affects timing when you have to handle hundreds of trees and plants as if they are fine china.

The stage itself was flanked by two large rear projection video screens that were planned to feature live footage of the concert and the audience during the night via a three-camera shoot as well as a jib which could capture shots from various angles. Previously this had only been used at very pricey rock concerts. The stage was dressed in foliage and vertical light towers to complete the funky jungle look. The sounds of the rainforest were heard until the concert began.

In the last days before the event, the clients decided to add a bit of patriotism to this night as a way of saying thank you to the guests who showed their support and bravery by attending. They wanted to play the live version of Simon and Garfunkel's *America* as an opening to the show. With visuals of the American flag waving on the video screens, vibrant panels of red, white and blue lighting washed the interior walls and ceiling as the film melded into images of America and its people. The overall effect brought the house to its feet with a standing ovation.

Then it was time for the B-52s, the headline act of the night, to take the stage and rock the "tent" playing all their hits and more. It was indeed a Love Shack!

Even the exit was patriotic as MAX created a thank you from Siebel to the guests over an image of the American flag on the back wall of the museum.

The event itself was a tremendous success, but not without some challenges ... read on.

Challenges and Solutions

Large events always create challenges. We knew by throwing in a prestigious museum, a public park and the City of Chicago that we were going to have a few extra challenges! We did.

Security. Security was a big concern, and it was our objective to get guests in and out safely while ensuring no party crashers. The client had zero tolerance for this, and we were instructed to take whatever steps necessary to make it absolute. We hired off-duty Chicago policemen who normally worked this beat, so they were intimately familiar with the surroundings. We hired more than we thought we needed, and then we hired more again. We had multiple pre-con meetings to discuss potential problems and to anticipate unforeseen issues. We had a vigilant force checking IDs at the entrance with security in the museum, at every exit, roaming the perimeter, in the tent, around the park and on horseback. When issues arose, and they did, we were ready.

Additionally Grant Park housed many homeless, and we didn't want them crashing the concert. So to prevent this, we created an area where they could hear everything and supplied them with food and beverage which kept everyone just where they belonged.

A few protestors arrived outside to stir up trouble and hand out their own propaganda. When they refused to leave peacefully and began to make a disturbance, our police officers made quick arrests and led off the perpetrators with minimal disruption to the evening.

Tight Time Frame. This museum was open to the general public until 5:00 p.m. the day of the event. Our guests began arriving at 6:45 p.m. This gave us exactly one hour and forty-five minutes to prepare for 3,000 guests. Quite a challenge! What did we do?

We began with negotiation. We negotiated with the venue to allow us access the night before to preset lighting and focus. We were also able to test all equipment for MAX the night prior, which was tremendously helpful. We started staging the caterers in the back exhibits and kitchens within the museum beginning at 2:00 p.m. the day of the event. These few changes were enough to make the difference and allow us to be ready for guest arrivals at 6:45 p.m.

Next we worked with the caterers and the lighting companies to ensure that we were able to make our visions a reality given the tight time frame. Everyone had the same goals, and we worked as a team to achieve them. Despite our best efforts at pre-planning, it was still a mad dash at 5:00 p.m. It was organized, well-managed and effective, but it was still a mad dash.

It was assisted greatly by the extensive production schedule (updated daily) that we created to ensure that everyone knew where they were supposed to be and what they were supposed to be doing during this time. Monthly, weekly and finally daily production meetings also contributed to the overall success of the event despite the challenges.

Now remember, while the mad dash was ensuing inside the museum, a second set-up was going on outside in Grant Park. And although our executive team oversaw both setups simultaneously, we treated them as separate entities providing full dedicated production support to each.

Grant Park. Our challenges with Grant Park were many and started early. In mid-July, we gathered for the first of several site inspections where full crews were in attendance. The last person to arrive that day was the city parks representative. As we all stood looking at the field and laying out the tent city on paper, the parks representative approached us and asked why we were all looking at "that" field. "Our" field was "over there" as she pointed to a hilly area with many trees about one-third the size we required. Due to a miscommunication in paperwork by the Parks Department, the wrong field had been secured. We did not panic. However, we were all aware that the deadline to file permits was upon us. The parks representative made the picture even bleaker by informing us of a series of city softball tournaments scheduled on the very field we thought we had booked during the dates we needed it. This is when it pays to have friends in high places. We immediately sent one of our local producers to the mayor's office. Over the years, she had become friendly with the office and, to make a long story short, we got the space we wanted. It took a few weeks of meetings with the Mayor, the city council and the police, but we got our space. By the end of August, we were ready to roll.

However, having a permit didn't mean that it was going to be easy. We had to ensure that we would return the field in the same condition we received it, or we would be responsible for damages. Realizing that we were erecting a tent the size of a football field complete with huge cranes, heavy trucks, forklifts and personnel lifts, we had to build a road. Not just any road, one that would handle a two-ton load. We created a road out of hundreds of feet of triple-layer plywood, and that was just so we could get started.

We built a chain link fence around the entire perimeter of our area to maintain safety. We brought in generators and work lights and crew restrooms. Security was on site 24-hours a day from the get-go. We built staff productions tents and brought in golf carts to maneuver around the site, and all that just so we could begin to build the main tent.

Power. By the day of the event, we were fairly confident. Everything was running according to schedule. We had had a few minor issues with power from the generators due to the very long cable runs, but our power company assured us they had worked out the kinks. In addition, we had insured ourselves by bringing in two dual-pack generators plus a separate generator, so we had a total of five generators just at the tent.

As guests began arriving at the tent and getting ready for the concert, one of the dual-pack generators failed taking video and audio out with it. The back-up generator quickly kicked in and just as quickly died. Due to fast work by our expert team, we thought we had solved the problem when the second dual-pack generator began to fail. This was unheard of.

There is always a chance that one might go down – that's why we had five (extra safe). But as our fourth began to go down, we had now lost video, audio and certain lighting with only five minutes to showtime. We needed to make some very quick decisions. We made a drastic one.

The generator that was powering the MAX technology in the front of the museum was identical to our dying ones at the tent. We made the call to quickly drive a crew of electricians over to it, disconnect it and drive it back to the tent. This was risky and stressful and time-consuming, but it was our only hope. Had it not been for our very professional and experienced team, this could have been a true nightmare. We were successful in the transition, and we started the concert only eighteen minutes late. Our team, however, only started breathing normally again an hour later.

The Lesson

First, never skimp on personnel. We had two experienced technical directors, and each of their teams had master electricians. While the generator people stood by scratching their heads, our team took over and rewired, re-cabled and solved our power issues. Additionally, our logistics and security teams (we hired an ex-Interpol security agent who was head of a unit of the Philadelphia Police Department and could react on a dime in any crisis) managed to cross highways and drive our generator to its new location in moments. Literally security stopped traffic and got the job done. (You had to have been there to see this in action.)

Then, there's honesty. I told the client what was happening minute-by-minute. But even more importantly is the trust I had in my team.

During our power issues, I asked our Technical Director, "Tell me the truth ... are we going to be able to fix this?"

Without hesitation, his answer was, "Yes."
I responded, "How long will it take?"
And he said, "We can do it within thirty minutes."

My trust in him allowed me to no longer visualize my professional life passing before my eyes! And this is what I reported to my client as I offered to open a bar in front of the tent and let everyone merrily drink until we were ready. Three thousand people drinking freely ... boggles the mind, but better than the alternative of an angry crowd, don't you think? The client was grateful not only for this consideration but also for being informed every step of the way. Honesty IS the best policy, but always have a solution in hand.

What Trust and Truth Mean To Me

Trust and truth are important to me in my business because they have been a part of my personal survival. I am able to take things in stride because I know that I can survive. As I mentioned earlier, when I was a baby my mother married and left me behind in Italy with my grandparents. Years later I came to the United States. I traveled by boat from Italy to New York with a total stranger, paid to watch over me. Then, from New York I flew to Los Angeles by myself. Another stranger awaited me at the gate. I soon learned that she was my mother. During my early years in the United States, I had to make do since my mother left me with other people much of the time. She had to work, and she worked long hours, far from home, in a city which at that time had no freeways. She took public transportation. We couldn't afford a car, and she at that time had not learned to drive. They didn't have driving lessons in a concentration camp. I had to fit in wherever I was, sometimes with strangers; so there was no other choice. Perhaps on some level I fear that I will get abandoned again; I don't know. But, I have always learned to cope. Part of coping has been surrounding myself with business associates I know I can trust.

And, if anything has influenced me, it is truth. Because I've been lied to so many times and in so many ways, nothing has become more important to me than honesty. In my heart I believe that truth and trust are the same thing. You will never truly again trust a person who has lied to you. Will you? White lies to serious disrespect have driven this home many, many times for me. Think about it.

Here's an example of a silly, white lie. When I met Mark, we got into a discussion about our birthdays. We were both Sagittarians, and he indicated that he was 32. I was 34 and somewhat embarrassed that I was two years older. When we opened a bank account together, I handled the details. While at the bank, the banker advised me that Mark's date of birth on the application and his actual Drivers License birth date were inconsistent. I called Mark and told him that his license date of birth was wrong! At that point, he admitted that he was actually two days older than me. Is any lie harmless? I don't think so because there is no reason for it. In order to create trust, you have to be truthful. If you can't tell the truth about something small, how can you ever be capable of handling it when it is even more important?

A more serious example: A woman who worked with me in my business looked me in the eye and explained that she was quitting because she wanted to leave the event industry and venture into a totally different career. The next day, she was my competitor. She had accepted a position as a top executive with a competitor and opened up their special event division using EE clients as her base. Again, that goes back to respect. If you respect someone, you are honest with them. If you respect yourself, you are honest.

A hurtful example: My mother has five version of who my father actually was. The first time she told me about him, he was a Yugoslav partisan. The second time, he was an Italian guard at the camp. Then it was her friend's boyfriend, and she just wanted to prove she could steal him away from her friend. There have been more versions since. She even lied to me about how she met my stepfather Peter. I was told she met him through a mutual friend, and then a friend let it slip they met through an ad in the newspaper! Again, not necessary.

The bottom line to all this is in order to feel confident in your career and in life, build a solid network of associates and friends that have a proven track record of honesty and that you can trust. And make sure that they know that they can always trust you equally.

11

Dealing with the Inexperienced Without Disempowering Them

Abu Dhabi

While attending GIBTM, a trade show and executive conference in Abu Dhabi in the United Arab Emirates, I was asked to do a site inspection for the Super Bowl of Rotax Go Carts (they claimed to be as big as NASCAR internationally) in nearby Al Ain.

I was escorted by limo about two hours out of Abu Dhabi into the desert where we saw some great museums and palaces and even the racing camel market and finally arrived at ... well, more desert with just a temporary trailer-type of building. I knocked on the door. No one answered, so I called the cell number I was given. No answer. We drove around looking for anything or anyone other than sand. Nothing. So, we drove back to the building. Finally, in the distance, I could see a Porsche racing toward me. In a flurry of dust, it came to a stop right where I was standing. And out of it, a young man. Gorgeous. Looked like the dictionary definition of a race car driver - tight jeans, tight t-shirt, glistening smile.

We shook hands. I mentally drooled a lot. We entered the "building." I began to ask about the event. Where was it going to be? He waved at the sand. How are you going to be ready in a few months? He shrugged. What would you like to accomplish for this event, and how can we help you?

"Just fill in what I don't have here and make this an event comparable to a Super Bowl ... exciting ... fabulous."

Music to my ears. But I've heard those words before. What's the budget?

"There are no limits."

Uh-huh. Heard those words before, too. So, a million dollars would be okay?

I revived him.

I asked for an example of what he thought was a wow. He started with lasers, but told me that there were hundreds of laser companies nearby, so there was no need for me to look for those. Hundreds? I told him that anytime anyone I knew had worked in his part of the world that lasers had been brought in from the U.S. or Europe. And then I realized what he meant and knew that he had no idea what he was talking about. But I couldn't resist asking, "Where are you finding all these hundreds of companies?"

And he told me, "In the phone book."

I replied, "Show me, please," very politely, of course.

He opened up the directory (aka phone book) and showed me. I said quietly, without cracking a smile, "You're looking under laser surgery." Then I immediately started talking about what other things we could do in which he might be interested.

The Lesson

It's impolite to disable people and not take them seriously, especially if they are inexperienced. It's particularly important not to embarrass or make them feel uncomfortable. It's up to us to educate kindly, just do our jobs and not laugh uproariously at some of the things we hear!

And, this doesn't just apply to the inexperienced. It's good policy no matter with whom you are dealing. During the 1988 Special Event in Los Angeles at the Bonaventure Hotel, Peter George, the hotel's Director of Catering, was serving as the event team committee chair. He called a meeting at the hotel, and everyone involved in the convention attended. I made a suggestion. Instead of taking it under consideration, he reamed me, dressed me up one side and down the other in front of all my peers. We all sat in stunned silence. (And anyone who knows me knows I am never at a loss for words. Some people are always thinking "Oh, I wish I had been quick enough to answer" but I NEVER have THAT problem. I always know exactly what I want to say.) At first, all I wanted to do was produce the perfect comeback to embarrass him in front of all. My second thought was to yell "F**K YOU!" but that would have been unprofessional, so I smiled like a lady and carried on as part of the committee. Afterward, everyone said they didn't know how I sat through it but confessed they saw each of us for who we truly were. Years later and everyone still remembers that interchange and how I handled it. So, no matter what you want to say to a client or an associate, you will always win if you bite your tongue and behave like a professional.

Another approach, particularly if you are in conflict with someone who is ranting and raving, is what I call the board game analogy. If you are playing a game with someone and pick up your pieces and walk away, they can't play anymore. Game over. That's my philosophy. Walking away disempowers that person. Use it only when you must.

12

A Man for Humanity

Walter Payton

I don't know much about sports ... other than figure skating. So when it was suggested I book a local athlete for a corporate hospitality event in Chicago, I didn't have a clue who the names on the potential list were. I booked Walter Payton of the Chicago Bears not knowing who he was, what position he played or really anything at all about him. Yet, meeting him turned out to be a pivotal business and personal revelation for me.

Walter showed up early for his call time for our event, dressed beautifully in a designer suit and immaculate in every way. He was extremely polite to me and my staff, charming to my client and gracious to all the guests (almost all male) who fawned all over him. He posed endlessly for photographs, signed autographs and chatted amiably the entire while.

When the event was over, he thanked all of us, shook hands with all the service staff on the floor and then exited through the kitchen so he could spend some time with the kitchen employees, just talking.

I followed him because I assumed he would need his car (thinking we had hired a limo) and stood by and just observed. He took the time to sincerely talk to everyone from cook to busboy to dishwasher.

Just as he appeared ready to leave, I approached him and asked about the car only to learn that he had driven himself to the venue. By now I knew he was not just a key celebrity, but a legend, and a much admired personality. Instead of hurrying away, he asked me where I was from, and we started talking, really talking. I am a far better listener than talker, so I began asking him about his life, his family and his world of sports. He glowed when he talked about his family. I told him how enthralled I was by his behavior, especially toward the workers, and he unabashedly told me that those were the people that mattered the most to him. We talked for a long time.

I was now a football fan.

Years later as I followed Walter's career, I learned that he had inoperable cancer and was dying. Shortly after hearing of his illness, I hired him for another show needing a sports celebrity that best represented Chicago.

Walter showed up, a shadow of his former self, but still as engaging and personable and so very attractive. He lit up when he saw me and called out a greeting saying, "Stick around, Andrea; we'll catch up later." I could not believe that he remembered me.

After the event, we sat together for quite a long time and talked. I'm not one for small talk, so I asked very directly how his family that he loved so much was dealing with his cancer. He was candid and sincere and openly talked about his illness, thanking me for not beating around the bush and avoiding the subject.

I again learned something.

The Lesson

Walter Payton taught me the depth of a true gentleman. He epitomized grace, graciousness, sincerity, courtesy and candor. He had great respect for all humanity, no matter the person's station in life. And in that I found a new role model.

When Walter succumbed to cancer, I mourned his loss. The dignity and sincerity with which he conducted his life is something that will never leave me. He was one of the greatest human beings of whom this world and my business in particular have given me the opportunity to experience.

The love he felt for his family and humanity is one for which I would have wished for myself. I feel that no man has ever truly loved me, and certainly not in the way Walter loved his wife. His love for her made me understand something about myself. Even though I lay down and took the abuse from the men in my life, I truly allowed myself to become the product of those looking for a victim. Why? Because I didn't feel worthy of anything better. Had someone with the grace and respect of a Walter Payton come into my personal life, I might have become a more completed human being sooner.

13

A Headliner (Among Other Things) Lost

Ford 2000, Nevis

When my client called about this event, my first question was, "Where's Nevis?" It was a new destination, and no one knew much about it. It had a Four Seasons Hotel on the island, no airport and no services, as we in the meetings and event businesses define services.

So here's how the story unfolded. A contact of mine from a large incentive travel company called me to provide a headliner for a meeting they were planning for the new CEO of Ford Motor Company in Nevis in the West Indies (as I later found out). I, of course, asked if my client needed anything else but was told that she only wanted a bid on a headliner from me. We sent her a list to consider.

We planned a site visit with the entire team who would be working on this, me to figure out where a stage would go for the headliner we would hire.

Just before our planned site survey, my client off-handedly asked me if I happened to know of any yachts in the area of Nevis, because the CEO wanted to host all 300 of his guests on board one for a sit-down dinner cruise around the island. Apparently all of her resources had dried up, and they had run out of options to meet this VIP's special request. No wonder. Try to imagine how much space it takes ON A YACHT to have a sit down dinner for 300.

Always an opportunist (and yes I think that's a positive thing), I said, "If I can find you a yacht, can I have the rest of the program?"

"IF you can find the yacht," my contact said, "yes, you can." And I heard in the subtext, "but you'll never be able to do it."

In addition to being an opportunist, I have never been able to resist a challenge. I'm a very competitive sort, even if I'm competing against myself! The gauntlet had been thrown.

In order to secure costs for getting my headliner to Nevis, I was working with a lovely lady from St. Kitts (where's St. Kitts?). So I asked her if she knew of any yachts, and she started sending me some information on possibilities. None seemed big enough or grand enough for this program.

A site inspection was scheduled to look at the hotel for all the other elements of the meeting, and happily my gal in St. Kitts called and said, "You're in luck; just when you're here a yacht from the Mediterranean will be nearby, and the captain said you're welcome to come take a look at it." I called my client to share this news (everyone was still skeptical). When we arrived in Nevis, the Ford representative and I took a small plane over to an adjoining island where we boarded *The Leander,* a ship that belonged to a former admiral of the British Navy.

Skepticism disappeared in the air as we looked down on the most magnificent yacht imaginable.

After boarding the ship and speaking with the captain, we learned that *The Leander* would be ending its season just at the time of our Ford 2000 meeting. Its crew would be delighted to bring the ship from Antibes to Nevis if we wanted them. How charmed could I be? The ship was a 246-footer with three decks and was the most amazing work of art and technology I'd ever seen. It had every toy on it I'd ever even imagined, from helicopter pad to various jet skis to windsurfers, wave runners and an assortment of smaller boats. It was so clean that it glistened, and the 25-person crew looked like the dictionary definition of British butlers ... all perfect ... all handsome ... all gracious. The captain was even more divine.

With pictures of the royal family and the Admiral all over the ship, fully-equipped sauna and gym and priceless antiques everywhere, what client could resist?

And the rest of the program was mine! And here's where the challenges began.

Challenges and Some Solutions

Remember that I said there was no airport? We had to fly into St. Kitts, and then barges from the Four Seasons would pick us up at the dock in St. Kitts and barge us directly to the hotel via a lot of Caribbean water. So our crew (equipment had been shipped weeks before) flew in and waited for a barge. Oops. The barges were all broken down, so we had to fly two-by-two to Nevis's postage stamp landing pad. We were so close over the water that we could almost reach down and touch the surf! Getting the entire crew over there in this manner was time-consuming.

One of my fondest memories was shared by Rob Hulsmeyer, our project manager, who told us of arriving at the front door of the customs office as a goat walked out the back door. The look on his face was priceless. Or the drive in from the airport with Rob where monkeys sat in groups on the road like packs of dogs. I never knew a human being could make so many jokes about a location or an animal! And just wait … the best is yet to come.

Now (because I was the heroine du jour), I was the only one who was allowed to stay at The Four Seasons, so the rest of the team was at a mini-plantation up in the hills next to the One-Hole Golf Course. Yes, a one-hole golf course where the owner cooked goat stew for dinner … and lunch … and breakfast.

We reconnoitered the next morning to look over things. We were planning on the major events taking place in a tent and had hired a local team as budget dictated that we could not bring too many people with us. Get the container and get started.

Okay, everyone's here so let's go get the container and get started WHERE'S THE CONTAINER? No one knew. We did know it had been delivered, but no one knew exactly where. This didn't make any sense since the island was tiny. Not being able to work that day since we had no container, we sent the crew home and told them to come back the next morning. One day behind before we even started.

We finally located the container on the other side of the island and sent a truck with a forklift to pick it up. The truck had a flat tire, and of course, there were no tire stores on the island. We sent to St. Kitts for a tire. The barges were up and running again, but it took a full day to get the tire, so we sent the crew home. Two days behind before we even started.

So, picture this next: The tire was on the truck. The container was on the truck. A fork lift arrived to get the container off the truck. The fork lift driver put the fork lift into reverse and backed it with the container into a ditch. We needed more heavy equipment to get it out, and, of course, there was no heavy equipment on the island. We found "island labor" to get it out and sent the crew home. Three days behind.

Then there was the HUGE generator which still had to arrive. It did, strapped onto the deck of a small boat with its operator from Miami. Unfortunately, he wasn't the primary. He was the last guy on the company's totem pole and couldn't figure out how to make the generator work most of the time.

This became an issue for our first night's event. Most of our lighting consisted of illuminating the many palm trees around the hotel's pool area. When it came time to power up, the operator threw the switch, and all 60 lights started exploding like flash bulbs. He had mis-wired the generator and blew all the lamps. And here we were on an island with no local options. "GREG!!!!!!!!!!!!!!!!!" With his expertise and his assistant's, our technical director rewired in time for the event to show off beautifully, but to say it was without cause for concern would be an understatement. A good lesson in why staff should never be released until the event is over.

The next day with everything operational, no crew. They didn't believe us anymore. We got them back, but when they arrived and went into the tent, they made a hasty exit and said they couldn't work. Why? During the night a donkey had died on the golf course next to the tent, and they considered it a bad omen. Plus, the hotel couldn't figure out how to remove the donkey without damaging the grass. The donkey stayed in place right until showtime.

Now remember, because of budget we had to hire local labor, and since we were assured that they were competent electricians, we agreed. However, we quickly learned that they were indeed electricians, but the kind that normally wired up houses and had no clue about our complicated lighting, sound, etc. So, our supervisory crew went on serious overtime to compensate, because we were stuck with them. Well, not quite; on the first day the crew chief said to Technical Director Greg Christy, "It's lunch time, mon, so I'm going to get a Guinness with my boys. We'll be bock." We never saw them again.

Mosquitoes were also a challenge. Now I'm so allergic to them that if bitten I go right to the hospital for intravenous cortisone. So Greg's Brite Ideas team bought electronic mosquito repellents. We were all eaten alive, so we came to assume that they acted as mosquito attracters.

And the stories just go on and on! *The Leander* evening was on the second night of the program. It had been made clear during many conference calls with the client and the ship's captain that the ship had to stay on the other side of the island until just before the event so that this magnificent yacht would be a total surprise to the guests. On the second morning of the event, I heard people walking by my room on their way to an early golf date. "What the hell is the *Queen Mary* doing out there?" were their exact words. Sure enough, there right outside the hotel was *The Leander*. Why, you may ask? The captain thought it would be nice to invite some VIPs out for afternoon tea.

All afternoon the tenders took people back and forth. So much for the surprise. Yet all went wonderfully well, and guests were bedazzled by *The Leander*, the captain and the crew. The former Admiral even gave each and every guest a sterling silver coaster with his personal monogram engraved into it. Added to that, since it was the end of their season, all the wine still on board (a ship's wine cellar ... imagine that!) became our bonus. It was all estate wines from France and Italy and much appreciated by our wine connoisseurs.

Then there was our headliner. Remember, that's where this all started. Al Jarreau was our choice. He traveled with 17 people in his entourage and landed at S. Kitts, just like everyone else, the night before our show. We sent the barges to pick everyone up while guests were partying on *The Leander*. I awaited the barge. Hmmm … I didn't see Al. But then a lot of the musicians were wearing hats. I counted heads - 17. Missing one. Who? Of course … Al. WHERE WAS HE? No one knew. But he sure wasn't on the barge. I traveled back to St. Kitts only to find Al wandering along the beach because the barge had left without him!

Departure? Another intriguing memory. On the barge back to St. Kitts, guess what? Yep, it stalled in the middle of the ocean. I was rescued by a boat passing by that was nice enough to take me and my extensive heavy luggage to the dock at St. Kitts. I checked in at the airport, and a scrawny little woman started shaking beads at me and screaming that I was the devil. She warned if they didn't want the plane to crash they shouldn't allow me on it. I boarded, and my last vision of St. Kitts was upon take off with this woman standing on the runway shaking her beads (and her fist) at me and screaming something that I'm glad I couldn't hear.

The Lesson

We had a lot of challenges on this one, but the client never knew about the difficulties, which is a lesson in and of itself. We will always inform the client of the challenge and our proposed solution if we feel the job or the timeline is jeopardized. However, if we know there are problems, but we can solve them in an effective and timely manner, we just do it. It's also important to point out that, had we not arrived days ahead of schedule, we never could have accomplished what we ultimately did because of the challenges placed in our path.

In total, the event was a huge success. People were awed by *The Leander* and didn't care if it was parked outside the hotel (in the water of course) since their curiosity was peaked. They didn't know they'd be on it that evening and figured it belonged to a Shah or Sheik at the very least. Our crew loved it because I tendered them all out to it, and they got a custom tour before any of the guests arrived. As for Al, he was found and delivered a great show for the guests in a tent without a donkey in or near it. Not knowing any of the obstacles, the client was thrilled with everything, though later I shared some of the stories. Since then, "donkey" jokes have been ever-present in our relationship.

The big lesson here is: Shit happens. Take it in stride. When I look back over my life, I had a lot of practice. Meeting a mother I didn't know; the abandonment I felt; the uncertainty of her marriage and remarriages; the volatility associated with her relationships and being thrown into a community where I didn't fit in taught me to take it as it comes.

And, finally, remember, in the tropics, carry bug spray and wear long sleeves, long pants and socks. And don't forget to bring Benadryl.

14

Disaster Management

Disco Inferno or How I Almost Burned Down Palm Springs

A few years back a fellow event planner invited me to become involved with an event held in the Palm Springs desert where her client wanted to have a fireworks show after a country western night. All elements had been planned, but they still needed fireworks. The client was a New Yorker; at the time my associate resided in Florida and I was relatively local.

The client asked me for a short and impactful show, and I hired a local and very reputable pyrotechnics company.

A few days before the show, the client indicated that he had seen something he wanted to hire: a bi-plane that had pyro on its wings. He thought this would be very cool to add. I had never heard of such a thing and said that unless I knew more about the company, the plane and their insurance that I could not take responsibility. The client insisted. So, I said he could hire this plane on his own but that I needed to coordinate it to make sure that all was going to go smoothly. That meant I needed to coordinate the plane with our pyro company, too.

When I contacted the plane's owner, I was told how great

and how safe the act was. Nothing specific was detailed, except, "Don't worry," which meant to me that I should worry. I let my client know that I didn't trust this addition and advised against it. I was pooh-poohed.

Let me describe the venue - a ranch surrounded on three sides by mountains of brush and only a one-lane road to get in and out. The center or eye of the keyhole was where the party took place.

To be on the safe side, I ordered two water trucks to be in the keyhole and on standby. My client didn't want to pay for this as he felt it was unnecessary.

All went well through dinner and during the entertainment. For the finale, we got our pyro team in place and called the cue for the plane to start flying. We saw it take off, and standing next to him, I heard my pyro chief take a deep breath and start muttering, "Go higher; go higher!" Then he took off at a flat-out run to the water trucks as pyro started spitting off the wings of the plane directly onto the brush. The hills on all three sides exploded into flame.

The water trucks took off, and my associate radioed the buses and started herding a panic-stricken audience of executives toward them. Immediately, I grabbed some blankets, and my entire team and I started beating down flames.

Fortunately, we got all the guests out and ultimately watered and beat down the flames. I lost my eyebrows, charred my face and hands and ruined my outfit, but at least no one was hurt.

Of course, during the time I was on the mountain playing fireman, my client was standing next to me screaming hysterically, "This is your entire fault!" Or best yet, "I'm not going to pay for this!" I chose not to respond as he stood there doing nothing but watching me.

Indeed, when I sent him our bill, he refused to pay it because our pyro had never been set off. It was a minimal charge, and I chose not to fight it even though I knew I had been wronged. And, yes, I paid our pyro provider in full. And, no, the bi-plane had no insurance.

The Lesson

When you know something is wrong, stick to your guns and don't give in. I should have refused to have anything to do with this job as it flaunted good sense and safety, and nothing good ever comes from that! But, I don't like to disappoint anyone. Why? Perhaps I'm still afraid people won't like me. You see, I'm still that fat, little wallflower inside, even though every trip I take I come home with at least one enduring friend. So, I need to work on this lesson with you.

15

Together We Build the Future

CEMEX Conference - Cancun, Mexico

A multiple-day conference held in Cancun for 300 top world-wide executives of CEMEX, a leading global producer of quality cement and ready-mix products based in Mexico, provided Extraordinary Events and me with a myriad of challenges, all of which resulted in innovative solutions that left lasting impressions in more ways than one. Given CEMEX's acquisition of RMC, an international ready-mix U.K.-based company, the main objective placed before me was to unite the two newly-joined organizations into one, through team-building, education, problem-solving and networking. My company and I took this objective, embodied in the overall theme of the October 2005 conference, *Together We Build the Future*, and artfully wove it throughout all aspects of the three-day, three-night event. With a significant amount of cultural diversity becoming a new reality within the company, this integration was quickly overcome by forcing the two groups to work hand-in-hand together for a viscerally heartfelt international cause. The conference theme became a call to action for my company and me.

Overview of Conference Events

Welcome Night. We set the tone of the conference at the welcome night, literally, with a performance by Mass Ensemble. This innovative group entertained the mostly all-male audience with alternative instruments such as a harp created from giant cables that, for this event, were strung from the ground to a fourth-floor anchor on one of the hotel's balconies. Performing from the middle of the hotel's pool, the musicians wore gloves to protect their hands as they "played" the harp with their entire bodies to elicit beautiful, ethereal sounds. Other instruments such as water drums and unique guitars were added to the ensemble. After dinner, guests were invited to experiment with these inventive instruments and were encouraged to interact with each other while doing so.

The dinner was seaside and planned to be a "bienvenidos a Mexico" with subdued spandex linens, classic local blooms creating elegant centerpieces, lovely lighting to create a moonlit ambience and a menu that combined classic Cancun cuisine with an international flavor. Even the way VIP guests found their pre-designated seats was creative. Beautiful models held up signs with key messaging words that identified corporate objectives. Each invitation had a different word, and guests found their seats by matching the word on their invitation to the area in which the model stood holding her sign with that same word.

Education. A top objective of the conference was to produce a high-level educational program that addressed real concerns of CEMEX offices worldwide. To do so, EE and I turned the entire educational experience into a team-building activity ... something that as far as we knew had never been done before by anyone, and certainly not by CEMEX. The client requested that the sessions "tell a business story." Instead of a series of disparate and unconnected speeches about specific subjects, we created an overall theme to the conference with one cohesive message to be delivered. The message or business story was to make the company into a cohesive unit with a global vision, embracing cultural differences and strategies that created one vision and ultimately unity. By building on this message, each speaker had a "chapter," all headed toward a mutual ending of "the story" and a sense of completion.

First, CEMEX leaders had hand-picked "teams" of executives to bring people together who might not otherwise meet. They would go through all sessions in these teams. At the end of each session, the teams were asked to relate each seminar's content to a question or issue that might be going on at their office or plant. This information would be used at the final session.

Putting together a roster of top-level business speakers from around the world to tell a whole story was another challenge. EE culled a list of leading business speakers carefully. Then, we went one extra step and gave them business issues that CEMEX was currently addressing or experiencing and asked them to custom tailor each speech based on this information. This took time and effort, but in the end, it resulted in presentations that had meaning for the executives. Additionally, each speaker had to attend the sessions of all other speakers in order to ensure continuity. In this way it became one cohesive "story." To me, this was completely innovative. It wasn't loose and disconnected but inspired by organization. When you have structure, it makes the possibility of free thinking even easier.

Topics included the global economy, competing for the future, organizational change, flawless execution and cultural diversity. Speakers were heavy-hitters -- authors, experts, consultants and professors from MIT, Harvard, the London School of Business and today's top international corporations.

The last session was formatted as a think tank for the teams. A professional facilitator asked each team to talk through the issues, challenges and thoughts brought up by the sessions and create a mini "white paper" to present to the group so each team could discuss the challenges and solutions of the others and benefit from the results.

As the final chapter to this "business story," we set up a question-and-answer session between the top executives of CEMEX (including its CEO) and the conference attendees.

The open discussion once again reflected the commitment of CEMEX to working together to build the future.

Team Building. Another major objective during the conference was to show the executives in a hands-on way how the products they manufacture and sell are installed and what impact they have on the real world. We needed to introduce the human element that so defines the CEMEX culture ... that of working with and giving back to the community. Additionally, it needed to provide a grass-roots understanding of the conference's theme *Together We Build the Future*.

To meet the overall objective of integration, EE and I set a bold, innovative goal – to create a truly powerful, unifying team-building experience for CEMEX by literally building a future for 600 children and their community in Leona Vicario, thereby forever changing the lives of all involved.

Working three months prior to the conference, EE and CEMEX began the transformation of a local Mayan elementary school in heartbreaking condition. The renovation culminated with the 300 executives working side-by-side in teams to complete construction on the poverty-stricken school while learning more about the CEMEX culture. For many, it was the first time they saw CEMEX products in action. The connection between the product and the difference it can make in the world was rock-solid. At the end, we had helped them build the foundation of a sustainable corporate future, and, more importantly, had helped build a future for a community and its children. This resulted in the most memorable moments for all attendees during the program.

This activity was much too significant (and close to my heart) to include as only part of a chapter. Therefore, the details of this team-building activity follow in Chapter 16.

Gala Night. Again, this event, prepared and executed with moments of hysterically funny situations, was too much of a logistical feat to just be a part of this chapter. But it provided tremendous networking opportunities, both planned and unplanned, for its participants. Look for details in Chapter 17.

Activities. One of the biggest challenges was that of Cancun itself. There was practically nothing that guests could do in the way of activities or venues that was acceptable to CEMEX's exacting requirements. CEMEX wanted to do "once in a lifetime" experiences which were not the typical activities one could sign up for with a tourist tour desk or concierge. Through research, EE discovered several unique, exciting activities well off the beaten path and exclusively available to this group. With a packed conference with little free time, we found ways to move 300 people to remote locations in the shortest time possible and give them even more opportunities to explore and relax together. The destinations included:

Hiking in Chikin Ha, an ecological Mayan reserve area. Attendees could swim, explore the jungle or take a simple nature hike accompanied by a guide who discussed the significance of the area to the ancient Mayans.

Exploring Isla Contoy, the best-kept secret of Cancun. At this bird sanctuary on an island sustained 99 percent by solar power, attendees received special tours and talks by the island's biologists on the ecosystems and the significance of wildlife in Mayan culture. This was the first time such a tour had been allowed.

Snorkeling in Punta Nizuc. An oceanographer led the group and discussed how the Mayans used the ocean to develop their culture and fuel their economy.

Learning about Mexican art. Attendees could learn more about Mexico's art from an expert art historian who discussed its influence on Mexico's politics and national culture using examples from famous contemporary Mexican artists.

Final Night. At the final night event, designed to promote camaraderie and celebration, EE brought in the tastes of Mexico with Chef Federico Lopez from Taller Gourmet and Gourmands y Gourmets in Mexico City. The event was held at Glazz, one of Cancun's most popular and classiest nightclubs. Lopez is one of Mexico's hottest chefs. At each buffet his selections were prepared before the guests and then fully plated on small dishes in a variety of shapes. Thus the food also became the entertainment. Again, the all-male audience was on EE's mind as it created tequila tasting bars to complement the interactive food presentations. A variety of interesting floral arrangements were set amongst lounge furniture groupings.

Revolving entertainment created by Luma, Theatre of Light, was placed throughout the space on platforms at varying heights to subliminally engage the audience but not distract from conversations between the now well-bonded group.

The Memento. Because CEMEX and its CEO are committed to the arts, EE devised a unique alternative to a traditional take-home gift, a hand-bound book featuring an artist's real-time renderings of every activity.

Onsite, using charcoal or water colors, artist Carol Wood created beautiful images of events, meetings and activities as the guests were actually experiencing them. Papers and materials were carefully selected to achieve the elegant look of a true coffee-table book. At the end of each day, these artworks were taken to the printer to be duplicated. On the final night, EE's team spent a sleepless night hand-binding each book in hard covers so that even the earliest of risers received one of these original books, hand-signed and numbered by the artist.

The book was a symbol for everything EE wanted to achieve. Like the program itself, the artwork took an idea to the next level, celebrated the human element and was highly personal as well as innovative.

This chapter has set the stage for the logistical challenges that EE faced during this conference to follow, but, from the conference framework itself, I took away value …

The Lesson

All of this might seem a little dry, but it's important to remember oftentimes in situations such as these that you need to be extremely creative just to make it creative at all. In this case, it was a stretch to work creativity into the business sessions and to make them the ultimate team-building experience. And, the value I took away? By helping another business achieve its goals, I, in turn, achieved many of mine.

From a professional standpoint, the education and format that was developed gave me inspiration as well as a true learning experience. I was allowed to create experiences in ways that other clients had never allowed. CEMEX truly embraced experimentation with a typical meeting format allowing me to create a team-building experience out of educational components as well as to create a social responsibility program that was magical to me as an event planner when I watched it unfold. Being respected and involved in every step made me feel valued and added value to my life and experience.

From a personal perspective, my goals flow back to my personal life. Years ago, when Jon's father Bob finally left me, he took all the money out of our accounts, leaving me with nothing. It was a horrendous time for me, so I flew to Hawaii for a week to stay with a high school chum to get away from the grief. While I was gone, Bob sold our house on a 30-day escrow, and when I returned I had two weeks to get out. So, I had a garage sale, doing all the work, and he came and took all the money from me. And, I let him! I had so desperately wanted to go back to school but was suddenly unable to do so. Then an angel intervened. My girlfriend Melba simply gave me the money as a gift. I never forgot it.

When Ron Rubin and I ended our professional partnership, I got nothing. Once again there was intervention. Mike and Julie Loshin of Parties Plus and Mike Stern from Regal Rents started sending me business. Sandy Porter from Maritz Travel gave me a Super Bowl job and sent the entire payment in advance! Andrea Bell gave me office equipment. I will never, ever forget those things. They asked for nothing and just offered their unconditional support. This industry gave me a life, and even with its minute challenges, has brought me friendship, respect and a way for me to give back. People want to know why I am so generous with my time in helping to educate others with seminars and workshops. When asked why, I simply reply, "That's what I'm supposed to do." And, it's what I'm supposed to do because it is my way of giving back – of paying it forward, just as others have done for me.

16
Creating a Legacy

CEMEX Team-Building Activity in Leona Vicario, Mexico

I've thought a lot about the true meaning of social responsibility and how it applied to re-building a school in Leona Vicario outside of Cancun to create the CEMEX team-building event. It was an event that succeeded so well that lives were changed forever. I want to believe that changing lives is something for which we all strive, and so I encourage all readers to copy, steal, modify ... but do it. Let me tell you what we did, why we did it and how.

After much looking around Cancun, we found Leona Vicario's school, about 45 minutes outside of the main town. The school was in heartbreaking condition when we first saw it. After weeks of site inspections at the school, meetings with contractors and suppliers of building products and internal CEMEX personnel, we began three months of hard work prior to the conference. The objective was to start to turn the school into a place of pride for the children and their town.

At first the requirements to start this project seemed insurmountable, since everything had to be accomplished while school was in session. For every item completed, 10 more appeared. The job required 36 truckloads of cement, 122 gallons of paint and 700 yards of grass sod not to mention plumbing, electrical, landscape, mortar and a variety of other elements. Our first major obstacle was the fact that, as with many small communities and their leaders, the school was very proud and the administration slow to respond to the offer of charity, worried that it would acknowledge they needed help. Discussions were handled with respect for the administration's concerns, and it was finally determined that the community and school leaders would take part in, and take credit for, arranging the event. Once this was agreed, we were able to move forward, now with the local police (for crowd control and safety) and the school's grounds managers fully on board.

It quickly became clear that not only was additional building necessary but the existing rooms and facilities also needed to be upgraded to accommodate the number of children attending the school. For 90 days prior to the conference, CEMEX and its partners did everything. Contractors poured cement, restructured plumbing, installed electrical, refurbished bathrooms, rebuilt the school cafeteria and began to construct a small library.

We immediately began by clearing the school grounds of trash, dismantling a dilapidated structure and then grading tons of dirt to accommodate a proposed new building and playground. As with most remodeling, it was easier to start from scratch rather than add to an existing substandard substructure. Because of this, when remodeling and adding multiple boys' and girls' toilets and stalls, all existing plumbing feeder-pipes needed to be ripped out and replaced, as well as electrical sub panels to accommodate the additional donated computer stations and Internet connections.

Because the school had no trash disposal service or facilities, all trash and waste had been burned in the play yard and behind the cafeteria. As a result, rats and vermin were attracted to the areas where the children ate and played. To resolve this challenge, CEMEX and EE built two enclosed areas to store new trash cans that CEMEX donated.

Access to the school for construction was another challenge. Because the town was very small and not built to any standard city codes, many of the electrical poles and power lines were mounted to large posts and, in some cases, large tree branches buried into the ground. This made access for our cement trucks and large buses used to transport the multiple CEMEX executives impossible.

To make access possible, we raised all power lines of the surrounding city block and all lines leading up to the school site from the main access road. Needless to say, this was not a simple task.

It was also very hard to judge how many supplies would be needed. The solution was having plenty of runners onsite. The overall productivity during the re-building was better than anticipated, and our runners had to sprint out for more plants, more paint … all in a town where none of those things existed. Ah, the beauty of cell phones. Call Cancun and rush those things back!

Another issue was making the project relevant to the executives at the conference. This was the first time CEMEX had ever initiated such a complex, lengthy community service activity. In order to understand what they would have to accomplish, the CEMEX executives needed to see the "before" pictures of the school. Because there were three months between the initiation of the construction and when executives would actually see and become part of its completion, a documentary film was created every step of the way, both for archival purposes and also to be shown at the conference. The objective was to bring attendees up to speed while tapping into their emotions. If they saw where the process started, and also where it ended, they would know what they achieved. Interviews with the town mayor as well as the school officials were ongoing as construction progressed.

As you all ready know, the work we began was completed by the 300 executives during our event. Now don't think that means 300 executives did a tiny bit of hammering and called it a day. They worked their butts off. Let me give you a glimpse of their day.

After a morning of intense business sessions, the executives were shown the documentary video taken of the school over those past 90 days. The first shots showed the school before CEMEX took hold. The horrible conditions of the classrooms, the kitchen and the playgrounds and the lack of athletic equipment, books and proper kitchen facilities were all visible. Then the video commemorated the activities leading up to this day with CEMEX trucks and contractors visibly laying the groundwork for it.

At the end of this presentation the executives were more than ready to pitch in. They were assigned to their team (electrical, landscaping, plumbing, carpentry, mortar, etc., all based on their defined skill set, a combination of EE's careful investigation and forms we had them complete). In teams they boarded buses to the school.

During the trip to the school, several planned activities were implemented. All were designed to create a spirit of "team." First they were given detailed printed instructions as to exactly what they had to do once onsite. They were told what equipment they would have and the task they would have to accomplish. Then they were told more about the school.

One man asked, "Couldn't you find a school that was closer?"

The guide's response set the tone. Here's the conversation...

Guide: "Who would send his child to a school without toilets?" (No hands went up.)

"Who would send his child to a school with rats running through his food?" (No hands went up.)

"Who would send his child to a school that had no playground, no desks, no library and no books?" (Again, no hands went up.)

Guide: "So, who would rather stay close to Cancun and paint a blue classroom yellow? Or would you rather ride an hour and change the lives of hundreds of children forever?"

The group started cheering and applauding.

As part of this special day, we had an additional challenge ... Mexico is known for its kidnappings, and we had 300 valued international executives from one of Mexico's largest companies in one rural location, surrounded by miles of jungle. We needed to make sure that the event was protected and that the executives felt secure in the midst of a highly-publicized crime area. After preliminary site surveys of the school and community with CEMEX's security detail, we positioned 11 security guards around the entire block of the school grounds during the event. Local police partnered with us to secure the event. On the day of the event, we received a police escort to the school, closed the streets upon executives' arrival and posted guards at the entrances and in the streets around the school. Nowadays, logistics and security are synonymous.

Once at the site, each of the 35 group leaders took their teams to preset tables holding all the tools, supplies and safety equipment they would need. Each team was then joined by one of the school's students and a parent. Together they painted, laid sod, planted flowers and trees, poured concrete, applied stucco, plumbed, finished electrical work and constructed the walls and roof of a new library, the first the school had ever enjoyed. To make the connection between CEMEX and the school rock-solid, CEMEX products were used. The sight of so many active CEMEX cement trucks was awesome to many of the executives who rarely had the opportunity to see their products in action, much less personally put to use in the field.

One final innovation was suggested by EE and quickly adopted by CEMEX. We asked each and every executive to bring a favorite book from his childhood to share with the children on the day of the event and then leave behind as the first contribution to the new library they had built that afternoon.

In a touching display, each CEMEX executive did share his own special childhood book with a student from Leona Vicario. These books, inscribed in more than 38 languages, were the very beginning of the new library. The emotional connection as grown men sat with small children on their laps telling them why this particular book had been so special was palpable. One man brought a book in Polish that he had translated by hand into Spanish. Another had done hand drawings of Black Beauty with an inscription to the children.

An official dedication ceremony ended the event, consisting of a speech by the Vice President of CEMEX, "Thank Yous" by school representatives and the parents of the students and a song performed by the children for the CEMEX executives. Additionally, gifts were exchanged between the school, the community and the executives.

At the end of the day, the executives had figuratively and literally influenced, if not entirely changed, the lives and education of more than 600 children and families as they experienced first-hand the core business of CEMEX. It was a lesson in the importance of their product. Plus, they had learned a valuable team-building lesson as they worked with one another across cultural and language barriers to achieve a common goal, one that was lofty and inspiring and immensely satisfying, while changing the lives of an entire community.

The Lesson

Community service events are not out of the norm but usually consist of a bit of hammering and perhaps some superficial painting. This project was entirely different.

From its inception to its execution to the lasting effect it left on all participants, this event was a powerful experiential manifestation of the message that the client wished to send. Not only did the community service activity serve as a team-building lesson, it also gave attendees first-hand knowledge of the company's product and illustrated its corporate culture to newcomers joining the company as a result of the recent acquisition. It also did something not every team-building activity does — it created a legacy for CEMEX.

The school's new buildings, library and grounds will be used for generations of children to come. The books that the executives left will be read by the children and grandchildren of those kids enjoying them today. And, best of all, the event launched a series of future events like it that CEMEX and EE will produce throughout the world.

Can an event's success be measured in emotion? Return on emotion might be a measurement for the future. We know that ROT (return on time) is now highly prioritized. I watched as 300 tired executives, hands filthy, splattered with paint and cement, sweaty and grimy, smiling, crying and laughing shared stories of what each of them did and what a difference it made. Carefully manicured fingernails were history; blisters were sources of pride. This was a true team of happy people who had bonded for a cause, one much bigger than themselves.

Without exception, every executive was engaged with the other executives and with the children. Because of their product, a world had changed. Together, they really did build the future, and, together my team and I did too. *Taking on projects that make a difference in the world is close to my heart, as it should be to us all. If each of us can leave even small legacies to others, we can change the world.*

For me, this started when I was at UCLA and started working with the mentally-challenged in half-way houses to get them back into society with jobs. There was no pay, but it was so enriching. Your behavior with other people makes a difference, and I'd rather make that difference in the world than have fame and fortune.

17

You Can't Stop a Hurricane!

CEMEX Gala at Zama Beach Club, Isla Mujeres, Mexico

The setting? A pristine stretch of beach on an island near Cancun miles from anywhere. The charge? Create Wonderland. Extraordinary Events transformed the beach into an event space that could accommodate a gourmet four-course dinner, a show by a major headliner and a fireworks display ... on the eve of an impending hurricane. Every single item had to be barged to the island. The caterer? One of Mexico's finest restaurateurs, who had never before catered an off-premise event of this size and complexity. The result? Wonderland.

CEMEX's "gala" evening, part of its multi-day event described in Chapter 15, had to be a wow. The previous "gala" had been staged in Barcelona's Palau de la Musica, a centuries old opulent and gilded opera house. CEMEX's gauntlet was thrown down as soon as Cancun was selected. "Create an event to rival Palau!"

Yeah, sure. Tacky theme parks. Spring break-style nightclubs. A huge pirate ship. These were the event venues available to us! Nothing like an opulent theatre existed in Cancun, so defining this resort destination became the solution. It was water and white sand, the most beautiful in the world. EE decided to make the most of it and secured the Zama Beach Club, a private and barren stretch of beach on the island of Isla Mujeres, a 30-minute boat ride from Cancun. Why? If it doesn't exist ... create it! *And if you build it, they will come!* We built it; they came.

And, we built it from the ground up, literally. There was nothing there. NOTHING. Nada. And that was the beauty as well as the curse. Every single item had to be barged onto the island, and barges did not run on any kind of regular schedule. There was no power. There were no toilets. There was no kitchen. Did I mention that there was nothing there? Well, to be totally fair, there was a palapa. And a pool. But swimming was not on the agenda.

We began by hiring our stars. We wooed and won world-renowned chef, Patricia Quintana. International talent was required as the male audience came from 38 different countries, so we hired Seal who has a dominant international presence.

With a crackerjack team in place (all of whom learned to dodge iguanas as they swatted the hordes of mosquitoes) and months and months of site inspections and intensive planning, <u>this</u> was the final result.

The Event

Three hundred CEMEX executives were bussed to a dock where a private ferry transported them to Zama. Read on, and then close your eyes. Imagine that as you head toward Zama you begin to see a bit of lighting in the distance, and, as you get closer, it becomes more prominent, now glowing in lavenders, mysterious blues and raspberries. The glow becomes more and more intense the closer you get. Suddenly like a mirage, the glory of the image becomes so vivid that your breath is stolen away. Where nothing formerly existed, there's a blazing wonderland with a surfeit of intelligent lighting creating movement and augmented with literally hundreds of custom-created pillar candles, and it's all been set there for you for this one night only.

The hundreds of "ahs" from our guests were music to my ears!

Disembarking, guests walked down the candlelit dock and crossed a glossy black wooden deck built on the sand to serve as the dining area. The gloss of the deck reflected more lighting. Their first destination was a giant palapa where cocktails were served and hors d'oeuvres were tray-passed.

Then guests were on to the newly constructed deck for dinner where the tables were dressed with floor-length sea green linens patterned with shimmery embroidery and anchored with fishing weights so they wouldn't blow in the wind. Centerpieces combined one of Seal's biggest hits (*The Kiss from the Rose*) with the lure of the ocean … glass bowls filled with shells and topped with a variety of perfect roses. Subliminal and effective. The entire area for cocktails and dinner was not only theatrically lit but also surrounded by pillar candles.

It was our objective to create opportunities for CEMEX executives to network. As at other events for this group, EE arranged seating which had the participants carefully selected so that they were dining with other executives with whom they had not previously been seated. Not an easy task, but ultimately accomplished.

Dinner was exquisite. Known in the food world for her ability to create menus that reach back into Mexico's history yet pave a way for its culinary future, Patricia Quintana was challenged to give attendees a true flavor of Mexico without offending their palates.

Quintana chose dishes from the Yucatan so the food would be relevant to the guests' experience. Using the freshest, seasonal ingredients, she selected Yucatan dishes that highlighted spices that were more flavorful than hot, herbs that were unconventional yet inoffensive and presentations that were interesting yet not threatening. During cocktails, her menu featured local delicacies from the sea paired with a variety of indigenous spices and chilies. At dinner, she served duck wrapped in Mayan banana leaves, a difficult dish to prepare off-site. It was done to perfection and served with her very unique tamales. Dessert offered a trio of traditional puddings. Everything focused on Mayan spices and ingredients. The result? A menu that was unique, innovative, beautiful and presentational, all prepared by a chef that is a Mexican legend and internationally recognized as one of the greats.

After Quintana's fabulous dinner, it was time for the main event, "the show." Even though EE had already faced many challenges, such as equipment shortages, missed deliveries and inexperienced local staff, the element of nature added another. Hurricane Wilma had begun to form off the coast several days before and was predicted to hit the day of this island event. Dark clouds loomed all day, and they finally did break open during the event, right as coffee was being poured. But more about that later.

The important point is that everything ended well. Seal was a tremendous hit, and an amazing fireworks show exploded over Zama for the evening finale. Once again, the Gruccis (remember … they did The Beijing Olympics) came through.

The guests were able to comfortably cruise back to Cancun on calm seas under clear skies, never knowing that all they had seen never existed prior to this event. Remember the gauntlet? Cruising back, the chief executive client smiled and said, "Fabulous! You did it! What will you do next time?"

Seems like it came together without a hitch except for the rain, right? No way! This event was filled with challenges galore!

Challenges and Solutions

Extraordinary Events transformed a remote private beach, with nothing around it for miles, into a true outdoor event extravaganza. All equipment and personnel had to be trucked from the Mainland either by barge (trucks) or ferry (staff and crew), as resources were limited or non-existent. When I say ALL, I mean literally every element of the event not limited to but including lighting, audio, video, staging, decking, tables, chairs, food, kitchen rentals, flatware, glassware, china, silverware, refrigeration truck, generator and florals. And, it was impossible to reserve space on the barge for the equipment trucks; it was a first-come, first-serve basis only, not a great situation when faced with a tight schedule.

So you STILL ask what challenges arose?? Here are a few that come to mind …

The client had selected world-renowned chef Patricia Quintana to cater the event. She is one of the favorite chefs of the CEMEX

CEO, a gourmand and wine collector. (You get the picture; the food and beverage had to be nothing less than spectacular.) The chef has written many books and owns a number of restaurants, including the primo restaurant in Cancun. She is known for her cutting-edge cuisine. However, other than culinary inventiveness, fame and an incredible personality, Quintana and her staff had never before catered an off-premise event this large and never one on a remote island on a deserted beach. Her experience was restaurant food service and management, which is quite different when it comes to menu creation, food preparations, organizing and ordering supplies and staffing. That meant that rentals, kitchen equipment and preparation techniques were a mystery to her assigned staff.

Now take a moment and realize that the venue was 45 minutes to an hour from the Chef's restaurant kitchen, and this venue had no kitchen facility or anything resembling one. To break it down simply, we were working with a first-time special event caterer on a stretch of beach with some sand and grass! We could not risk anything going wrong, especially not the food.

EE solved the problem by bringing in as a consultant, Joann Roth-Oseary, owner and CEO of Someone's In the Kitchen, a top U.S. catering firm. Roth-Oseary would combine her logistical skills with her ability to instruct and would teach them how to do it.

Once she joined the team, Roth-Oseary was sent to Cancun and Isla Mujeres to assess the true capabilities of the chef and her staff with regard to supplies, off-premise food prep and what, if any, of the china, glassware, flatware, etc. that was used in the restaurant could be used for the event. Rentals, staff and a plan would be ordered based on her findings.

From the beginning, before arriving on-site, Roth-Oseary encountered obstacles from the chef and her staff. For starters, they spoke only Spanish, and Roth-Oseary does not. When Roth-Oseary asked in advance for a list of all equipment, a plan for loading the trucks and a production schedule, what she received was in Spanish, and once translated, it had more omissions than inclusions. And then, add a bit of resistance to being educated in how to do "it." Both EE and Roth-Oseary worked hard to point out the greatest advantage to the consultancy. When done, Quintana and staff would have a blueprint on how to accomplish such events in the future. But, they initially seemed to think that Roth-Oseary was overly anal and did not want to be bothered with all of "the details" because they knew what they were doing.

In her first face-to-face meeting, Roth-Oseary diplomatically began firing away questions about supplies, kitchen set-up, guest tables, china and flatware. When she asked about table sizes, placesettings and how many guests were going to be seated per table, it was evident that nothing had been well thought out. For instance, the tables they owned, and always used, were too small and would not fit the china and glassware that the menu required. The kitchen area that had to be constructed was quite a distance from the guest seating area. This meant that if, for example, shot glasses were going to be placed on a charger, they had to be affixed to it in some way. When asked what they were using, the chef's lead person just stared blankly.

Due to the kitchen situation, Roth-Oseary suggested that most of the food prep be done at the restaurant and transported via refrigeration trucks. One would think that a food service organization would either own one or two of these trucks or at least have rented one, but this was not the case. After five minutes into this initial meeting with Roth-Oseary, they understood her role.

Almost everything from the guest tables and chairs, kitchen equipment, banquet tables, flatware, china and glassware had to be ordered. Step one was to break down the menu and gain insight as to how things were going to be prepared and served. Once that was done, supplies were ordered. Step two involved syncing vendor deliveries with the barge schedule. Now keep in mind that we were not the only ones using the barge and space was limited, and there was a charge for each round-trip barge transport. In addition to the actual food, kitchen equipment, table settings and staffing, Roth-Oseary spent time working with the chef and her staff to order tenting, food prep tables and create entry and exits to this make-shift kitchen.

Day one of load-in involved installing the kitchen tents. The kitchen equipment arrived two days later and posed myriad challenges. Although Roth-Oseary had ordered what she understood to be catering equipment, what arrived was intended for use in a permanent kitchen. Electric boxes and plate holders weighed thousands of pounds! With no wheels, they immediately sank into the grassy area they had to cross to get to the field kitchen. This called for a feat of engineering better known to the *ancient Egyptians* who had to haul heavy objects across sand! A board of plywood inserted under the equipment *with each step* allowed the heavy load to be moved slowly but surely to its place of rest.

And remember that pesky barge that only operated intermittently? Now imagine getting flooring, rentals, kitchen equipment and trucks laden with thousands of pounds on them to this area. Many boats. Many challenges. Many round trips, with the second leg of the last one occurring while the harbormaster closed the seas because of Hurricane Wilma.

In addition, Quintana's staff, unaware that catering is all about pre-planning, was reluctant to set up the day before the event. After much discussion, Roth-Oseary got them to show up, which they did, fours hours late. Luckily, she had taken care of other details while waiting for them and had created an exact diagram of where tables and chairs were to be placed while she was back at the hotel taking care of another challenge. The linens that had been ordered with pockets for weights to keep them anchored in the wind were wrong. There was no time to get new linens, so Roth-Oseary had to find weights that would fit (not an easy task). Upon her return, she discovered that her diagram had been reconfigured into something that would not work if the catered event was going to be successful. Much to the chagrin of the staff, every table and chair was moved once again.

Finally on event day, the remaining equipment, along with the florist and the guest table centerpieces, arrived. Of course, at that moment the winds picked up higher than usual, and the linens threatened to float away. Both the catering and on-site EE staff spent time affixing the fishing weights to the custom-made linens. No spandex for CEMEX! We needed to sew the weights into pockets built into the linen to weight them down against the breezes. Finding the right weight was a bit of a challenge on our breezy remote island.

Once the weights were on the linens, the staff then placed them on the tables and began to set them. From the moment the army of catering staff set foot on the Isla Mujeres, they were put to work per a very detailed plan written in two languages.

And now I'll give you a giggle and a bit of creativity. The beach was overrun with giant iguanas, and as interesting as they can be in broad daylight, running over your feet at a dinner like this could be disconcerting. So we carefully planned to rid the area of them by researching their favorite foods and planting them (literally) away from the area where the guests would be.

But meanwhile back at the airport ... Upon arrival, Seal and his band made it through the customs and immigration check points; however, problems arose for his technical team. Evidentially, we were using a permit form that was so new that the Cancun immigration department didn't know it existed. Obtaining permits anywhere is always a long arduous process, and Cancun is no exception. Add to that the lack of communication between the customs and immigration offices at the airport and downtown Cancun, and it's a whole different ballgame. For months prior to the event, our local EE production assistant played by the rules and followed the "steps" to secure permits for Seal and his group, yet hours before showtime the star's technical team was still sitting in the Cancun airport with no sign of movement imminent.

When the EE team was alerted, its producers spent several hours on the phone with the office in the United States and with the Mexican government and airport officials to resend and verify documentation as needed. Imagine explaining to your client that his expensive act couldn't appear because of some minor technical dispute at the airport! It took time. It took finesse. It took patience and professionalism. Because EE followed the rules to secure the permits, as well as invested time in developing relationships with the customs and immigration agents, the technical team was finally cleared and allowed to enter Cancun.

Back to the beach. The month of October is the beginning of hurricane season, and we were in mid-month. The weather was constantly monitored, and we were fairly confident that we would not encounter rain on event night. Even if the hurricane hit the day of the event, there would be no way to get all the equipment off in time, and there were no other suitable locations for the event. And although staff had been trying to wrangle one for days, no tents were available. In talking it over with the client, EE decided to soldier through. Although hurricane warnings were issued as the event was being loaded in, we had made it through three days without a drop of rain or high winds. We attributed that to the production team's prayers to the Mayan Rain Gods that took place each night before leaving the venue and our fork ceremony! There's a superstition in Cancun that in order to avert rain you stick forks in the sand. EE commandeered hundreds of forks, and the entire staff, by now numbering in the hundreds, ceremonially stuck forks into Zama Beach. (We bought out Cancun's fork supplies ... true story.) Did it work? Not quite. Our guests were seated al fresco at an amazing dinner. The setting was magical and the meal amazing. The skies were clear beneath the stars. What a night! Then, five minutes after dessert was served, the client looked up at the sky and said, "I see a cloud." The team laughed, and suddenly the sky opened up and the torrential downpour began!

Before dinner, guests had enjoyed cocktails under a palapa on the second deck that had been closed during the meal, but as the rain started falling, Roth-Oseary yelled to the bartenders to open the palapa and the bars again. Because there had been so much pre-planning, the entire staff sprang into action, handing out 300 rain ponchos (bless forethought) in under three minutes and directing guests under the large palapa and other covered areas. Drinks were immediately tray-passed. The team was ready for anything, and covered, dry and with drinks in hand, the guests were not discomforted. Whew! Once again, the value of hiring the best professionals money can buy proved a wise decision.

Do you think we were safe? No, of course you don't. Soon after the guests were out of the rain, the generators went out and all power was lost. *Drowned.* Though it seemed like an eternity, in about 20 minutes the power was restored. During the power loss, the rain stopped and all available event staff used whatever they could to dry off the 300 chairs so that guests could sit down and enjoy the show. Another team drained the stage's roof of all water and tested the stage gear to make sure all was operational and dry. By announcing updates every few minutes, guests were reassured that all was well and the show would indeed go on. And it did.

Both Seal and EE received several ovations, and an amazing fireworks show concluded the evening.

Some Uninvited Guests

As a sidebar, I must tell you about the inclusion of some unexpected guests. Next to Zama was a private residence that had been rented by a couple to celebrate their wedding, and they became quite a problem for us, especially our technical team. Here's what happened as retold by Technical Director Greg Christy:

"The beach club in which we were working had private residences on either side of the event site. Early during the load-in, we received a visit by a bride's father who had rented one of the properties next door for his daughter's wedding. He saw our huge setup and expressed concern over the outdoor beach wedding. He mentioned that his group had some flexibility in their timing, and we advised him the best times to work around our event. He happily left, only to return the next day to let us know that his daughter REALLY wanted her ceremony on the same day as our event. Again, we tried to accommodate him by outlining some times during the day when we thought it would be fairly quiet for them. Once again, he left happy, and we thought the problem was solved. But, again, he returned to tell us that his flexibility apparently had vanished, and his daughter had to have the ceremony exactly at the time of Seal's sound check. Still not wanting to ruin someone's wedding, I took the dilemma to Seal's tour manager, and we created a 30 minute window in the Artist's schedule for the wedding to occur. Again, we thought – problem solved – win, win for everyone.

"We are now on a hair trigger schedule, with no time to spare with losing the 30 minutes of quiet time. I am monitoring my watch minute-by-minute, waiting to see the bridal party. Five minutes late, ten minutes late – no sign of them. I run over to the house and confront the father, who tells me: 'Well, you know, brides are always late' ... by this time, I've lost my patience.

"'Look, I've got a rock star to keep happy, and a very important event to stage – I've bent over backwards, and you are about to lose your window.'

"I headed back over to the sound desk. Just as the 30-minute window was closing, and the tour manager was ready to crank up the sound system, the father rushes over and tells me they are ready! I have a decision to make. Knowing that I have done everything I could to not ruin this couple's most important day of their lives, I give the okay to begin the sound check. A beautiful wedding ceremony on the beach begins, amid the ear splitting sounds of guitars tuning, drums pounding and 'check one, two – check, check!'

"I noticed a flurry of unhappy people in the wedding party, but I turn my attention to the sound check and move on with my day.

"A couple of hours later, and after the bridal party has had quite a time celebrating the nuptials, the groom spots me on the beach and starts running directly toward me, screaming, 'You ruined my wedding, you bastard; I'm going to kill you!' I grab my radio and call for security, as the groomsmen tackle him to the sand.

"I then reinforce the perimeter with a security team and continue preparing for the event. Then, about an hour before guest arrival, loud rap music begins emanating from the wedding party property. The bridal party had taken their stereo speakers, pointed them out their windows and turned them up to the point of blowing them out. I received a message saying: 'You ruined our event, so we plan to ruin yours.'

"Now, I am a very calm person, by nature – virtually unflappable in any situation. But this was one point in my life that I just snapped. I was pissed. I called my electrical team on the radio to organize an assault on their house to cut their power. And then, the voice of reason, Andrea, stepped in to attempt to orchestrate a diplomatic solution to the conflict. By this time, the ferries were in route, and the guests were expected within the next 15 minutes. I told Andrea she had 10 minutes, and then we were going in.

"Ten minutes later, the music abruptly stopped. I heard something about a pick-up truck full of beer, wine and champagne on its way next door, and I never heard anything more from them!"

To add to this description, earlier in the day when the bride and groom heard that CEMEX's evening was featuring Seal, they invited themselves to attend. Rather than totally discourage them, I invited them to sit on the beach behind our area and listen. This was apparently not a good enough solution in their eyes as they ignored the invite and started the nonsense with the loud rap music. My crew wanted to kill them. Not a good start for a marriage in my mind.

So I had cases of champagne delivered to the bridal couple, thanking them for their cooperation. Then we created a seating area for them (not in our guests' view) close enough that they would feel part of the concert without CEMEX being aware of it. Additionally they got Seal's autographed CDs. It could have been a disaster, but, instead of arguing, I solved the problem with liquid diplomacy.

The Outcome

The expectations on this event were high. The objectives were many. The challenges were daunting. While this might be said of many events, few teams take on the task of fulfilling a client's request for a spectacular evening by staging it at a venue on an island with no water, no electricity, no easy access and no buildings. We didn't take the easy road by settling for a mediocre venue and run-of-the-mill food.

Creating a true fantasy island for 300 executives so that they experienced something that could never be recreated was the only way to meet the client's objectives. And even a sudden rainstorm and impending hurricane did little to dampen the event. In fact, because EE handled it with a calm hand, the small bit of adversity actually helped achieve one of the client's biggest objectives. CEMEX wanted to bring its executives together even more by having them realize that adversity and challenges could be met. By accepting this as a team, together they could build the future of CEMEX and face all challenges. CEMEX used our hurricane challenge as a point of discussion for the next day's general session.

The Lesson

This event was successful because we fostered teamwork, promoted innovation, honored cultural diversity and rewarded resiliency – the exact objectives that CEMEX was trying to create within its own team. The entire event focused on team work. Every obstacle possible (including bugs, bugs and more bugs that bit) challenged the team. By working together closely (catering with technical, logistical with catering, airport staff with customs and immigration, Zama with transportation), a detailed production schedule (which would be longer than *Gone With the Wind* to read) was created that outlined every element, every contingency and every possible plan.

Of course, Hurricane Wilma did not help. Every day was spent checking out the Harbormaster's findings, on an hourly basis, 24-hours-a-day. The client was very nervous because this was a *very* expensive event. Should we or shouldn't we go ahead? Would it rain or would it not rain? And ultimately, the client did not want to make the decision, so EE made it. Go!

The team worked around the clock to accomplish the seemingly impossible. The sun and the humidity made the effort tiring and not always comfortable. The communication between the team on the island and the team in Cancun was constant, even though phones often did not work because of the satellites being affected by weather changes, especially the winds.

No one element could be accomplished without consideration of every other element. So everyone had to work together and did. The organization and the specific delegation of responsibilities made this possible.

Where there might have been adversity (the caterers and the consultant from afar), there was none for even this was pre-planned. When the rain storm hit, the truest spirit of teamwork came into play because every staff member, from Patricia Quintana to generator operator to producer, worked in tandem to hand out rain ponchos, serve drinks, wipe tables and chairs, sweep water off the stage and keep everyone calm and happy with constant announcements. Every step of the way guests were informed and, as a result, the happy and competent team created a delighted and satisfied audience.

And why was the team successful? My college days working with the mentally challenged at Duarte taught me how to figure out where I was going and how to get there, because one is not in control when working with mental patients. Did you know that I am a trained psychologist? (I went for my masters in criminal psychology because I was fascinated and really wanted to help people who they said could never be modified; people that seemingly couldn't be helped, who wouldn't be helped. I found that there was a disappointing inevitability in it all. I had thought that I wanted to be Sidney Poitier in *To Sir, With Love* until my lofty ideas were squashed because no one cared. So, I stopped pursuing the ideal and stepped into reality.)

And to take it all one step further, I'm a good listener because as a child it was all about what *they* said, not what I had to say. Being shy made it so much easier to be a good listener. Most people I've met think I'm a brilliant conversationalist because I get them to talk. That's why I've been successful at teambuilding. I listen, figure out at what they are good and then let them do it. I'm also a successful mediator.

Thinking of teambuilding as cheers and rallies is ridiculous. I could never be a cheerleader, can't think of anything less I would want to be. Teambuilding is so much more than getting people together to do something inconsequential. When you get them to work together to discuss strengths in each other and give them a vehicle in which they can truly communicate, that's what I call teambuilding. That is why I developed the concept for the school. Everyone did something greater than self and had a role that was pivotal. In the end, the act of generosity makes people proud and allows them to share their vulnerabilities as well as their strengths. That's teambuilding.

The moral of this story? You most certainly can't stop a hurricane, but you *can* create a team that can pull off miracles, in life or in events, even in the most adverse situations!

18

Cultural Diplomacy in Three Languages (And Some Interesting Logistics, too)

Asience Shampoo Media Launch - Yokohama, Japan

As the final step in a major media campaign to launch Asience Shampoo Extraordinary Events projected images of universal beauty choreographed to music onto a 30-story hotel in Yokohama, Japan!

Not only did we have to implement technology never before seen in Japan, but we needed to do so in a manner that saturated the media and launched Asience Shampoo by linking the product with the concept of universal beauty. This was underscored with the images from Asience's advertising campaign, incorporating them into an incredible event that was artistic in intent, massive in scale and impossible to miss. The client wanted to present this product in a BIG way - a tall order in any culture, a much taller one in Japan.

Logistically, this involved balancing the creative vision of our artist with that of the client to ensure all images met everyone's *concept* of beauty. It also included: obtaining all necessary permits (not easy in Japan); a total lack of rehearsal time; shipping projectors that looked like thermonuclear weapons around the world; two earthquakes; layers of cultural differences complicated by language barriers and more – you get the picture!

The logistics were fierce. Truthfully, the tales would fill a book. A psychiatric book.

The TOW Agency of Tokyo came to EE with a challenge. We need to present our clients with something new and different. What can you do for us (meaning the Agency and ultimately the client).EE met with TOW to present what was, in our eyes, "new and different." Our idea was to project MASSIVE and unique moving imagery onto a 30-story tall building! TOW loved it, but at the same time, they feared it. Our client was especially intent on embracing technology that, while seen and done in the U.S., was completely unfamiliar and brand new in Japan. To their credit, they were willing to risk the unknown and plunge ahead to provide this uniqueness to their client.

Complications

To say that this event was fraught with complications is a mild way of putting it! To start, we had *layers of clients* that we had to please, the first of our many logistical challenges. The chain of command went like this:

End Client: the cosmetics company - They needed to approve everything.

Next Tier: the ad agency, all powerful in Japan - They needed to approve everything and could never say "no" to their client (part of Japanese culture).

Next Tier: the Japanese production company/our client - They needed to give everything to the ad agency for approval and could never say "no" to their client.

Next Tier: EE (the actual producers) who said "no" a lot but were never listened to; we had to mediate between the Japanese production company and the Next Tier, Max Johann (the artist and projectionist) who said "no" to everything all the time. Sometimes justifiably, and sometimes not. But after all, he WAS an artist, and he was protecting his art.

Challenges and Solutions

Once the concept was accepted, the first challenge was to find the right building. Projections don't work well off glass, and most tall and well-placed buildings in Japan are constructed with many windows. Once a number of potential sites was located, they had to accommodate an area that was at least 50 yards away in order to place the projectors in a position with enough of a clear throw. That meant no city streets with heavy traffic, no buildings in the way, no signs, banners and other corporate logos in plain sight, among a lot of other criteria. Plus, the building needed to be seen from all over this greatly spread-out city in order to maximize the launch.

For us, that represented a whole lot of site surveying, thousands of miles and time zones away from our home base in Los Angeles. Then, approval of the site was needed. There are very few office buildings in Japan (where people work 24/7) amenable to bright lights being cast onto their building and windows.

Another arduous and intricate challenge for us was obtaining permission to stage the show. In the U.S., getting permits to use buildings, block off streets and the like have become second nature to EE. Not so in Japan! It took literally months of hard work, back and forth across the continents, to obtain all of the proper and necessary permits to pull off this magnificent event feat. Not only can you not park a truck in a street without the correct permit, God forbid if the truck's wheel base is six inches larger than originally thought — time to apply for a whole NEW permit!

To accomplish the artistic part of our task, we hired Max Johann/ Artist Projectionist, who creates expansive works of moving art by choreographing film of original photographs and art to music. Superimposing these images (one over the other, and with the ability to move up, down and side-to-side at will), they can move across any surface through his hand manipulation — a gargantuan moving painting. (I've described his work in previous chapters.) The client had seen the work of one massive projector, and this is what they bought off on. One projector. This is what was permitted.

After several site inspections in Yokohama, and given the client's requirements, Max decided he needed two projectors. The results of his decision? Months of "negotiations." Enter the art of communication and of finding a way to accomplish a complex job, all the while dealing with two different cultures (who are <u>never</u> in the same time zone) and two different ways of doing business.

The bottom line: The client didn't want to pay for two projectors. Yet the show could not be produced with merely one. TOW didn't get it. They smiled and nodded and said "yes" but meant "no." Finally we compromised. In order to ensure the integrity of the show, we paid for the additional projector ourselves. And still they argued, because it meant revisiting the permit issue situation. Even though it would result in a way better show, they didn't want to go there. To translate this into easier terms: We knew they couldn't accomplish this show with one projector, but they were never willing to understand that concept. The phone calls and emails took on a wearisome, grievous life of their own during these bilingual discussions until we accomplished the task.

Choosing all of the thousands of Asian and universal beauty images was another complication in that we had to make sure that everyone's concept of beauty was portrayed. EE spent many hours sending images to Japan and awaiting approval from all members of a 20-person Japanese committee – resulting in a seemingly endless slew of meetings to view each and every slide and image planned for the presentation.

One problem EE overcame was balancing the creative vision, ingenuity and artistry of our designer with the vision of our client. Max is an artist and wanted artistic control. The ad agency for Asience considered that THEY should have artistic control. Imagine Michelangelo being asked to paint the Sistine Chapel, only to be told how to paint it, which size brushes to use, how many hours a day were to be spent on his back and, by the way, absolutely no scaffolding is allowed in the Vatican. The middleman, the Japanese producer, tried to mediate. EE tried to mediate.

It was difficult because of the linguistics and cultural diversity. Add to that the fact that English was a first language to only one party (we at EE), and the entire picture gets even more complex! We were never sure who understood what. Everyone smiled and nodded, or sometimes screamed and nodded and shook fists and stamped feet, but what was truly understood? Always the voice of reason, it was usually me who had to take both parties (the Japanese producer and Max) aside, and never together, and calm them down. There was a lot of: "Yes, I know you are right, but you have to understand the needs of the artist," followed by, "Yes I know YOU are right, but you have to understand the needs of the client."

Max constantly threatened to quit the project. Add to that a distinctly Japanese concept that everyone should work 24 hours a day without eating or sleeping. Now further add the fact that one can never say "no" to a client. Deadlines were given by Max and EE. The client smiled, nodded and said "yes," but not one deadline was ever met. How was this resolved? In a nutshell, I begged. I begged Max a lot, and he wanted to do this project so much that he agreed and worked tirelessly to accomplish in very little time what should have been leisurely. Images were being re-edited and rephrased almost right up until *showtime*. Since the "show" was choreographed to music in order to achieve artistic flow, this caused more difficulties.

I said psychiatry, didn't I? Well, as I mentioned earlier, I'm by profession (yes, really!) a trained psychologist, and I employed everything I'd ever learned in soothing very ruffled feathers as much as humanly possible.

I wish I could tell you that this was resolved, but it never really was. What we did resolve was that everyone needed to stay calm, and since editing would be done onsite, we would have group meetings and come to as much of a consensus as we could. Additionally, the Japanese producer flew to Los Angeles several times (usually to pose for photos with the projector with which he was enthralled) to review the images. Max shot so many that it was difficult to narrow down the choices.

The thousands of images finally chosen to be projected onto the exterior of the Yokohama Intercontinental Hotel (all 30 stories of it) were of Asian and "universal" beauty -- from nature to man-made landmarks to people. Max had spent a considerable amount of time in Japan, along with EE staff, photographing Japanese people, landscapes, florals and art ... anything that spoke to beauty. By combining these images with the Asience campaign photos, a final "show" was created. One that was approved, or so we thought.

Given the scale and the length of this two-hour show, the people and media of Yokohama would have seen it without any pre-marketing. However, TOW ensured that crowds and media would turn out in droves by creating a buzz weeks before. The most important issue was to make sure the media understood how unique this show would be, so TOW flew the press to Max's shop in California to interview him at work, photograph the projectors and preview the show. They then created and sent specialized Web clips to them that provided parts of the show, images and the interviews with Max. As a result, we were under the gun for time. The projectors needed to be shipped. Yet the ad agency brought in press for this media conference that kept Max and his team and his projectors from working. It also meant that the projectors had to be *rush* shipped by air.

One bonus that helped ensure that crowds and media would attend was that Yokohama was celebrating its 150th anniversary at the time of our launch. Ultimately, this brought in many guest VIPs, including the city's mayor who served as MC, and who hosted a pre-event press conference with the traditional exchange of gifts. (Unfortunately, at the very time Max needed to be setting up and getting ready for the show, it was required that he be available for this ceremonial exchange.)

To celebrate the anniversary, images of Yokohama and its people were incorporated into the projection show, which helped audience reaction dramatically as they could see their city and themselves portrayed in such a positive way. This also helped achieve the client's objective of total media saturation.

Of course, on the two nights of the events, it rained. Since the projectors were situated 50 yards from their projection surface, this provided yet another set of challenges. But due to the high intensity of the projectors, the resolution on the building was perfect anyway. We had made the right choice.

Oh and, as if the logistics and challenges so far weren't enough with which to deal, Japan experienced two huge earthquakes during the event set-up! Not that our equipment was affected, but the team was constantly wary as the media insinuated "disaster" at all times.

The projectors, though huge, are delicate and need coddling; natural disasters don't blend well with fragile equipment.

Another interesting challenge: Ethics. When we first introduced Max and the concept to the client, Max displayed images of international icons ... Rome's Coliseum, the Eiffel Tower and the Kremlin. After our contract was negotiated, we had a surprise coming. We had been told that our show needed to incorporate images from the ad campaign, created by a famous Japanese photographer. We viewed the images. It was of their model superimposed on ... you guessed it ... The Coliseum, the Eiffel Tower, the Kremlin. That was the moment our project acquired yet another phase — that of calming down OUR artist, Max.

Heard enough? Oh, that's only scratching the surface. Now let's talk about equipment. Utilizing the special projectors necessary to create a show of this size posed a unique challenge — shipping them to Japan! The projectors were HUGE, just like the show. They weighed tons! They needed special crates. Getting them to Japan was continuously challenging, because as long as the client was changing the content of the show, the projectors were needed in California to test out the images. And they kept changing the show. Ship? Don't ship? Change images? Set deadlines, knowing they'd never be honored? Finally, these very, very heavy projectors (each the size of the Hubble Telescope) were shipped.

Shipping them halfway around the world posed a unique challenge, as they resemble doomsday weapons! Enter customs, which held them up for days. EE hired a shipping agent specifically to handle this task. Even with a dedicated person keeping track of the projectors 24/7, the costs involved were astronomical and the weight and dimensions of the shipping crates significantly enormous. The paperwork we were buried under was substantial.

A Unique Event

New technology played a large part of this event, but it was not just the mechanical aspect of the projectors that was important. The artist operating them was a much more important and unique element. Max Johann's large-scale projection shows are truly one-of-a-kind art pieces. This brought an air of legitimacy to what might have been too commercial of an endeavor in someone else's hands. Plus, the fact that it could only be seen for two nights ensured large crowds of people and media.

The most unique elements were in content. Not only did the advertising images need to be incorporated into the artful construction of the project, but new images had to be captured that fit the client's specific needs and tastes (and it was next to impossible to figure those out cross-culturally, since there were "rules" that we never did understand). Because Max's projections rely upon movement, it was critical that the still images projected showed motion and progression, particularly of the key model as she literally walked across such icons as The Coliseum.

Color was also important, but since colored tints and hues have different meanings to the Japanese than to us from the U.S. and Europe, many images had to be scratched or re-colorized so as not to offend anyone.

In essence, to once again refer to the Sistine Chapel imagery, Max had to create art out of culture and advertising, make it "move" to music and do it all while working until the eleventh hour while trying desperately to interpret three layers of clients' wishes.

But he did it, and so did we. EE's hard work dramatically achieved the client's objective of total media saturation. The results were phenomenal; the show a complete success, and Max became a local celebrity.

The Lesson

We overcame the logistical challenges of this event and took away an education in how to do business with another culture. And if you are working in another country, you must respect the culture and its ways of working. There's really no choice. I learned that I might never truly know or understand my Japanese clients' agendas or why they do business the way that they do, but I can be assured that it will be difficult. When working internationally there is no right or wrong. There is only different. So accept it.

Part of my willing acceptance goes back to my upbringing where my parents, friends and peers were different and truly not accepted. Remember, many of my formative years were in Burbank, a city with no minorities except Jews. (And I was Jewish, and we numbered in single digits at that time.) My parents were from Europe, had accents, had liberal political views (oh my, they were … hush … DEMOCRATS … oh, no!) We were not easily accepted. And even in school there were church days. And so we few had to hang out in the cafeteria while everyone else went off to their churches for the morning. There are so many stories of prejudice that in today's world are hard to believe, but they happened.

When I went to Berkeley in 1961, my first boyfriend was from Iran, and I hung out with a crowd that was either foreign, gay or black. I had read a book, Five Smooth Stones, and really related to it. (Little did I know that later in life I would be living out the black man/white woman relationship that seemed too exotic when I first read about it.) In 1961, there was something very rebellious going on with me. I had been such a very good girl at home, in school, everywhere. But in that one year at Berkeley, I started spreading my wings. No curfews. No rules. No supervision. By today's standards I was a prudish conservative in most ways, but I thought I was not.

Then, very quickly I came home on summer vacation, fell in love and a few years later married Bob and became a conservative housewife. Very conservative. I became a good wife, stayed a good daughter and then wanted to be a good mother. When Bob and I separated in 1972, after years of being good, I branched out into some unsavory relationships, surrounding myself with people who thought and acted differently than I did. It was very educational. What some youngsters experience in their teens, I lived out in my late 20s and early 30s. That was my time to explore different cultures, different people and varied ways of life.

Then, in 1978, I moved on to musicians, a different group all their own. Every experience enriched my life because each opened me up to new thoughts and ways of communicating. Believe me, when you can talk to a black man who is a total radical and feels oppressed by everything you say, you learn to listen differently and communicate back skillfully.

I love anything that teaches me something I don't know, even when that learning accompanies a painful personal experience. When dealing with people of different cultures and values, it is all a learning experience that I love (except when they don't wear deodorant, have bad breath or dirty clothes, and then I hate them!)

19
Patience

Duskin

At this point, it should be obvious that this book illustrates that over time I learned that international communication styles and expectations are quite different, but those challenges can be overcome with asking persistent questions and a lot of patience ... on both sides.

To further illustrate this, I want to go back to 1994. By then, I had been working with Japanese clients for a few years on small to mid-size projects. I was hired to do a large show for a company out of Japan at the Universal Amphitheatre, a very large space converted from an outdoor amphitheatre to a fully enclosed theatre seating thousands. Set in the heart of Universal City and home to Universal Studios, it was a union facility with a lot of rules and regulations. And with those rules there was no flexibility.

We progressed in creating a stage set and a show, hiring talent and a production team and negotiating with the union. Then ... the earthquake ... and I do mean THE EARTHQUAKE, the Northridge Earthquake which brought all of Los Angeles to its knees for a long time.

At the time I lived in the mountains above Los Angeles, an hour away from our office which was on the second floor of a building in the San Fernando Valley. If you remember the story of the police officer who was killed on a freeway off-ramp, that was the only road leading from my home to the office, and it was no longer accessible. Electricity was out; phone service was out. It was a disaster, literally.

The earthquake was in the early dark morning, and I had no idea if I still had an office. Since my family had a shortwave radio, we were able to get the news and found out how serious the disaster was. VERY serious.

Mid-morning one of my employees reached me on my cell phone to tell me he had driven to the office. All he said was "Don't come in. There's no office left." I hung up pretty depressed.

Shortly after, my cell phone rang again, and it was my client from Japan. "Oh, Mr. Andrea," he said, "so sorry to hear about earthquake."

I was so moved. How nice that this client cared how I was.

"Do we get script today?"

I was stunned. I explained that I had no office, no computer, no electricity, no road and no way to get anything to Japan.

"Oh. So sorry. So we get script today?"

I tried again."Oh. So sorry. Okay. Send script today," was his response. Needless to say, I didn't. I couldn't.

Once we found roads and resettled our office (fortunately I backed up the computers every day and kept the back-up in the trunk of my car), we went back to conducting business.

Additional Communications Challenges

Another call followed shortly from Japan.

"So happy you are good, Mr. Andrea. Client want blimp during show."

I thought of those wonderful little inflatable blimps that could fly around the Amphitheatre and said, "Of course. We'll send pictures." And we did.

The next call brought, "No, we want blimp."

It turned out after much dialogue that he wanted the Goodyear Blimp, which is bigger than the Amphitheatre. Of course, I tried explaining. We even tried to have it "flown over" the amphitheatre, but later learned it couldn't be done because of Federal Aviation Administration regulations. But, again the client really wanted it. So, we secured letters from the FAA, the police department and the venue denying us the right to fly the blimp.

But still, "Oh. Yes. We want blimp." That went on a long time until I told a little white lie.

"I called President Clinton, and he said so sorry, no blimp."

"Oh, okay," was the response. And this response was final. The client finally accepted that "no" was "no."

Sorry, President Clinton. I didn't mean to use your name in vain.

Odd things were introduced on an almost daily basis, which to this day I cannot explain. The opening for this show, attended by 6,000 Japanese ladies, was a military color guard with weapons. The client requested a 21-gun salute (with four guns), but I wouldn't agree to this, saying it was against military policy even if they used blanks.

Then, one of the chief executives, who was a saxophone player, wanted to play *You Are My Sunshine* with the 48-piece orchestra we had hired to do play-ons and play-offs. We started with a two-hour rehearsal. It went on for eight hours as the executive could not play along with the professional studio musicians who were getting annoyed, though being union, they were handsomely compensated. The client had a lot of difficulty embracing the concept of union overtime, which was astronomical, and asked me to try to negotiate with the musicians and stagehands to bring the costs down. Of course, this was impossible. I finally came up with a line that worked perfectly. "I will lose face with the entire orchestra and employees of the Amphitheater if I try to go against their strict rules." This the client understood.

Finally, the client insisted on posting Japanese counterparts (none of whom spoke English) with our sound engineer, lighting technician, video engineer and even the orchestra conductor! As their director called the cues to his Japanese staff, and then a translator called the same cues to our team, can you guess what happened? Every cue was late. So the emcee would call out an award winner, the director would call a cue in Japanese, the translator would repeat it in English and the appropriate U.S. person would react. In the case of the orchestra, by the time the conductor got his cue, the award winner would be on stage waiting. The walk-on music was playing after the winner had already arrived. The same thing happened with the walk-offs. And though we tried to explain this to our client, he was upset that our cues were so late!

We eventually worked out the timing issues, and all in all it was a successful collaboration. It was challenging but fun to see the whole show come together, especially after all the obstacles.

The Lesson

As you can see by the way I ultimately had to make the client understand my meaning, I learned a lot about communication. I learned even more about patience. If you aren't born with patience, it takes a healthy amount of discipline to acquire it. Working with international clients will teach you to put away your temper and negative body language expressions and hold your tongue and think of reasonably acceptable logic to deal with what the client doesn't understand. Being patient without being condescending will show your client the proper respect he or she deserves, and the rapport that you will build as a result will come back to you in dollars and cents.

I am prone to patience because I was alone so much as a child. Sharron used to say, "You are really a wise old man in the body of a little girl."

Patience is the only way I know. It has much to do with why I don't stress out easily. There is no sense in getting stressed over things out of my control, but one thing I can control is my patience. This serves to keep the people around me calm. Think about it in terms of personal relationships. What do you accomplish when you nag? It doesn't make anything happen any faster.

I remember asking one of my staff once what she does when things are falling behind, and she said, "I get angry and yell at everyone to make them react quicker." I asked her, "And what does THAT accomplish?" and she responded, "I guess it doesn't accomplish anything." And she's right. It only creates tension.

It's just another lesson in how to communicate and allow people space and time. Then, when you really do need something, you are taken seriously because not everything in life is so urgent.

I can equate it to a staff member who needs something on Wednesday because the client insisted it be that day. I always ask, "Did you ask them when they are going to read it?" And, I encourage them to offer, "I'd like to get it to you then, but it won't be as good. Give me a few more days, and it will be embellished and excellent."

During one of my divorces, my attorney took his time with things I needed but one afternoon wanted a response from me in 30 minutes or less. My reply was, "You've had plenty of time to ask me, so don't expect me to respond instantaneously."

When you respond with patience and calm, people will respond in kind. The attorney apologized and said I was right. "My inability to deal with you in a timely and considerate manner should not create an emergency for you."

This is a very telling statement for anyone.

20

Producing for an Audience That Had Seen It All

The Special Event Los Angeles 2007 - *Special Events* Magazine's Gala Awards

The Special Event Gala conjures up an awards show for the elite of the elite in the special events industry.

More than 5,000 professionals from the special events industry traveled to Los Angeles, California, from all over the globe for a tradeshow, educational seminars and a series of events that culminated in *Special Events* Magazine's Gala Awards Ceremony and Celebration.

The Galas, an industry icon, was in need of revitalization, a face lift so to speak. What better city for an aging star to get a nip and tuck than Hollywood? Let's think Oscars. Or Emmys. Or MTV. And then let's create a show that takes all the same components and personalizes them specifically for our industry. We needed to produce a show that truly reflected the creative industry it was honoring – an audience of our peers who do this very same thing for a living - and to offer a new standard of innovation for an audience that had seen it all. How do we impress them, entertain them, engage them and *wow* them? But the ultimate goal (which was achieved) was to do what had never been done before – to create such a buzz that the event sold out.

Daunting task, right? Daunting might be an understatement.

All of that and more was the charge I set forth as the show's executive producer. With little budget and a challenging venue that allowed for no setup or rehearsal time (see Challenges), we set out to create an evening that would theatrically entertain as well as form a well-planned show while creatively presenting awards.

I convinced event partners, Brite Ideas, Entertainment Plus Productions, Inc. and GOWest Events and Multimedia to work with us to produce a theatrical stage show that combined awards presentations, multimedia and live customized performances on stage.

To achieve these objectives, EE restructured the event while retaining the essential, expected elements: a stunning event environment with an elegant dinner celebration; a high-tech, high-impact, multimedia awards show with 32 categories and multiple nominees plus several special awards, seven live production numbers with a cast of 28 and an exciting after-party on par with a major Hollywood-style event. All this while meeting the challenge that there was no time for rehearsals onsite and only one day to load in a show that would normally take a week.

To turn a tired format on its head, we began by changing the venue type. No more hotels and convention centers. This year, our challenge was to find an enticing and exclusive venue that could hold an audience of more than 1,000 people and still have the cache of "Hollywood."

Though not an easy venue to secure, The Shrine Auditorium, a historic, Moroccan-inspired theater and event space, fit the bill. The site had been home to the Academy Awards and its elegant Governor's Ball for years; just the connection we wanted to draw between the two awards shows.

However, the Shrine's Expo Center where the dinner would take place had seen better days. To discover how we tackled that, read on.

Event Description

For the first time ever, this event SOLD OUT! Tickets were actually being scalped until the last minute. This was an event no one wanted to miss. Hyped for months on the magazine's Web site, the event promised to deliver a standard of excellence and innovation that would give the audience something to take home and emulate ... how to do an awards show.

As guests entered the lobby of the Shrine auditorium, they stepped onto the red carpet, experiencing what generations of stars had turned into the legendary "walk." Even though all attendees were jaded event professionals, the venue itself caused a stir. As waiters handed out champagne, the attendees took in the surroundings. But not for long; the evening's itinerary was a full one, so EE wasted no time getting everyone to dinner on time.

Guests entered the Expo Center of The Shrine through a sea of red fabric with moving fiber optic stars surrounding them. Using the theory of selective visibility, we utilized draping to focus design attention on the positive while hiding the negative. And the ceiling was all but hidden by the installation of huge imported Moroccan lanterns in all shapes and sizes; an effect that worked not only to make the cavernous space more intimate, but also to create a dazzling and magical atmosphere for dinner. This was also a nod to the Moroccan accents in the Shrine's architecture. Bars and tables became miniature Moroccan museums filled with authentic artifacts, some created from ornate, hand-carved doors.

Metallic linen, created to complement the Shrine, sparkled in the light of individual pin spots. Centerpieces of candles, vases, urns and bowls from Morocco finished off with exotic floral work were each one-of-a-kind art pieces. The beautiful Spanish guitar of the world-famous performer, Benise, created a relaxed atmosphere. Dinner was catered by one of Los Angeles' most high-profile firms, Patina Catering, who designed a gourmet menu that perfectly complemented the jewel-tones of the placesettings.

After dinner, guests entered the theater for the awards show. Traditionally Galas had been long and drawn out and sometimes even (dare we say?) boring. If you are not an award winner, it's a long time to sit, right?

Instead of a mere awards evening, we created a theatrical awards "show." With the philosophy of theatre in mind, we created an overture. Then a few middle acts. And, a finale that tied it all together and made it cohesive.

The Show

The Overture: Massive high-definition projections created a dynamic backdrop for the main stage. A personalized pre-recorded video filmed by Jay Leno welcomed the guests, the perfect beginning to any Hollywood awards show.

Act One: From out of the audience two dancers appeared. Two lovers. Joining together on the stage, a marriage proposal in dance was simulated, and as the curtain of the majestic Shrine Auditorium rose, the wedding took place. On stage, two extremely talented singers performed *The Prayer* while 16 bridesmaids and groomsmen joined them in an elegant dance. The stage was a beautiful wintery set where snow fell softly across it in animated effects on the huge screen. The audience was hushed, but there was a tangible tingle of emotion that filled the theater. Then came "the moment" as a Cinderella-style carriage, encased totally in twinkling lights and drawn by a handsome white horse, entered onto the stage to deliver a "bride and groom" (our two first presenters) to give out the awards for the Wedding Categories. Goosebumps were felt throughout the audience! The stage was set for the caliber of the evening and what was yet to come.

Act Two: *Here for the Party* introduced the Fair and Festival category as hay bales and a western setting were the backdrop for a S*%#!T- kicking song and dance number that shot a burst of energy into the room! The production was completely customized for this series of award winners with perfect lyrics, contemporary choreography and HOT costumes.

Plus, no world-class awards show is complete without capturing the audience in real time. Just as the Academy Awards does, EE used a jib camera to follow nominees up to the stage and back to their seats.

Act Three: *Putting It Together* introduced an event planner (our talented lead female singer) and her team of decorators, vendors and assistants. As she sang, the customized lyrics and precision choreography literally followed her as she put together a party right before our eyes! This production introduced the Event Planning Categories. This was a truly perfect representation of the delicate balance of an event planner and all that he or she must accomplish to "Put It Together."

Act Four: This production exemplified a new direction for entertainment where entertainment met technology. GoWest created an amazing backdrop of hip-hop dancers in a cityscape on the main screen in pre-production. Perfectly executed choreography was combined with live dancers on stage to create a "hip hop battle." It was an amazing piece of entertainment and one that is virtually impossible to portray in words. Achieved with GoWest's trademarked "Synchronology," it is multiple synchronized video sources with live elements combined. Dancers interact with themselves, wrapping imagery around a space using projections. Synchronology uses the endless possibilities of the virtual world in an unprecedented fashion, and in this show, we demonstrated to the audience that the only limitation was their imagination.

Act Five: We wanted to make sure that our discerning crowd got a taste of everything possible for entertainment - next up was Bollywood. The performers took the stage with authentic colorful and amazing costumes. The choreography by Emmy winner Fred Tallaksen was a perfect blend of contemporary and Bollywood. We added specialty drummers with oversized drums all in full harem costuming, and the stage exploded at the end as the performers flew kites above the audience.

Add to all that a bit of invention. To introduce the category of Best Rentals, we brought our presenter onto the stage on a genie lift.

The **finale** featured *Baby, You're A Star* with the whole cast and a surprise appearance by Rock and Roll Hall of Famer, Solomon Burke, who closed the show with custom lyrics that paid a special tribute to the audience, an audience where everyone indeed was a star of the events industry.

The After Party

After the awards show, guests re-entered the Expo Hall. A dessert of gourmet sweets was served family-style at each table. A rousing performance by Gary Sinise and The Lt. Dan Band added the Superstar component to tie in the Hollywood element, electrify the room and rev up the energy for a crowd ready to dance, once they finished their slack jawed, "Oh my god, do you know who THAT is?"

As expected, Sinise held this jaded crowd enthralled as he not only played but engaged the audience in friendly banter making this superstar accessible to the attendees. Again, a major feat, as Sinise did not normally perform for this type of event and had to juggle his filming schedule to accommodate this date.

The results? The client's objectives were indeed met and exceeded. The event elevated the awards show to its highest standards, got the industry talking and most importantly, honored the award winners in the style they deserved. This was an event that could only happen in Hollywood and was deemed better than the Oscars by the folks at The Shrine, who have indeed "seen it all!"

Planning and Preparation

When we began, we knew that each and every performance had to be unique. No one in the audience could have previously seen anything we were going to show. The costumes had to be created for this one event. And it had to flow to keep the energy of the audience up at all times. To make that happen, it had to be all about THEM. We hired the best talent in Hollywood from dancers, singers and choreographers to show director and stage manager to costume and makeup personnel. Every element was carefully scripted and pre-programmed. Technology ruled as can be evidenced by the first-time major usage of I-tiles as a staging element and the large screen which had choreographed graphic elements with moons moving over the Manhattan skyline, birds flying over pastoral settings, snowfall and even an endless table of delectable treats for the introduction of the food categories. All of the technical components were integrated into the production so that each enhanced every other element and showcased not only unique performance but also innovative technologies used as entertainment pieces. We wanted every aspect of what was happening on stage to make sense, to have a purpose and to be meaningful to the event and to the audience.

This show was extremely experimental and had a large impact on its audience. There was little budget to accomplish it all, but it set a new standard and was highly-touted in the industry for being equal to any major awards show.

The entire event was an exhilarating challenge because we set out to entertain, but most of all, to make the audience the true stars of the experience. After all, this was their world and their moment to shine on a stage and in a theater where the greatest of the great have been acknowledged, and now it was their turn.

And it was pure theatre at its best.

Challenges and Solutions

The biggest challenge, and a huge one, was the audience. Imagine an entire theatre filled with "we've seen it all and done it all" folks that HAVE indeed done just that! We did it by giving it our all and pulling out the stops. We continuously had "wow" moments, and throughout our show we appealed to their emotions and not just their senses. New technology was not enough; it was in how it was presented ... with meaning and in context.

I demanded an event that was completely in good taste, and while giving everyone creative leeway, also firmly kept control over each and every element so that the variety of providers was kept in synch, communicative and cohesive. The challenge was that everyone who provided a service had different ideas of what they wanted to showcase. The entire team was made up of companies that could take on this challenge on their own yet I remained responsible to create an event where disparate concepts were all being taken into consideration. However, we all had the same goal and that was "show 'em!" Therefore we all worked hard to accomplish what we finally delivered.

Another test was that this extremely intense show in a very challenging venue took up an enormous amount of time and came right on the heels of New Year's Eve, when every performer was maxed out; yet we were requiring them to do a lot for virtually nothing. Technically it created a situation where vacations had to be suspended, which didn't make anyone happy. But we emphasized that this was an opportunity to "audition" for the top event producers from around the world!

Money. There really wasn't much. (Surely some of you have worked on The Special Event before.) And for sure there wasn't enough. So everyone had to dig deep for the betterment of the show and do what it took to make it absolute perfection. It became a matter of pride to inspire our peers.

Time in the Venue – okay, imagine the Super Bowl half-time show, and you cannot get into the stadium to rehearse! Or the Oscars being loaded in, *in one day with virtually no sound check.* That was our situation. We had one day to load in AND rehearse because *The People's Choice Awards* was on stage until one day before our show and loading out during our load-in! This for a show that would normally take at least a week to set up. So with technical and staging loading in the night before and day of, there was no time to block, rehearse or run through the entire show cue to cue. We were only able to rehearse through the fifth award. Everything else was done on the fly. How was THIS challenge met? With the most professional team ever assembled and an unflappable stage manager who created a secure and steady approach to what could have been a disastrous situation and lots of run-throughs at offices and rehearsal studios. It's all in the pre-production, right? (Ah, if only clients understood the true value of pre-production!)

EE pre-programmed and pre-recorded large portions of the complex show. Virtual scenery (which took less time to install and added a new, cutting-edge dimension) was used. Techniques such as snow actually falling during the winter scene helped hold the audience's attention during the long show. It helped to change the show's pace, feeling and look at appropriate times. With video, music, dance and custom musical numbers expertly choreographed, the audience never knew what to expect next. And, EE used NO POWERPOINT to ensure the awards had an innovative feeling. While challenging, it made us rethink every element, making the show fresh and exciting. And one huge solution to keeping people in their seats was met with low-tech – EE closed the bars in the lobby during the awards!

Okay, here's the nightmare. Two hours till doors and the computers lose the entire show. Solution: A competent team that knew the show so well that they could reprogram instantaneously, and, of course, a team that could handle stress well. And a stage manager/director who didn't cry when this happened!

We had a lot of people who wanted to participate and sponsor, many of whom were not qualified to be in a first-rate production, yet saying "no" to our peers, fellows in the Los Angeles community and friends, was difficult. But we did it. Most shows in the past have just been too complicated to be effective, and we aimed for simplicity.

We also had to address the length of the show when determining when dinner would be served; before, after or during the awards?

EE made the bold move to serve dinner first. It worked. Before the awards, guests had ample time to enjoy the gourmet dinner which has been taste-tested over and over again to ensure that it could be delivered well-presented to this very discerning audience from a field kitchen (the Shrine has no permanent kitchen). Why? So that no one would sit through hours of awards either hungry or thirsty.

And lastly, we had a 600-pound Rock and Roll Superstar who was to appear for our finale, and at the last minute we had to figure out a way to get him on and off the stage and the dancers around him (remember … no rehearsal). Again, the success of professionals won out as we could choreograph on the spot.

The outcome? I'll just share with you the comments of a few highly-respected event peers:

The Gala Awards were THE BEST EVER!!!!!!!!!!!!!!!!!!!! I am speechless (and that tells you something!) The Golden Globes, Oscars, Grammys and more could learn a few things from you!!!!!!!!!!!!!!!!!! -Steve Kemble

For the first time ever, this event sold out! Attendees were part of history, and not just because they were at The Shrine. They have called it "the best ever," and have said: "Now, that's the way an awards program should be produced." Extraordinary Events has raised the bar to new heights. -Kim Romano, Penton Media, The Special Event Show

The Gala event was an amazing evening; perfect from beginning to end. Congratulations! You and your team outdid yourselves. It was a once-in-a-lifetime, flawless, entertaining, well-produced evening. -*Janet Elkins, EventWorks*

You and your team created the most fabulous evening to cherish for a lifetime. No one will ever be able to duplicate the essence of last night. You really out did yourself; take a bow. -*Cheryl Fish, High Rise Events*

Finally, a Gala Awards show that was tasteful, clever, beautiful, enjoyable and had the correct pace. From the moment we arrived we knew we were in good hands; it was apparent someone had thought through every detail, every moment. For attendees, this night may have been the best educational session of them all. -*Jeff Kalpak, Barkley Kalpak Associates, Inc.*

The Gala evening was elegant, sophisticated and worthy of our industry. I have been to many industry conferences, and this was the finest production of an awards show I have seen. -*Jean Vivrette, Pacific Partners*

The Lesson

You need to believe in your own good taste and your sense of integrity. And sometimes you just need to say "no." And say it a lot of times and stick with it.

Thanks to my mother, I grew up with great taste. God bless her, Lelja's appearance was always perfection. She wouldn't go to the mailbox without being perfectly groomed. Style, hair and grace all became important to me because I wanted her approval, and it has helped me carry through all these years. Because of it, I have a firm belief that I am my own best discriminating audience, and if I can please myself, I'm for sure going to wow everyone else.

As for my sense of integrity, well, I (in the past) surrounded myself with so much low life that I think integrity became important. Case in point – two husbands and a boyfriend with none.

So in this case, keeping a firm hand and never caving in to anything or anyone made this the stand-out event that it became.

21

Improvisation

Car Manufacturer's 25th Birthday Celebration - Las Vegas

The Situation

There are a variety of stories and experiences all woven into this one grand event in Las Vegas during this client's annual new car show.

Months before the actual event, my client (a travel company) asked me to prepare a bid based upon some very exacting specifications. It was a "25th birthday" celebration, and the focus *had* to be on *past and future* (remember that). And by the way, since I was such a good writer, could I prepare the entire proposal?

Flattery will get you anywhere with me (a flaw I'm working on), and I agreed. I wrote. I rendered. I planned. I created. And the end result was a dynamic celebration that started 25 years prior with entertainment and themed décor and ended with the future. Think two rooms, each distinctly different with an exploding birthday cake (five tiers of balloons all of which would explode on cue to reveal a Happy Anniversary logo) dividing them.

A beautiful presentation, my client confirmed. Perfect. So perfect that since I understood the project better than anyone else, he wanted me to do the pitch to the actual client though he was a seasoned and highly-paid sales executive. More flattery, so. I agreed.

I walked into the manufacturer's headquarters to meet three planners for the first time. My client was sitting at a conference table, chit-chatting, feet up on the table. I was introduced rather informally and with no set up by my client told to begin. I hadn't yet put down my purse. I began with, "To meet all your specific requests, here's the concept ..." Before I had finished the words *past and future*, the head planner stopped me and said, "Didn't they tell you *that* concept is exactly what we don't want?"

My response: "Then it's a good thing that's not the only idea we have."

Snappy response, right? Didn't mean a thing since I was quickly ushered out while my contact continued to stay and schmooze, yes feet still up on that table.

Weeks later, not having heard from my client, I called and said, "What are we going to do?" The key word here, folks, is "we."

The response? "Well, since we've changed direction and are not using your concept (MY concept?), we're going to pull it in house and produce it ourselves.

"So you got the business?" I asked.

"Yes," he replied.

"Then I think I'm entitled to the business, too." Silence on his end. Obviously he didn't agree.

Normally that would stop someone, but it didn't stop me. I went to the head of purchasing, and after a lot of conversation pleading my case, my client agreed to pay me a considerable and generous amount for my time. I agreed.

Let me digress. I didn't "plead." I rather explained what I thought was a fair and honorable solution and presented my case clearly, with facts and timelines in place. And then I insisted on being paid for my time and efforts. So now let's fast forward.

Months later, my client (someone new in the process but whom I had known well for years) called and asked me to do the project again. I asked if he knew the history, and he said, "No, but it doesn't matter because you are perfect for the project."

I offered to apply some of my settlement but in the end didn't have to do so since the entire project was now new and we had to start from scratch. Persistence had paid off with no repercussions.

Unplanned Situations

The venue? Las Vegas. Home to the very first permanent "Cirque du Soleil" show. And this time my client wanted to do a Cirque show. It was prior to any now well-known Cirque shows and before any were available for corporations. No one was doing "cirque"... things have really changed, haven't they? With a nice décor package for this sit-down dinner and a center stage to allow for performance in the round, we hired acts from Cirque du Soleil (across the street from our hotel) and carefully coordinated performers so they could appear during their breaks. We constructed a detailed and versatile show that with split-second timing (Vegas shows are predictable for their timing) could be a smash for our car manufacturer.

Well, that was the plan. We coordinated with the hotel to see how long dinner would take. One hour and 45 minutes we were told. Okay. That allowed for our acts to perform in-between courses, with a finale, and then the band. Like all plans, this one went south quickly.

Dinner took only 40 minutes. Other problems plagued us, like the hotel staff wheeling tables and chairs through our room as the performances were happening and the wait staff practically throwing the food at the tables. The first two acts performed, and then the whammy ... the head client contact approached and told us, "Cut the final acts; let's go right to the band, or we'll lose them to the casino."

Now we really had a problem.

The next act was Chinese Acrobats waiting backstage. Not one of them spoke English. We literally had to take their unicycles, bicycles, chairs and equipment and carry them to the loading dock to make them understand that they were not going to appear. Challenging but accomplished.

The second problem was that the band was not onsite, and we had no clue where the musicians were! They were at a hotel down the strip, and everyone knows Vegas traffic. Fortunately at that moment the drummer showed up, and I grabbed him. Throwing a bit of impromptu costuming on him, I told him to take the stage and do the most energetic drum solo anyone had ever heard and to keep playing. He was amazing. Unusual, but amazing.

The bass player turned up next, and I had him parade down (playing acoustically) one aisle and join the drummer. The dynamic was getting better. As each musician showed up, I had him come down a different aisle, and the beat kept getting stronger as one-by-one the musicians joined together to become a dynamite band. When all were in place, they were joined by their singer. Everyone thought this was orchestrated and choreographed to give a huge energy to this evening. Whew!

The Lesson

Besides learning to speak Chinese, there are really two lessons here. First, don't be afraid to ask for what you deserve. Truthfully, you will be respected for it. And in all likelihood, you won't lose your client by firmly valuing yourself and your time. If clients don't value you and won't pay, you won't see them again anyway.

Next, don't give up when things go against you. There's always a solution; think on your feet and make the best of every situation. Sometimes it can be much better than originally planned.

I always look at getting the outcome that I want as a game. I am the ultimate test taker. I went all the way through school really not studying. In college I hardly attended classes or read the required books and still maintained a 4.0 average. I just knew how to take tests, particularly if they were essays. I could always figure out what the instructor wanted.

For instance, I took Physics at Berkeley in 1961 (Oh, my God! Could ANYONE be that old?) from Dr. Edward Teller (you know, the father of the hydrogen bomb).His class was so popular that EVERYONE took it ... thousands. Instead of tests, he assigned us to read four books and produce book reports. Science was never my forte. I didn't understand a single word and still got an "A" in the class. How did that happen? One of my reports was to be delivered to the famous Dr. Teller himself. I tried to read a book on magnets. And the operative word here was "tried."

When I met Dr. Teller, I had learned one page of my book but didn't understand how magnets worked, so I began to ask him intelligent questions about his theories and about why these things were so important to magnetic fields. Surprisingly he was delighted to answer me. I then led him into a conversation about his emigration to the U.S. from Germany and told him a bit about my similar background (or at least my stepfather's). We had a delightful chat until his next book report student arrived, and we parted with a nice hug. I ended up walking out of his office with him saying I had presented an excellent report. I received a passing grade (it was just pass/fail) on a subject about which I knew nothing. I'm not really proud of this but learned from it, and the same technique has served me well in business.

I listen to my clients and ask questions, deep and probing questions about which I am sincerely interested in the answers, much more interested than talking about myself. It has gained me much business and found me many delightful relationships. I thank Dr. Teller for teaching me the value of this.

I'm sure you are wondering how this fits into the car story with which I began. Well, if my client had listened to his client he could have saved all the money he paid me for what he never needed and given the client what he asked for on the first go-round.

The life lesson? The best friends are those who listen instead of talk.

Providing Real Meaning

Miki's Dream Passport - San Francisco

In early March, 2000, I received a phone call that changed life as Extraordinary Events knew it for the next two months.

"Hello, Andrea. Tim here. I have a project you might be interested in. I'm flying from Tokyo to Los Angeles later this week. Can we meet?"

Later that week, the visit. Tim Lemon, representing Japan Travel Bureau (JTB) Communications, was asked to produce a show for Japan-based Miki Prune (Health Food Supplements Company). They were bringing almost 2,000 Japanese award winners on an annual incentive trip to San Francisco in May, and JTB had presented a unique concept to them for consideration. Create an original one-hour musical that would target the specific objectives and messaging of the client and deliver it in a motivational way to strengthen the sense of team and stimulate sales. Miki loved it.

Tim: "This sounds right up your alley, Andrea."

Andrea: "Let's do it."

And thus, the *Miki Dream Passport* Musical was born. At a round table in the Extraordinary Events conference room, three men from J-Com met with my team. Tim (an Englishman now living in Japan) was both translator and interpreter, two terms that became mutually exclusive.

The challenges included: a limited budget; a more limited time frame (less than 60 days from first meeting to execution); the language barriers (the audience spoke no English); the cultural differences in show structure and the fact that JTB had not attempted something like this show before, therefore, taking a great risk with an important client.

Being a firm believer that challenges are dreams waiting to become reality, we took the plunge, picked up the gauntlet and dared to dream. In less than 60 days we conceptualized and created a one-hour original musical (which became 90 minutes when implemented) and which delivered a specific message to the audience. We collaborated on a bi-lingual script (being written in Japanese) which we adapted to English lyrics and dialogue. We wrote original music and lyrics; choreographed a Broadway-style show; cast and costumed over 30 performers; rehearsed and performed it. We communicated with a client in another country with different hours, different holidays, different culture and a different language. And, finally, we executed all of this in a union facility with a short load-in schedule.

So the final night, following meetings with motivational speakers, education and hospitality, we produced a wonderful dinner with pretty tables, lovely lighting, a parade of the executives and top awardees into the ballroom and a laser show with the Miki logo. It was followed by our custom Broadway-style musical delivering Miki Prune's business message to motivate its all-Japanese-speaking sales force through the story of a young woman who had a series of adventures, meeting friends along her travels, all of whom have a business problem to solve. In song, dance, magic and circus-style performances, these problems were resolved to show that every salesperson has the tools within to succeed. The custom musical score, innovative scenery and bi-lingual script delivered the message to perfection in a highly-entertaining fashion.

The Show

House lights dim as the spotlight focuses on a glorious large stage. Could it be an entertainer like Art Garfunkel, the 1999 headliner? Maybe a few entertainers as opening acts?

Dessert is cleared, and the adventure unfolds. One of the executives from Miki steps forth and introduces a pretty assistant. Together they explain that this is an unusual show. It's the story of a person, just like them, and her adventures in becoming the person she's always wanted to be. To help her conquer her fears and overcome the obstacles in her path, each seat has a bag under it. In that bag is an assortment of hand props for guests to use during the show, when instructed. The bag has flowers, a mirror, a disposable flash camera and glow sticks.

Musicians in place, the overture begins. Beautiful music swells in a compilation of original and traditional show tunes to produce a lovely medley. At the crescendo, the tiny tinkling music signifying the unifying theme of the show plays, and from the side of the stage, we meet our narrator, The Prune Fairy.

In a theme park-style character costume, The Prune Fairy introduces the plot (in Japanese), and as he finishes the monologue, lights come up on a homey living room where our heroine, Mary, is talking to her Auntie Emily. She expresses her wish to become a great musical star. Auntie Emily tells her that her dreams can come true. She can be whatever she wants to be, and there is a way to make her dreams come true. If she follows the Prune Road (somewhere just outside of San Francisco) and meets the Queen of the Prune Orchard, the Queen can grant her dreams. But how does she get there? All she has to do is sing.

And so Mary's dream journey begins. She falls asleep in her big easy chair, and the Prune Fairy once again appears to narrate the next sequence of events, the journey.

Mary dreams of wonderful Broadway dancers in a chorus line, beautifully costumed, perfectly choreographed and performing to music from A Chorus Line. Leaping, twirling, they are glorious. Between the dancers a lone figure seems somewhat out of synch. Lost, perplexed, he tries, but he can't seem to get in step. As the chorus line exits, he remains behind, sad and forlorn. Mary, now awake, greets him and asks him if he is one of those wonderful dancers. He introduces himself as Jack, also known as the young Bojangles, a wonderful dancer as long as he performs solo. He demonstrates his talent to her with a magnificent version of *Mr. Bojangles*, done Fosse-style with stylized lighting effects. Our Dancer is sad because he wants to be able to perform with his friends, TO BE A PART OF A TEAM. So Mary invites him to join her because she believes that the Queen of the Prune Orchard can grant his wish.

Mary and Jack dance down the Prune Road by a stunningly colorful field of flowers, as our cast of dancers (now in the audience) encourages the audience to wave their flowers in the air to *Ease on Down the Road*. The Prune Road curls through the center of the audience with a few twists and turns to keep it interesting. The music ends, and we hear the gong of mystical music. Two giant cards are then set on stage, and in Japanese, we hear the dramatic and theatrical introduction of Master Magician Greg Wilson, bilingual and internationally-renowned illusionist. He performs his amazing show with the assistance of three helpers, calling upon members of the audience to complete his act on stage. He takes his bows, and one of his assistants remains behind to "clean up" the stage.

Mary and Jack introduce themselves, meeting Sam, the assistant. Mary asks him to do a trick for her.

"I can't," says Sam. "I'm only the assistant."

He is not INDEPENDENT enough to perform by himself. So, he, too, is invited to join them as they continue down The Prune Road and by another floral field as our guests wave more flowers in the air to help them on their adventure. Once again, the threesome "eases on down the road" with the encouragement of our dancers.

A calliope signifies the circus theme that follows. In the background, a big top is projected onto the stage with circus performers everywhere. Clowns in brightly colored costumes playfully cavort on stage. Four acrobats leap onto the stage. In a display of strength and skill, they perform a hand-balancing act that is truly stunning. One of the acrobats seems to want to join in, but he stays on the sidelines. The act over, Mary, Jack and Sam meet him. His name is Thomas, and he's very sad. He does not have the COURAGE to join his team. Mary, discouraged by his sadness, tells him to *Put on a Happy Face* and sings and dances with him until (clowns pratfalling and making merry) he finally laughs. Thomas is now invited to join them, too. Clowns help the audience wave flowers as yet another field is displayed, and our adventurers continue to sing and dance down The Prune Road in search of the Queen of the Prune Orchard.

As they turn on stage, the set is now the dungeon of a dark Gothic castle, fog rolling out around a large cauldron. Ominous creatures surround an ugly cackling witch who tells our cast that they simply cannot go to meet the Queen because she won't let them. She and her horrible assistants intend to trap them all in the land of darkness. And so a chase begins. Mary is captured and held captive. In Japanese, the cast instructs our audience to take out their cameras and use the flash as the witch is afraid of light, and it will disable her. As the audience flashes their cameras, our cast becomes momentarily enthralled by the cameras, posing for the guests from on stage and in the audience. Even our witch gets caught up and poses prettily. Mary, incensed, demands that they pay attention to rescuing her, and so her recovery continues. The cast has our audience pull out mirrors, and with our intelligent lighting reflecting off them, the witch succumbs. Finally, Mary is rescued. All four congratulate each other on their courage, their independence and their sense of teamwork.

Once again they *Ease on Down the Road* finally emerging in a beautiful orchard where they meet The Queen surrounded by living foliage. She introduces herself to the four adventurers, and happily Mary asks her to grant their wishes. Alas, she cannot.

Graciously she explains that all along they have had within them the ability to act out their dreams. They never needed her. "If you focus and if you believe," she tells them, "your wishes will come true." She sings to them as she departs the scene. *If You Believe* becomes a true show-stopping moment of heart. Miki's philosophy is never more evident, because at its base is the Japanese character for "heart" underlining their human approach to business.

It's time for our travelers to say goodbye to each other and go their separate ways, having learned their life lessons. Jack dances off with his chorus line, happy to be part of a TEAM. Sam performs some magic all by himself, for he is now truly INDEPENDENT, and Thomas joins his acrobatic friends in feats of COURAGE and skill. Mary waves goodbye, then drifts off to sleep in her comfy chair, which has reappeared as if by magic.

The Prune Fairy returns to explain what has happened, and as Mary awakens, she sees her Auntie Emily. She tells her about her wonderful dream. Aunt Emily advises her "to focus and to believe in herself." Mary ponders, for those words sound very familiar. Auntie Emily departs, and Mary sings *Over the Rainbow* to close the show.

Curtain calls and bows proceed with the entire cast. All except Mary. To a thunderously powerful musical moment, Mary appears, only now she is decked out head-to-foot as a famous, glamorous Broadway star. She, too, has realized her dreams, and as she belts out *If You Believe,* the show closes with the audience waving glow sticks in unison.

The cast holds their position on The Prune Road, and everyone joins together for the *Miki Prune Song* orchestrated for this one moment in time to unify the entire sales team and cast. Challenges met. Dreams realized.

Results

EE was charged with promoting the Miki Corporate Philosophy to motivate staff to "challenge" *ambition, team spirit* and *independence* as individuals. And to achieve it by creating *moriagari* - a Japanese word which has no one-word equivalent in English but means something like creating "an escalation of lively enthusiasm and excitement."

Participants fully identified with and became a part of the event. They integrated the specific business messages into their own lives and experiences and left motivated and excited to be a part of Miki.

Individual cast characters challenged the separate aims of the corporate philosophy, with the key characters representing the program guests. This challenged the audience by identifying business problems and offering a tangible solution in a palatable manner.

Enthusiasm and excitement were created by incorporating three short shows within the story and using audience participation and interactivity. Each time the audience participated in the show, they were drawn further into the story line and its challenges and identified with the "team spirit" presented on stage.

How do we know they were thrilled and moved by the experience? One of the most gratifying experiences of producing special events is that we producers are in the unique position of being able to see first-hand the audience's reaction to our work. This was the crowning glory of this project. In this case, we saw it not only once, but twice. The exact same show was being performed for two divisions of Miki on two consecutive nights.

We had no way of knowing whether the audience would understand music and dialogue that were not in their mother tongue. But, song and dance are comfortable mediums for the Japanese audience. We hoped that the music, the "acting" and the familiarity of some of the songs would make the performances accessible and enjoyable.

The audience was comprised mainly of women, many middle-aged. The creative solution therefore became creating a homey and friendly main character who was our Japanese version of "Everyman" and who had the same dreams most middle-age women have or have had.

The character's adventures were whimsical and lighthearted. Because the Japanese are enthralled with magic, we included it within our adventures, as well as circus, which is very popular. Working the script around those acts, with new twists, was a creative way to utilize what would work with this audience. We threaded the package together to make a cohesive and entertaining whole that always, in every way, drove home its unique message.

We succeeded beyond our wildest dreams. The audience sang along with many of the songs. At times, during some emotional segments, many were crying. They laughed at some of the jokes, even some impromptu plays on words. And when our cast spoke to them in Japanese, they were enthusiastic and receptive.

We had designed many interactive elements into the show but again we could only hope that they would choose to participate.

Without exception the entire audience took part in these activities, waving flowers to encourage our star along her journey through fields of flowers, flashing cameras to kill our evil witch who was afraid of light and joining wholeheartedly in the antics of the magician who demanded audience participation. All souvenir program guides were kept as keepsakes and used for autographs by the cast after the show. All guests enthusiastically joined in singing the company song at the end of the show.

At the cast "party" at the very end of the performance, transportation departure was delayed as guests gathered to meet the performers and warmly thank them, get autographs and pose for pictures before leaving. Tears of joy and sentimentality were much in evidence, and it was obvious that every guest left with a sense that they had taken part in something special.

As the Miki executives formed a receiving line at the exit, the normally reticent Japanese guests were overt in their praise that this had been an overwhelmingly meaningful experience to them.

In the words of EE's associate producer and logistical coordinator, "There was a time when you just knew and felt that the audience understood the effort, artistic as well as logistical, that went into this show. They felt what we and the cast felt. And that is something that doesn't require any language to communicate, because it is not about words; it is about human feelings. We all tried so hard and talked and planned so much about how to make sure that they would understand English. They probably didn't understand that much English, but it didn't matter because they felt the emotions in their hearts and souls that no language can express. They *experienced* the show."

Challenges and Solutions

The challenges were numerous on this production. I've outlined a few of them.

International Client. The client was in Japan, and the production was in the United States. This challenge was met with constant and intense communication that meant no one observed evenings, weekends or holidays. Whenever someone needed to talk, we talked. Email, digital photography and Federal Express were our salvation.

Union Venue. The venue was a union facility and had not been booked with enough load-in time for the project. The solution was rehearsing in rehearsal studios instead of onsite, therefore, allowing more time for technical setups and rehearsals.

Business Philosophies. The United States team did not understand Japanese philosophies and vice versa, oftentimes making communication difficult. Respect. Trust. Faith. Cooperation. That's how we met that challenge. It is rare that a Japanese company, much less a production company, takes the leap of faith shown to the Extraordinary Events team. We talked through every element upon which we did not see eye-to-eye and came to mutual agreements.

There is a great difference in the way production is done in both countries, and we simply eliminated the word "why" from our vocabularies. "Why" didn't matter. For instance, JTB wanted the main talent to have their "big" moments (magic act, acrobatics and big dance number) during the first half of the show, and we strongly disagreed, feeling that they made a stronger finale. We conceded and saw that they were right because it created more dynamic and involvement right from the onset. We, however, felt strongly about the final moments of the show. The lead character wanted to be a musical star, but in the original script she just woke up in her house with her dreams and did not actually realize them. So, we wrote her appearance as a Broadway star into the finale. All agreed that it was the perfect surprise ending for the show.

The Language Barrier. They spoke Japanese. We spoke English. Tim Lemon. Tim Lemon. Tim Lemon. That's how we met the challenge. Tim worked tirelessly to interpret and to communicate, never seeming to take a side as he made us feel productive and creative. I'm sure he kept his Japanese team feeling that they were getting their needs met at all times. Hats off to this man. He was the consummate communicator.

Every single detail was attended to with care and precision to execute a worthy stage show. Both on stage and off stage, all cues were executed beautifully. All lines were delivered without fault. At moments where ad-libbing was appropriate, the cast had learned enough Japanese phraseology that they could "play" with the audience in an impromptu fashion, and the audience loved it.

The Cultural Differences in Work Ethic. There is a difference in how people in these two cultures work. We have worked extensively with Japanese clients, and, therefore, not only acknowledge but respect their way of working. However, we had many new vendors working under challenging time constraints, and this made it more difficult, because we had to educate them.

To quote Tim Lemon, "There is a Japanese joke about the typical Japanese work week. In Japan people are used to working Monday, Monday, Tuesday, Wednesday, Thursday, Friday, Friday."

To the Japanese, deadlines must be met even if unreasonable. In the U.S., you simply do the best you can. To the Japanese you cannot say "no" to your client. In the U.S. if you are faced with an impossible task, you tell your client it is impossible.

The Japanese attention to detail is beyond that with which any U.S. company ordinarily deals. This means that in the midst of last minute casting, writing, problem solving and communication, we had to clearly and in great detail produce documents that we deemed unnecessary, yet were very necessary for our Japanese clients.

Even two weeks prior to the show, decisions were being made about last minute additions, opening acts or laser modules, and for each of these, tapes had to be submitted and overnighted. It was hard for the Japanese to understand that if they asked for information on a particular act that they might not get an immediate answer. In Japan the timelines are immediate. It was hard to explain that various magicians took days to return phone calls or create pricing.

It was all about communication. And logistically, that was a challenge.

The Limited Budget. Because the show had a specific and limited budget and the venue was a union facility, dollars were closely watched. The Japanese team could not make frequent site inspections; therefore, rehearsals were videotaped for their review. Music was written and samples overnighted to Japan for approval, as the musical element was very important to the client.

Staging a show that is not written or choreographed in its final form is a unique challenge, so we had to create staging and scenic that could be adapted to a wide variety of scenarios. Every inch of stage had to be usable. Set pieces were minimized and easily movable. Visibility from every corner of the room was a paramount consideration.

As the show evolved, it became more and more complex. Scenery became a key issue. There was very little money for it, and it could also have become very expensive. It was decided that scenic elements would be brought to life through Pani Projections (large-scale projections), so that, as our lead character traveled through her various adventures, the scenery would be in a state of constant change and keep the environment interesting. A theatrical trick and a very effective one.

Rehearsals took place in Los Angeles as well as San Francisco, but because the primary cast came from Los Angeles, preliminary rehearsals were held there. Flying the director back and forth was more cost effective than traveling and housing the entire cast. As soon as a piece of music was written, rehearsals began. We never waited for the show to be complete before rehearsals. As soon as we cast one lead, we costumed that person. Each element completed was one less about which to worry.

The full cast was assembled only for the final three days in order for rehearsals to take place in its entirety.

A show such as this one could have been enormously expensive. Instead it was clever. Utilizing the concept of audience participation made it feel "homey" and familiar to the audience. It was not filled with glitz and tricks and expensive laser and pyro. Instead it had great personal meaning and integrity delivered through talent. It featured no expensive *names*. The acts that were used worked for lesser rates, because they were allowed to customize their performances and participate in the creation of a script which showcased their individual talents to their fullest. For instance, Greg Wilson became an integral part of the show when asked to create magic tricks for Mary and Jack and the witch who needed to appear and disappear at various points. It was not part of "his" show, but he directed those illusions for the betterment of the entire piece.

In other words, we negotiated each and every element of the show to maximize the budget. No one element was sacrificed at the expense of another.

The Logistics of the Show. In a word, difficult. As mentioned before, rehearsals could not take place on stage but instead in rehearsal studios. Los Angeles cast members were rehearsing with blocking that was somewhat different from what was being rehearsed by the San Francisco cast members. Patience. A professional cast. Temper-free technicians and stage managers. Adaptability. We went into the show with a caution for all those participating. Either be flexible or don't be a part of this show. There was no room for drama, except on stage.

The Lesson

This was a bi-lingual production with original music and ideas, and, more importantly, it was message-driven. When there's a message involved, I'm always on board. It's the stuff of which my personal dreams are made. How can it get any better when I can do what I love and help other people understand how they can succeed? I was entertaining and informing all at once.

And herein lies the true lesson. Make your productions (and your life) meaningful to your audience (and friends and family) while you entertain and touch them right to the core of their souls. In other words, provide real meaning in everything you do.

I don't know what else there is. It goes back to small talk and my mother not wanting to discuss important topics. I don't live a shallow existence. Everything in my personal and professional life is important and meaningful to me. This became important to me in school as the editor of the school paper for years. I became involved in issues, such as racism, before it was popular to do so, and I wanted other people I knew to be concerned with me. I encouraged it in them then, and I still do.

The phrase, "Do Everything with Intent," means much to me. It all ties into my philosophy of generosity and paying it forward. It's important to show people who you are. And doing this has involved me in social responsibility projects and finding ways through my business for people to have real communication and not just be inundated with smiling, motivational speakers. It is my goal in business to make people belly laugh from joy or cry because something has been so beautifully touching. It can't happen every time. In my very rich fantasy, I wish that it could.

23

Lessons Learned

Ask the Right Questions and When You've Asked Them ALL,

Ask Some MORE and Never Proceed with Verbal Acceptances

Years ago *long* before I had experience producing major events (well, to be fair, neither did anyone else so there was no such thing as a mentor), I was asked to produce a series of events for a large automotive-related company. The client ... let's call him "Jack" ... was a big, tough, aggressive man who had strong opinions and shared them openly. He was a bit scary to me. *That'll show you how long ago it was.*

He wanted two events, each done twice for back-to-back programs. One was a reception in the exhibit hall of a Southern California Hotel (which shall remain nameless), and the other was a headliner for the final wow night.

I signed on The Pointer Sisters and was really excited. This was big time! I planned a fun kind of "country" night for the reception. I called the hotel, and they gave me the hours I could get into each room and when I needed to strike. Now remember this was a *very long time ago*. No fancy production schedules. No computers. Just legal pads with handwritten notes and phone confirmations. Good enough.

I hired a decorator, a technical team and confirmed with my client and my hotel contact when I'd be arriving, what rooms I would need and what I would be doing. All was well.

Until I arrived.

There was no room for me. I went to Jack who was supposed to make the reservation. "I thought you were making your own arrangements" was his response.

Going to my hotel contact, the only room left was the living room of a suite with a chair that made into a bed. Supposedly. When I opened the chair, it stuck half way, and that's the way I slept for a week. Scrunched.

That was the *best* part.

When the decorators arrived to set up the country-style reception and I met them at the exhibit hall, it was filled with huge tractors. WHAT? I called my hotel contact and asked when they would be moved out. "Oh, they're not being moved out," he replied. "They need to stay."

I went to Jack. "That's your problem; you're supposed to take care of that." Well, I COULDN'T move the tractors, and the hotel WOULDN'T move the tractors, so the best thing we could do was either disguise them or use them. Hay bales, fencing, anything and everything we could think of to make them fit into our scheme. Can you imagine if it had been an elegant motif?

Still not terrible. YET.

Time for The Pointer Sisters. I had to send three limos for them instead of one, because they weren't getting along. Not a good thing, do you think?

At least they were on their way. This was also before cell phones. I was being paged continuously along their route from Los Angeles to San Diego, because the drivers had to keep stopping for various foods and were running late. See's Candy, Kentucky Fried Chicken, Barbeque … each time they delayed (one at a time, no less), I was called at the hotel and paged.

All this was happening simultaneously with setup for the ballroom, or what SHOULD have been setup. I had been told (verbally) that

I could have access to the ballroom at 8:00 a.m. So that's when my crew showed up. Guess what? There was a breakfast in the ballroom. Yes, I had confirmed it over the phone, but in the words of my shrugging Convention Services Manager, "Someone else must have booked the space, but you'll have it by 11:00." So knowing how little time we had, I called in some extra crew. I again went to Jack who said, "You should have checked." It was useless to tell him (again) that he had told me he had everything arranged in advance or that it was his information that gave me the setup and strike hours in the first place.

Okay, we can make it happen, I thought. At 11:00, I showed up at the ballroom. You've guessed it. They were setting up for a lunch featuring Frankie Laine, a legendary entertainer. I again went to the hotel management, and now it was the fault of yet another salesperson and "Oh, well, things happen, but you can have the room by 3:00." Sound check had been scheduled for 3:00, and we were not yet in the room. I added more crew. When I told Jack that this would be an extra expense, he got very loud and told me he was not paying for it; it was MY problem.

On with the show, and we started setup at 3:00; sound check at around 7:00; doors at 8:00 and showtime. That went off without a hitch, and I went back to my scrunchy chair to get some sleep before the second group of guests arrived the next day.

The next set of shows was easier. Tractors stayed in place, but there was no breakfast, lunch or Frankie Laine.

The Lesson

Don't ever, EVER, accept anything verbally. Get it in writing, signed off by your client and by your vendors. Do disclaimers ... "If the room is unavailable when promised and extra crew is needed, there will be additional charges."

Put EVERYTHING in writing. Do a detailed production schedule and have everyone initial every page.

24

Never Assume!

Los Angeles' Bid to the Democratic National Convention Committee

Extraordinary Events was hired to come up with an innovative method for Los Angeles to present its bid to The Democratic National Committee to host the convention (which incidentally L.A. won). So, here's our presentation at the South Hall Lobby of the Los Angeles Convention Center.

The DNC arrived by limo into an empty convention hall. Committee members walked a red carpet which led them to a loooong balloon wall that spelled out *Los Angeles*. Where were they supposed to go?

With a rousing fanfare of unseen herald trumpets, the balloon wall burst open in one magical explosion and revealed the entry to the South Hall Lobby where a long line of faux paparazzi applauded them into the hall. Down an escalator they went to join the executives and VIPs of the Los Angeles Visitors and Convention Bureau and the city. Music. Morning fare. Very nice. And angels, lots of them. And then ... from 400 feet overhead, accompanied by a beautiful piece of ethereal music, an angel descended and performed an aerial ballet until she landed at the feet of the DNC members and handed them Los Angeles' bid. Magically, she arose again to disappear 400 feet above. It was a moment that the press wrote about and photographed for print and live television.

But, that's not all they wrote! They *also* wrote about the angels that were already in the room, and herein is our story.

We had specified to our talent coordinator that we wanted a room of angels to circulate. I had great faith in his judgment. But I should have said, "Describe every person and every costume," but I didn't. So here's what I got. One angel was in *scarlet red lingerie and sequined wings.* Another wore a Frederick's of Hollywood *black bustier with black feather wings* (think whips and chains angel), and it went on from there. Yep, there was plenty about which to write!

The Lesson

Never make an assumption. NEVER! Check every detail. Ask for write-ups and *descriptions.* Ask for photos. Don't ever feel too secure. Don't *assume!* You know what that makes out of you and me!

Even though I slipped this one time, I usually never assume. This stems from my upbringing, which taught me never to feel secure. There are always going to be things out of my control. Right now do I have control over the economy or war? No, there's nothing I can do, so I roll with it. I am comfortable being insecure. It gives me momentum. In fact, I don't think I've ever felt secure about anything, because, unfortunately, I always want what I don't have. I love what I do have, but it is never enough. That goes back to the wallflower in me. Being insecure is all I have even know. It's like anorexia of the brain. At age 65, it isn't going anywhere, but the little fat girl and I have made friends with each other now, because if I can overcome a challenge and achieve, then I have a much greater sense of my identity.

25

Lessons on Learning What We Don't Know – The Hard Way

Lore of Ireland - Dublin

July: My Irish lore begins with a blur of words from a client I had not spoken to in years. "This is right up your alley. We're doing a program in Ireland, and we need a WOW." My heart soared. I loved Ireland, what little I had seen of it. And I was dying to work with friends of mine over there. We had been talking about it for years.

The background: A Media Broadcasting Company with 200 well-traveled guests - last year at a Sporting Club in Monte Carlo; the year before a Palace in Spain. The client didn't like anything she had seen in Dublin. Blah. Boring. Find a place. Find something to do. No parameters. But she wanted an evening of "magic" for a group that had experienced some incredible international trips.

Email – such a blessing. I wrote my friends. They had several possible venues. They sent me photos and described them. I used this information (and my imagination) and sent off some ideas combining theme and a theatrical show to the client. She liked them all. I had also sent estimated prices. She didn't like *any* of them. Cut backs. Needed to economize. Oh, dear.

As it happened, I was in Europe a short time later, so I offered to go to Dublin and look at the venues. She said, "Pick one. We trust you." (I nearly fell over!)

I went to Dublin for a day and a half and saw impossibilities. It can rain any day in Dublin. We had to be indoors. No place could hold all 200 people in one room. Nothing felt special.

Our last stop was The Round Room, possibly the ugliest room I had ever seen and our only viable possibility. It was part of the Lord Mayor's Residence, and it was built in the 1700s. It was our solution, albeit a depressing one. The walls were the most disgusting shade of green I had ever seen, except for the other walls which were ochre. Now I've used ochre when I oil painted, but never as a décor element. I asked the lighting director to bring me some lights and see what we could disguise. Nothing! They remained just *hideous*. I met with the team of technicians, directors and choreographers and brainstormed, and things fell into place. Here's what we finally did.

The Lore of Ireland

August: Guests received a beautiful and formal invitation from the Lord Mayor of Dublin to a cocktail reception at the beautifully elegant City Hall, a domed room with exquisite marble statuary, columns and remarkable history. The mosaics alone were stunning. Here we held a champagne reception, and each couple had their photo taken. Golf awards were given out, and our finale was the appearance by the distinguished Lord Mayor of Dublin who welcomed our guests, and seemingly overcome with the spirit of hospitality, invited the entire group to his home for dinner.

Guests boarded the coaches and arrived at his home where he ushered them through the front entrance, down a long art deco corridor and into his banqueting hall, The Round Room of the Mansion House.

At the threshold, they saw nothing, absolutely nothing, except ancient pillars of stone with Celtic carvings, all lit mysteriously with smoke whirling throughout the room. Low-lying sounds of birds and animals softly called from the stage, also dramatized with more pillars, while four ancient drummers beat out Celtic rhythms. All were body painted blue with Druid symbols. As they entered the room, adorable Irish children handed each guest a simple votive candle, almost the only illumination. They were told to find their seats, and 200 votives wended their way through the tables and created an enchanting sight.

Each table was draped in floor-length black satin. Each centerpiece (an original creation of stone, floral, water and candle representing Druid elements) was pin-spotted perfectly. The idea was to make everything disappear except what we wanted to highlight - the stones around the room, the stage and the centerpieces.

Lighting was ever-changing, appearing as if through a mist as if part of an enchanted forest, ever-illusive.

As all guests were seated, the drummers accelerated their rhythms until they turned into a wild frenzy. As they stopped, an ancient Druid priest in flowing robes stepped forth from behind one of the pillars and incanted a welcome in Gaelic to our guests. He then pointed skyward and called forth "The Spirit of Ireland." That brought attention to the single redeeming feature of this venue, the magnificent domed fiber optic ceiling. From 40 feet above, an aerialist dropped down over the stage and performed a dramatic aerial ballet to an ancient melody. She suspended herself over the stage as the Druid once again called out to her, and she danced around him and exited as he bid everyone to enjoy the upcoming feast. The meal service began.

The musical history of Ireland was revealed in between courses. After the first course was served and cleared, our Druid stepped forth once again and the show, *The Lore of Ireland*, which had been created for this one client, began. Every moment was designed to stir the senses, create emotional responses and bring forth the magic of Irish music in a unique performance. It was my goal to create the equivalent of *Riverdance*, and I did.

First our narrator introduced The Anuna Singers, multi-layered vocalists in Gaelic and English who were the original voices of *Riverdance*. In their velvet robes, they entered through the audience holding candles. Their voices, spiritual and plaintive, brought forth tears from moment one.

After the second course was completed, the narrator reappeared now in the garb of a 19th century dandy. He introduced the history of the times and brought forth The Three Celtic Tenors in a 20-minute tribute to the working-class history of Irish music. The group began with an Acappella version of *Danny Boy* and closed with the moving *Ireland* to bring the house down.

Dessert, and onto a rousing finale. Once again, we found our narrator, in a U2-type of modern dress with the requisite sunglasses, lounging on one of the pillars. He spoke of the progression of Irish music and dance and brought forth a children's group of costumed dancers (some as young as five years old) who led into the Anuna Dancers in a stirring display of soft shoe and hard shoe step dancing. (All of the dancers had been leads in *Riverdance* and *Lord of the Dance*.)

Our Druid priest returned in his original robes to give the entire group a blessing in Gaelic ... "in Ireland there are no strangers, only friends who have yet to meet." The Spirit of Ireland rejoined him to do another aerial ballet as she was lifted back into the ceiling, not to be seen again. The entire cast was choreographed into an emotional finale with bows.

What I had wanted to achieve, and did, was a magical moment in time when reality could be suspended, and emotions could reign. The absolute stillness of the audience during the entire performance, as well as the teary smiles as people rose to exit, told me a message had been delivered and appreciated for the beautiful memories that would last and last.

The entertainment encompassed all of Irish history and was presented in a very unusual and creative way. The use of a T-shaped stage allowed us to bring it right into the heart of the audience. Unusual exits and entrances involved the audience in the drama. The beautiful costuming was authentic, and every element was customized just for this show.

Surprising the guests by allowing them to think that the event would take place at City Hall and then having the Lord Mayor escort them to his home was a real "WOW" and an unforgettable moment for all.

Even wait staff was rehearsed so that they became a part of the event.

The entire evening was about detail and split-second timing. No one element was more important than any other. And it was entirely Irish, which meant that it was emotional, tasteful and literate.

With a limited budget and few venues that could hold 200 in one room available in Dublin, there were many challenges. However, Extraordinary Events created an evening that was filled with surprises, drama and the magical music of Ireland in a custom-created revue. The venue was decorated to symbolize ancient Druid times, and every element was authentically Irish, including a menu of local delicacies. The objective was to give everyone a unique experience. The reviews came in high ... the objective was accomplished.

Objectives

On a limited budget ($98,000 for two shows a week apart – not much for an international event), we needed to create a "WOW" factor for people who had seen and done it all. This was accomplished through clever thinking and attention to detail, as well as creativity in planning. If you don't have the money for all kinds of special effects or headline entertainment, you do the next best thing. You make people invest themselves into the evening. We created an emotional evening of spirituality and brought the guests into the experience in a non-silly, non-thematic way. We reached for the highest denominator and brought the audience right along with us. We never allowed ourselves to believe that the evening would be too high brow. We believed in our audience and trusted that they would recognize good taste and quality, and our faith was rewarded. The "WOW" was created by talent and sentiment and creative presentation instead of artificial effects.

We also needed to create an evening which would earn our client the business for next year. This was the final night, and the final memory. It had to be perfect. We had our audience leave enthralled with the creativity, the customization and the attention to detail. The client believed that if we could make this kind of event happen in Dublin we were indeed makers of magic, and next year was confirmed.

Challenges and Solutions

There were limited venue options in Dublin to fit our bill. There were limited funds for site inspections, so everything had to be accomplished in a one-day trip. We found a location (after looking at many analytically), and thus the second challenge arose. It was the ugliest and dreariest room we had ever seen. We overcame this challenge by getting creative and basically hiding the entire room by draping it floor to ceiling in black fiber optic drape.

The next challenge was that the Irish, as lovely as they are, had a difficult time not doing things the way they had always been done. In other words, I was creating a show from my own fantasies, trying to bring wonder, history and magic into this event. Well, *it simply was not the way it had always been done*, and there was resistance. My solution was to create their investment into the process, and by collectively brainstorming, everyone finally began to participate in the creative solutions and production, rather than the resistance. We empowered the entire team, and it worked.

Then there was the HEAT WAVE … in Dublin where they had never seen one! Therefore, a quest for air conditioning ensued. To say that there are not many air conditioning units in Dublin would be an understatement. Yet at the first wave (We did this event for two entirely different groups a week apart), guests were sweating and drinking water by the gallon which kept the wait staff very busy refilling pitchers. When the heat wave struck, every business and event tried to capture whatever units they could. They were priced at a premium, but necessary. Side note: Having well-connected local vendor/partners pays off. We got the unit, and everyone during the second wave was comfy.

The currency fluctuation was another challenge as it was unpredictable to estimate what anything really costs in U.S. dollars from day to day. Unfortunately, when the job was booked, the dollar was much stronger. The dollar became weaker between planning, execution and final billing; therefore, we lost money ($30,000) in the process! And when I told the client (optimistic to the last), I was told, "It wasn't in your contract." C'est la vie. Sometimes you win; sometimes you lose.

And finally, just a fun story: In the middle of the performance, one of the guests (wearing a "rock the size of Gibraltar" on her ring finger) came up to me and said, "I have a cute idea ... my husband is wearing a kilt; have him join the *Riverdance* group ... people will love it."

Let me note that it was said as a command, and not a request.

My reaction (in my head), "Let me guess, you're the woman who saw *Phantom* and said, "Hey, Mikey, I think it would be adorable if you did a duet of *Music of the Night* with my husband" ... and of course asked this while he was in the middle of singing, right?"

My answer (out of my mouth), "I wish we could, but we can't. Let me tell you how a show is created and produced. This is a fully-staged and rehearsed show, timed to the second, Though I think it's a FABULOUS idea unfortunately your husband wasn't available to rehearse with us, so it won't be possible this time."

And did I tell you about the mischievous leader of the Anuna Singers? After Wave One, we had to cut some time from his group, and he agreed. Then, when they took the stage for Wave Two, he had indeed cut out a couple of songs *but added others* as he winked at me from on stage! Ah, the life of a theatrical producer!

The Lesson

Several.

First, *always* have a local partner who is "connected." It never fails to pay off.

Next, *never* issue an international contract without acknowledging what might change, such as the currency exchange rate, and account for it on every page of your contract and budget. *Always do your homework! Why didn't I think of that when I met each of the men in my life?*

Never assume that there won't be a heat wave or a cold spell, "just because." Plan for every contingency.

Always bite your tongue before answering a diva with a big diamond who acts imperiously.

Never assume that all Irish *don't* have a devilish sense of humor.

26

ZZZZZZ....Don't Sleep Through Reading Your Contract!

User's Week Conference Wonder-ful Night - Santa Clara, California

For the opening night of an annual User's Week Conference in San Jose, California, Extraordinary Events, in partnership with our client The George P. Johnson Company, created *A Wonder-ful Night* featuring Stevie Wonder. Completely transforming the Santa Clara Convention Center through innovative design, décor and lighting, we set the tone for the conference week. The decor featured metallic bead waterfalls, original furniture and spectacular florals. Local jazz musicians and a finale concert with the incomparable Stevie Wonder added the entertainment element. Over 3,000 guests were moved seamlessly through a space that was used effectively and creatively to accomplish the end goal of welcoming guests to a "Wonder-ful" week.

The Event

In October of 2000, the location selected for the conference was San Jose, California, the genesis of high-tech America. Due to the location, we expected a high turnout of industry professionals, and we knew that we had our work cut out for us to impress these guests in their own backyard. And we were to accomplish this goal in the Santa Clara Convention Center, a nice but rather small and unassuming venue that many of these guests had been to several times for similar conventions and meetings. In order to make this night memorable, we would have to make it "Wonder-ful." And that's just what we did.

Unlike other companies who choose to save the best for last in a multi-day event, this client likes to pull out all the stops right away. The goal is to make an immediate impression and create an atmosphere of excitement that will keep guests anticipating the next big event. Knowing this, we had to find the perfect entertainment. Entertainment is a large part of the client's events, with emphasis on high-profile acts ... entertainers who are in keeping with its image. This year we selected Stevie Wonder, and from there we created the theme of *Wonder-ful Night*.

Our biggest challenge was using the space creatively and efficiently. With over 3,000 guests expected and only one main entrance that featured a small lobby and several off-shoot areas, our flow was going to be very important. We had to make sure that the first few thousand people, most of whom would be arriving within minutes of each other, would proceed to the areas we wanted them in a quick manner without feeling like they were being rushed. We needed to take special consideration with the 150+ VIPs arriving throughout the evening that had to be escorted upstairs and kept "separate, yet a part of the party." They required their own top-level security and service staff and constant attention. We also had to be very careful about how many people we had in each area (including the entrance lobby) at one time as the fire marshal was ever-present and very strict. So our mission was simple ... move them in, move them on and do it quickly ...just don't let them know it. Sounds easy enough, but sometimes guests have a mind of their own.

We accomplished our first initiative by creating a nice, but simple lobby. A place where guests would take notice and enjoy, but not necessarily feel obligated to stay. The sponsors of the evening were well-branded through the use of huge moving lighting gobos, so they had the instant recognition they wanted and deserved. The huge, gray concrete structural columns that filled the lobby area were made more attractive by custom-created fabric "sleeves" that accepted light and added design to an otherwise sullen architectural feature. These were accentuated by additional fabric structures that were stretched over metal frames and arched in unique fashion throughout the high ceiling and unusually shaped lobby. These pieces curved off of the high soffits and over archways that were otherwise plain, unattractive concrete. They added warmth to the cold room and created canvas for the dramatic lighting. We succeeded in making this an attractive "hallway" through which guests could pass.

As our guest count began to rise and the date of the event approached, we realized we actually needed to use this entrance lobby as part of the event space or we would run out of room. Every inch of space became precious. But there was a problem. The large structural columns, which occupied most of the floor space, were not budging. And the fire marshal was very clear about the pathways that must be left around them as they served as the main exit from the building. And so we worked around them. *Literally.* We built buffet stations around them in a circular fashion so that they hugged the actual columns and served up easy finger foods for guests to nibble on as they walked by. A double bar was tucked up underneath the escalator shaft to conserve space and satisfy thirsty guests while not impeding traffic flow. It all worked, and everyone was happy. We added staff to assist with "moving" guests through this area and enticing them to investigate the other parts of the building. We utilized signage to reaffirm that there was always more around the next corner or down the next hallway. Everyone moved according to plan without suspecting even once that they were doing just what we wanted.

Building on the theme that was started in the lobby, we needed to decorate the main function hall that would hold the majority of guests for the dinner portion of the evening. This was a cavernous exposition space (over 45,000-square-feet) with tall, unimaginative ceilings and a variety of unattractive walls, each one slightly different in color, texture and size. We knew that even the best lighting would not help detract from these walls. We needed to draw guest attention away from them and onto something better ... but what? Our team came up with the perfect solution. A room filled with such innovative decor that no one would even notice the room itself! Creative theatrical lighting would enhance the entire effect. And it worked perfectly.

We started with the concept of metal. Three shades of metal to be exact: copper, bronze and aluminum. All décor was created using these three shades of metal. We eliminated the typical brights and concentrated on earth tones and metallics to create a Zen-like atmosphere in an ordinary space. The use of intelligent lighting fixtures allowed everything to continually change throughout the night, moving through the full color spectrum.

Capitalizing on the high ceilings, we created very tall décor that would run down the center of the room and draw the focus here and not to the sidewalls. A series of metallic beaded "waterfalls" were hung from the ceiling in curvy angles and dangled just above the heads of guests. These unique pieces captured light in new ways and constantly changed in tone and texture with the aid of intelligent lighting.

To complement these waterfalls, huge floor-to-ceiling fabric cones emerged out of custom-built, metal-colored sofas positioned down the middle of the room. These square sofas provided comfortable lounge seating for guests while creating beautiful décor visible throughout the room. Each of these enormous columns stretched up to the ceiling and held an intelligent lighting fixture within so that their own inner light continually changed throughout the evening as well, setting the tone for the entire space.

Scattered throughout the rest of the center of the room were different sizes and shapes of seating tables. We wanted everything about this night to be different from anything anyone had seen before. One of the ways we accomplished this was to use custom-designed seating tables. Tables were crafted out of brushed metal and topped with frosted Plexiglas and lit from within so that each one glowed. No linens necessary, just clean, glowing metal. Some were in the shape of triangles and some were squares. Growing out of the center of each of these tables was a completely unique centerpiece. Wheat grass was used as a base and then exotic florals "grew" out from there. Each one just slightly different from its neighbor ... and there were hundreds.

Complementing the custom tables, three sizes of cocktail tables were added for diversity. Highboys as well as 48-inch and 36-inch round seated tables were covered in three shades of custom-dyed spandex. Chairs were covered in matching spandex as well. Smaller versions of florals were added to these tables, each displayed in custom-built metallic containers which were pieces of art in themselves.

But we still had the problem of the ugly walls. Our focus was definitely on the center of the room, but the walls were not going away. We had darkened them but they remained ... we could not ignore them. They were persistent. To cover them would have eaten away the entire budget. There was a lot of wall space to cover. And so we put our heads together and did the next best thing. We covered "part" of them. And in a very artistic way. Our design team created panels in our three shades of metal that were placed at intervals around the room. Each one of these panels featured a sconce that held a floral vase. A beautiful and artistic display of florals emerged out of each vase and was spot lit for emphasis. Again, each one was completely unique and created out of all white florals and accented with fresh greens and fauna. Our ugly walls disappeared and in their place a lovely display of innovative art.

Food was served up from lavish buffets that were covered in custom-created, matching spandex and topped with more incredible floral artistry. Each buffet display was featured in another custom-created metallic sculpture, some reaching as high as eight feet.

To spice up the air in each room during the dinner portion of the night, the client wanted live local jazz. But not just any jazz ... the best. This is a very discerning client, and we had our work cut out for us. We actually attended the Monterey and San Jose Jazz Festivals just to source out the best local talent for the night. Canvassing for agents backstage, we found the perfect groups and contracted them for this special night. Each room featured a different local artist playing a distinct sound.

The second half of the evening took place in a totally separate portion of the venue. This meant quickly and efficiently moving all 4,500+ people (Oh, yes, the guest list exceeded the initial 3,000) into the concert hall for a performance by Stevie Wonder. Quite a feat made even more difficult by the fact that we had to move 150 VIPs in first and allow them to take their seats before opening doors to the rest of the crowd. Under tight security, we accomplished this and then proceeded to move the rest of the guests into the concert hall.

To build excitement for the concert, we created special banners that were hung down the center of the hallway leading into the concert. Each featured a picture of Stevie Wonder modeled after the theme of *Superstition*. These five-feet-by-eight-feet banners were digitally imposed onto brightly colored scrim fabric and then lit. They offered a contrast to the metallic colors from the first half of the evening. They added excitement to an otherwise bland hallway without taking up needed space, and they were highly visible to all.

Once inside the concert hall, the look was completely based on Stevie Wonder's mega hit *Superstition* which set it apart. The room was saturated in colors of red, purple, magenta, violet and hot pink. Huge gobos with the client's logo swirled around the room getting the crowd excited. Additional client and sponsor logos were seen on the video screens as guests entered. As the crowning jewel to the night, we not only carpeted the 45,000+ square feet of space, but we set the stage with a beautiful treatment to back Stevie's show. Custom wrought iron spirals wrapped themselves around sheer gatherings of fabric at different levels making a beautiful canvas on which lighting created a constantly changing backdrop. This was going to be a concert to remember, and the guests could feel the energy.

Stevie preformed a record multi-hour concert to the delight of the fans that watched him not only on stage but also on two huge I-Mag screens (20-feet-by-40-feet each) on either side of the stage. Two additional sets of 10-feet-by-13-feet screens were hung halfway back in the room along with delay speakers so that every guest could enjoy the show up close. The room was completely alive, and guests were dancing in the aisles. It was a true concert environment that gave the client the kickoff to the conference it wanted.

And as guests departed the venue, we provided the final touch to the evening. Desserts and coffee were served as the many buses lined up to take guests back to the eighteen+ hotels at which they were staying throughout the area. This was truly a "wonder-filled" night to remember.

Challenges and Solutions

Challenges are many when you are dealing with such a large guest list and such high-profile clients and entertainers. Some are within your control while others are not ... you just get to deal with them. The challenges started with this event in the initial design phases. The client had elegant expectations, and we were dealing with a non-elegant venue. This was a very nice but ordinary venue with convention center catering and décor. We had to change all that and meet our client's very high expectations.

We accomplished these goals by working with and not fighting what we had. We built décor that enhanced the environment without trying to "cover it up" which would have been both time-consuming and pricey. We emphasized what we wanted and downplayed what we didn't. We also challenged the executive chef to be creative and to design his dream menu, and he did. The entire staff of the convention center became excited with us, because they realized that we were going to showcase their venue in a way it had never before been shown. They were proud of their venue and worked diligently with our entire team to please us. This was the little venue that could ... and did.

Our other major challenge was guest flow. We addressed this through signage, both living and actual, as well as creating exciting environments that would attract guests to circulate and investigate.

One major issue beyond our control occurred the day of the event when the first 1,500 guests arrived early. Not five or ten minutes early, but *forty-five minutes* early. We still had food in the ovens and bartenders getting dressed. We still had last-minute florals being addressed and scissor lifts running around doing final lighting focuses. Our solution? We asked the coach drivers (who had all left their positions early "to be punctual") if they could "get lost" for five minutes. They agreed, and this allowed us to hide last-minute crew and bring out the bartenders and whatever cold hors d'oeuvres we could find. We opened the doors forty minutes early, and guests never knew it was not planned that way.

Another unplanned challenge occurred during the show seating. Once the doors were opened to the concert, it was a mad dash for the best seating. As we all know, VIPs are often the hardest ones to "move" and yet the most important to get into place. Several VIPs had elected not to come down early with the security escorts we had arranged for the priority seating upfront. As guests entered the hall for general seating, many tried to sit in the reserved VIP section where they saw empty seats. Unexpectedly, they got very angry when asked to move as the late VIPs arrived to take their reserved seats. Special security was immediately brought into this area to address the issue and avoid unpleasant behavior. The "tardy" VIPs were escorted to their seats, and all was well.

Because of Stevie Wonder's very serious policy (it's in his contract) against photos being taken during the show, we also had to take extreme measures to ensure its enforcement. But no matter how many measures we took, the worst happened. During sound check, one of the waiters walked in and took a picture on his cell phone. Stevie's manager took away the waiter's phone and let us know firmly that we had breached our contract. It was not an auspicious beginning.

We hired additional security as well as used many of our own crew to monitor the audience. Despite multiple announcements and signage making the no photography/no video taping policy eminently clear, we were still forced to take away several cameras from guests. This led to a series of backstage dealings after the show to ensure return of said cameras to the proper owners.

But guests didn't remain upset about their cameras for long. Stevie put on a fantastic show and was having such a great time that instead of the contracted 45 minutes he did almost three hours. And our client went nuts as all buses for 4,500+ people were now on serious overtime. The quandary? When in a lifetime will people ever get to see such a show? Do I insult the act? Do I anger the client? I decided to just let it play out.

The Lesson

Every event provides an opportunity to learn. In this case it was to read our contract carefully, to make sure our client had read it (and initialed it) too and to include contractual responsibilities over which we wouldn't have control in our agreements with the venue and contractors. We had a hefty charge for the waiter who took the photo. Our contract with the act said we had to pay a substantial bill (and we left that one paragraph out of our contract to client) so we did. Personal lesson? Don't whine when you get caught with your drawers down. `

27

Know Your Audience

My Big Lady Clothes

A few years ago, I made a life-altering decision. I was obese and self conscious, so I signed up for gastric bypass surgery. Vanity and health-related issues like diabetes influenced this decision, but in all honesty, vanity was the primary contributor. My reason: Just once in my life I wanted people to look at me and say, "My, she has a nice figure."

I was a size 22/24. Yep, obese. I'll skip the details, but the end result was that I lost almost 100 pounds and was not only "normal" but better than normal. Clothed, I had a great bod. Unclothed, another story. But I later fixed that, too, though it has nothing to do with this story. Now between sizes six and eight, I had a lot of "big lady" clothing in my closet. It was designer stuff (Yes, they have designers for large sizes) and expensive. By now, you already know that my great love is, and always has been, shopping.

This information is important to my story because my medical group offered support meetings every week, and part of its routine was to have people bring in the clothes that they had outgrown so that those losing weight wouldn't have to buy new clothing as they down-sized. Some of the ladies were almost 400 or 500 pounds, and I decided to bring them my clothes, thinking that by the time they got to my size 22s they could have a glamorous wardrobe.

So, I attended one of these meetings with bags filled with my lovely offerings. To kick the meeting off, the facilitator asked, "So what's the best part of losing weight?"

One lady responded, "I can walk into K-Mart and buy anything I want now."

I should have grabbed my bags and run at that moment, but I didn't. At the end of the meeting, the various bags people had brought were opened, and clothes started being passed around. I happily anticipated the joy of watching women seize my designer clothes, ranging from evening gowns to business suits. It didn't happen. These women were almost repelled as they handled my clothing. They snickered at the evening wear ..."Where they hell would I wear THAT? When I shoveled horseshit?" Business suits were almost as denigrated.

I was aghast. I knew I (and my clothes) didn't belong there.

The Lesson

So, how does this relate to business? Any business? It's a simple lesson: *Know your audience.*

28

When There's <u>NO</u> Money

Annual Awards Ceremony

For all of you who have had a client asking for the moon while telling you there is no money, this is dedicated to you.

The Background

Let's start with this premise, reader. You've been hired to do an awards show for an audience of 3,000 during an annual conference you are producing at a convention center. There will be lots of awards, perhaps 600 or more. Move it along and get it over with quickly. Make sure the names are right; I-MAG it; stage manage the executives; line up the presenters - just ordinary, everyday stuff for a production company. End it with a very popular late night show host who knows his stuff. Nothing to do there. Just light him, make him sound good and make sure his private jet arrives on time and is ready when he leaves. He's a pro.

The Challenge

In addition to the other elements, the client had a convention committee, and almost everything was decided by committee on extensive conference calls. During one of the calls, the "entertainment" for the awards was brought up. WHAT ENTERTAINMENT?

"Something like the Oscars and Emmys; you know, something like that."

We patiently explained that there was no budget.

"What is the set going to look like?" they asked.

WHAT SET? There was no budget. It soon became clear that the client expected both and was fearful that the audience would be bored if there was no entertainment. When we explained where the budget was going, what we heard were sighs of deep disappointment and the references to the fact that "Extraordinary Events is doing the speakers, the late night host, the food and beverage for 3,000 for five days, the tours ..." The unspoken message? For all we're doing for you we expect you to do something for us. We agreed to try to come up with a plan.

Several conference calls later, ideas were bandied about by the committee. They included production numbers worthy of a Vegas showroom, a celebrity emcee/impressionist like Danny Gans ("Is he available? How much is he?"), laser light shows and the city symphony. But mostly, the committee wanted production numbers. *The budget? Zero. Zilch. Nada. Nothing. Get the picture? NO MONEY FOR THIS ELEMENT!* Again, more deep breathing across the phone lines and reminders of how "next year" in Vegas they would know to increase *our* budget.

We wanted to make them happy. Wouldn't you?

The Solution

Since we had no set and no entertainment during awards and no money for either, the challenge was great. We decided to create a set and provide entertainment that would change the look of the stage during each performance number, providing literally a new set for each group of awards. How did we do this?

From the front box truss that was 40-feet-wide-by-40-feet-deep-by-28-feet-high, we suspended sixteen 40-foot dark blue sparkle knit fabric panels. These hung directly from truss to floor and were lit so that the iridescence of the material created an opening look as guests entered the area. The blue panels complemented the overall color scheme of the room. From the back truss, we attached two triangular white spandex panels that criss-crossed from one side to the other. We lit these back panels with colored light.

After guests were seated and before the initial group of awards started, we began the first performance set. Our cast of six dancers appeared from between the panels, and as they danced, they moved the panels from their straight hanging position. While they weaved the panels about and around their bodies, a rhythmic gymnast augmented the group with a stunning display of Olympian dance/ribbon/ball performance until the dancers brought the fabric into a new position, creating an entirely different stage look. In the back of the stage, two huge spandex panels were stretched to create a backdrop as well as a surface for some creative lighting elements.

With this new look in place, the first set of awards began. Forty minutes later, we did the next performance/set change. This time we added the element of a huge piece of fabric that the performers used in an Alvin Ailey (modern dance) type of look as they danced, creating the illusion of appearing in and out of the fabric. By the end of the dance number, the stage and fabric had yet another look to it.

During the third and final dance performance, the fabric was woven into yet another look and then ended with a kabuki drop (all fabric panels simultaneously were dropped and whisked away by the dancers as they dramatically exited) to reveal a clean stage in preparation for the final award, the big winner of the evening. Here, too, we added a little bit of drama. Performance artist Zoey Stevens took the stage, and as clues about the winner were given, he painted. As he painted, more clues were revealed. And more clues and more painting until the clues began to be less and less broad and the painting became more and more clear. When the final clue was given and the name of the winner was announced, the portrait (of the winner) was complete, the winner brought onto the stage and the award presented.

We spent $15,900 on stage design and entertainment, including set design, fabric and six dancers, with choreography, costumes, travel, rehearsals and the artist to paint the final award winner.

It was an innovation and creative solution for very little money to make a client very happy.

Side Note

Until we actually started rehearsal, we never quite knew if this would work. We did a scale model in our office using fabric strips and a model of the truss and stage sculpture. Then we pretended to dance (using our fingers) and moved the fabric around as we imagined it might look. Originally the spandex also was moved into new positions. Well, onsite there was a lot of adjustment. The dancers did not move as our fingers had planned. The spandex didn't move to the positions that had worked so beautifully on the model. With a lot of laughter and even more imagination, we went back to the drawing board and recreated until we had the look we wanted and needed.

One More Serious Challenge

On show night, our lives were threatened … The real story behind this event was that we worked in a venue that had never before been used. It was a new area at the convention center, and we were assured it was "sound" and that meant that the "sound" would work. The client signed a contract that stated construction work could continue throughout setup and load in. This meant that jackhammers were on during our sound check, *and we were not allowed to turn them off.* The end result was that we were not able to do a sound check. The construction noise was intensified by the glass surrounding the venue and continued during the beginning of the show. Here's Technical Director Greg Christy's account of what followed.

"When it came time for the headliner to perform, he walked out on stage, delivered his first joke – and silence from the audience. Another joke – no response. CAN YOU HEAR ME????? From the star. NOOOO!!! From the crowd. For a comedian, a definite show stopper. Our entertainer walked off the stage … a first for him, I believe, and he was pissed. In the tech booth, we could hear a litany of expletives through our headsets. He wasn't going back out, and the 3,000 attendees were getting restless. Our tech booth was in the middle of the crowd, and soon the audience around us was glaring in our direction. Of course, with open bars, people's inhibitions were lowered, and it quickly started to turn nasty. I was reminded of a scene in a movie as the angry villagers descended on the castle with torches and pitchforks to vanquish the perceived evil. Unfortunately, our castle was flimsy black drape. As the Technical Director, my mind was racing, looking for solutions. I have been called a *MacGyver* on many occasions, with the ability to get an event out of a tight spot. But I quickly realized that this was unsolvable. There was just nothing we could do to fix the sound at that point. The show was on the verge of failure, and in my many years that just wasn't an option.

"It suddenly dawned on me that there was a complete general session set up downstairs in another room. We ran downstairs, ignored the security guards in the room and proceeded to hijack the lighting and sound rig. None of the technicians from another company hired by the client were onsite or expected until morning, but, after all, this was for the same client and our technicians were top pros. *This was an emergency.* We moved the guests as soon as we had sound and lights up and cajoled our late night host into agreeing, which he graciously did and for more than hired to do. Andrea opened the bar for all 3,000 people at her own expense while guests waited."

To top it all after the team's Herculean effort to save the show, the client sued me for the entire night, claiming incompetence – saying I should have known that there would be sound issues. Oddly enough, prior to the event, I had apprised them in writing of exactly that potential problem. And, guess what, I won the suit!

The Lesson

It was one of those distinct financial challenges that Extraordinary Events turned into an opportunity. For next to no money, we got creative (isn't that the best time for creativity?) and figured out a way to entertain the guests, change the look of the stage by creating a variety of sets within one and fulfill our client's request without impacting the non-existent budget. We gave our client entertainment that was functional as well as a display of interesting and professional talent.

This displays to perfection that there is always a creative solution to every problem. And the solution was simple. My friend Patty Coons summed it best for me when accepting an ISES award for the most innovative solution. It was for a solution that was so simple that most people wouldn't have seen it. Patty said, "Sometimes the best solution is the most simple." That's something I'll never forget.

Think about the best food you've ever eaten. Is it a dish with a lot of sauces or a juicy steak or lobster where the primary ingredient is what is to be savored? Life is a lot like that. If you are talking to a friend, the simplest communication is the best. It's how you reach out heart-to-heart.

People often say to me, "You ask the most direct questions, and no one ever gets offended." But don't you get to the heart of the matter by asking the pointed questions, and why would anyone be offended by that? People who speak in circles have no point. Why look for complications when it is the simple things in life that truly matter?

And there's another major point in this story. Yes, the client sued me. But I didn't cave in. I stood up for what was right and, just because they were "the big boys," was neither intimidated nor cowed. I was direct and honest *and got it all in writing*, and the mediator totally ruled in my favor. I'm not going to describe the legal setting and the posturing of "their" five lawyers accusing me of heaven knows what, but, believe me, that alone is a good story.

29

Ask for Help when It's Needed

The Gatlin Brothers

I am often asked, "How did you get started?" Or, "How did you get to where you are today?" My answer is simply, "I never believed in limitations." When I entered the world of special events, the medium didn't exist in any form we would know today.

One of my very early experiences was The Biltmore Hotel asking me if I could book a headliner for an incoming conference. I had never done this before but said "of course." *A reply I would still make today no matter what the question.*

The participants were all men, lots of them. And after researching a few options, I settled on Larry Gatlin and the Gatlin Brothers, a hugely popular country-western act at that time. On the day of the event as the band was setting up, one of Larry's brothers told me that Larry was a bit difficult because he required total quiet during his performance. He was known to walk off the stage if the audience was rowdy, which he considered disrespectful.

I watched the audience before showtime. They were drunk. They were loud. Beer bottles were flying across the room. Oh, boy! I walked up to Larry backstage and said, "Larry, this is the first time I've ever booked a headliner. I hear that you walk off stage if the audience is rowdy. Please don't do that. If you do, I'll lose my job. My career will be over. Please."

Larry smiled, turned, took the stage with his group and started his show over the cacophony of hoots, hollers and loud, loud, loud drunken men. Suddenly, he stopped playing. I was in the front row growing more and more despondent by the minute. Surprisingly, Larry motioned for me to come onto the stage. Reluctantly, I did. Then, he took the mic and said, "I promised this lady that I wouldn't leave the stage if you all were loud and rude, because she said it would be the end of her career. So help me out here and settle down." And he continued his show to a hushed audience.

My career did not end but actually began that night.

The Lesson

People appreciate honesty. They like to have all the information they need to make choices. Not giving Larry the facts about my situation could have taken my life in a different direction. Because I swallowed the fear of how he might react and just explained the situation, he worked with me.

Don't ever be afraid to ask for help either on a business or personal level. Most people are afraid that they will appear weak, but when you ask for help, you invite people *in*. People love to be helpful.

All three times when my personal relationships were severed, I immediately asked for help from friends and business associates, and everybody was there for me as I would be for them.

I remember a business speaker who knew a competitor needed something, so he offered it. His competitor was astounded. The speaker replied, "I know you would do it for me." This of course implied that when he needed the competitor's help, the favor would be returned.

Keep in mind as well that people often don't know when you need something. It is your obligation to let them know. One of the most powerful statements is, "I need your help." When that is your opening statement, they not only listen but cooperate, and their defenses come down.

30

Unifying a Theme in Challenging Economic Times

Atlantis Resort, 2008

The objective of this multi-day incentive trip held at the Atlantis Resort in the Bahamas was to create one unified theme and message while acknowledging the uniqueness of the destination and speaking to, rather than ignoring, the challenging economic times.

The client required a program that tempered the serious business objectives facing the group with the fun they had earned. More importantly, the company wanted to acknowledge this group of special people as treasured members of the team. Thus, Extraordinary Events clearly identified the objective to communicate to the attendees that they were indeed *treasures*. This theme was threaded through every meeting and event and verbally declared in scripts written by EE. The company president's speeches, as well as dramatic voiceovers, complemented the meeting content and graphics with this specific messaging.

Cost Management and Budget Maximization

This year it was crucial that we find creative ways to maximize the dollars spent. In past years, one logistical objective with this annual event was to maximize the use of the host hotel property by creatively using all of its many locations. But times, they are a-changing, aren't they? So, to maximize our budget we strategically convinced the client to re-use one room three times. This saved additional labor costs that would have been incurred with striking and re-setting equipment and décor to accommodate various locations. This also greatly saved on the technical equipment and staging required. We now didn't need one stage at General Session while another stage was being set that same night for the Awards show. This was a huge savings that allowed us to stretch the budget and our creativity – we took great satisfaction in facing the challenge to transform "the look" completely for each event.

The next area identified to save cost was the entertainment. So, although the final night band had to be imported per the client's music needs, we used all local entertainment for the welcome night. Because the locals had no flight, ground transportation or work permit fees associated with them, we could now afford to bring in that final night band.

Additionally, the events we designed relied on versatile actors/ singers who could also be living statues; not an easy thing to find, especially in the Bahamas. To maximize our entertainment budget, we brought in multi-talented entertainers who could play one role at one event and another part at the next. Thanks to costumes and make-up – and the multi-talented entertainers themselves – guests had no clue that each actor had appeared at another event. This once again was huge in helping us keep transportation and workers' permit costs down in addition to the talent giving us a cost reduction for a multi-event job.

As always, we put money where it meant the most. As an example, we chose a theme for the Welcome Night that showcased the island and what it does best. A local "fish fry" enabled us to use minimal decor and local talent to authentically attain the look, the feel and the food of this regionally-inspired theme. By not designing over-the-top decor and rather playing off the natural environment, we could allocate more money into the other events.

At the General Session, we avoided the cost of a hard set by achieving the effect we wanted in other ways. For instance, we wanted to create the feeling of being under the sea. Instead of building a truss and rigging divers to actually "swim" overhead, we attained virtually the same effect by using special lighting and soundscaping to simulate the divers swimming overhead. The cost difference was significant, and the impact was just as strong.

Since the client was very conscious of "green," we kept our focus on decreasing waste, containing costs and remaining eco-friendly by virtually eliminating floral at the overall program and instead using recyclable materials to create décor. Walls were covered in reusable fabrics; linen, props and hand-painted backdrops could all be used again.

Finally, we worked hard to present budgetary reasons for doing things differently this year. Traditionally the "blow out" night was in the middle of the program and the awards night on the final night. This meant that what we call the "Blow Out Night" was on the same day as the General Session. This is a HUGE event, and we would have had to double our labor to make the change-over happen in time. Knowing this, we pressed (and won the battle) for the Awards Night to take place after the General Session and the Blow Out Night to happen two days after this, the last night of the program. We were then able to work two regular shift days, working through the "dark day" to set up the Blow Out Night on time with an hour to spare! And thus, we dramatically saved on labor while improving the overall program content and look. By not putting the awards on the final night, we accomplished two things. First, guests had more time to bask in their awards, which meant they could congratulate each other on their achievements for days instead of hopping on a plane hours after receiving their recognition. Secondly, we allowed the attendees the chance to simply kick back, have some fun and leave the event feeling that business is serious but serious fun always helps keep everything in balance.

The client had only our word that we could so completely transform the ballroom that guests would never know they were in the same place they had been before. It was blind faith, and we achieved everything we said we would, including an authentic pirate experience.

In the past, the program's theme was focused on a couple of the events, but we turned that upside down so that everything had one cohesive message: YOU ARE THE TREASURE.

Creativity

The Atlantis Resort itself was the inspiration for a theme that was ambitious and fun and also extremely relevant to the program's objectives. Atlantis is already a destination that is deluxe, innovative and imaginative. Though the hotel is themed, it is not "messaged." That became our task as we developed a program that took Atlantis' mythology and wove it into a highly customized program that met the specified requirements of this company. The client said, "I want our guests to become emotionally involved; I want them to feel like a part of the program, not be observers, but be participants in every element." And we delivered just that!

Since the key was to send a strong message to the attendees that they were the highly-valued jewels of the company, we jumped on that imagery because what better place to weave the theme of *treasure* than Atlantis? And, of course, the Caribbean itself is rich with references to pirates and stashes of bullion, gems and silver. That was the starting point to create days that built and built and built emotionally, intellectually and imaginatively.

Thus, *treasure* became the thread that held together every element of the days ahead. Our passion for this theme paid off as not only our client but the attendees actually embraced our concepts (especially the interactive pirate party) with full abandon.

Welcome Night: Local Treasures

The guests' journey began in familiar waters – a relaxing welcome night. The Bahamas has a great hang-out area for locals; it's called "Fish Fry," and we found this on our site visit when we were looking for somewhere authentic to eat. Simple, and in our words, "cheap and cheerful." But where to have "our" Fish Fry?

We located a beach near the hotel which was relatively undiscovered for events and there this informal evening set around the theme of an authentic Caribbean Fish Fry introduced people to the island, its laidback pace as well as its local fare and entertainers. It was a time for old friends to greet each other and for new friends to meet.

With local music drifting through the air, the fragrance of grilled and fried local fish intoxicating the hungry guests and the colorful yet simple décor, it was relaxing after a long day of travel. Culminating in a Junkanoo parade (energetic parade of brightly costumed people) to bring the VIPs on stage, the evening ended early to encourage guests to rest up for the next day's most important meeting.

By bringing in local flavors and products as well as entertainers, we revealed the island's *treasures* and creatively used little of the budget. The island elements were good enough on their own.

The General Session: Revealing Atlantis

The mystique of Atlantis – both the mythical land that was lost in time and this hotel property – was impossible to ignore. And we didn't want to. The story about this culture and this lost land was the springboard for an exciting General Session and, from there, the events that followed. We played off the legend of a highly evolved culture that attained its wildest dreams and then experienced great loss. It's a story that holds great romance for every generation – the possibility of a treasure that has yet to be rediscovered; and in these financially challenging times, clearly alluded to the fact that Atlantis would indeed rise again. A powerful and meaningful analogy to the business climate of 2008, don't you think?

The story began as attendees entered the ballroom in almost total darkness save for a light that flickered over the chairs like sunlight filtering through the sea. The sounds? Softly drifting surf, an intermittent wave and the subtle songs of a whale in the distance. While the room remained dark, a diver's light appeared above the heads of the seated guests. Slowly it began to move overhead as it searched the waters and slowly moved towards the stage. Bubbles and breathing could be heard ... it became clearer that the light was from a diver's helmet as he swam through the currents and that the attendees were now in the middle of a diving expedition. We heard the diver's voice as a solemn voiceover began to share the story of searching for the lost city of Atlantis. Around the room pieces of the lost city were slowly revealed as the light from the diver's helmet passed over them. The voiceover played off the client's key messaging in an extremely targeted analogy that told of today's business climate and compared it to the story of Atlantis' greatness before it disappeared. The story culminated in the theatrical discovery of the buried city as the diver figuratively landed on stage. At this point, a dramatic custom music score, created for this one meeting, began to swell as the entire set was bathed in bright underwater lighting effects. With the story told and the lost city discovered, the lead executive took the stage to address his audience.

In his opening remarks, his custom-written script (a collaboration between EE and the client) imparted the message that just as he had led his team to the lost city, he, their president, would also lead them to find the treasures within themselves.

Because of the drama, the specific messaging and the involvement of the audience, it became a fully integrated and exceptionally emotional moment for the guests. Mission accomplished … so far.

Read on.

Awards Night: The Treasures

During the highly inventive morning session, the attendees found the lost city of Atlantis and with it discovered that they themselves were the treasure of their own personal and professional lives.

But there was going to be so much more.

That evening for their Awards Night they entered the same ballroom. But was it? For what was hours ago the ruins of Atlantis was now the city in its full glory – a sparkling environment with accents of Grecian beauty everywhere. For this was Atlantis once again risen. This glorious Atlantis now embodied a place in which dreams can be realized; an appropriate theme for a celebration that recognized the achievements of the past year.

Every table was ethereal perfection. Lighting was magical. In addition to the stage set comprised of hand-painted backdrops, columns, silk hangings and foliage, four vignettes were placed in the room. These sub-stages around the perimeter were set with columns, fabrics and a beautiful statue of an ancient Greek god or goddess. These complemented the main stage on which a statue of Poseidon, God of the Sea and Ruler of Atlantis, was center stage ... a major focal point.

Minutes into the awards show, the lights focused on Poseidon and a deep-throated voiceover announced, "Tonight we pay homage to Atlantis and its ruler, Poseidon, God of the Sea." What had at first seemed to be a marble statue as the centerpiece of the stage now slowly began to come to life. Poseidon (a Broadway Tony winner) belted out a song that captured a whimsical element for the evening ... *If My Friends Could See Me Now*, which because of the surprise element, got a roar of appreciation from the audience. At the end of the song, he returned to his original pose as a statue, and the awards resumed. Sheer magic as living statues are nothing new, but *singing* living statues are truly unexpected.

These bits of magical realism were sprinkled throughout the awards. Remember those four vignettes that met the client's criteria of getting the audience involved? No one was less than a few feet from one of our statues. Statues? No, during the awards each of our gods and goddesses came to life to sing a song that related to the award being presented. Not only were the performances imaginative, but they also served the very real purpose of breaking up the awards show. Because they were highly touted Broadway stars in their own right, their voices were not only entertaining but inspirational.

When the awards were over, Poseidon left his pedestal along with the other gods and goddesses. Together they performed one more highly energetic ensemble piece, *Let's Get It Started*, to lead guests out of the ballroom and to the hotel's Aura Nightclub that was exclusive to the guests on this night.

It was a true wow...but not the last one.

There's more ...

Final Night Blow Out - Pirate's Bounty

In Atlantis, one discovers treasure everywhere for the Bahamas' history is well known for housing pirates. For years we had tried to sell our client on a pirate party. The answer was always "no." But hey, this was the Bahamas, and we finally said, "Everyone has done one but not like THIS. It will be reality, not a décor job. The pirates will be authentic. The décor will be authentic. The menu authentic. We don't do parties; we do transformations; we do experiences; we do time warps." We told the client (and meant it) that this evening was going to transport guests to another place and time; their reality would be Blackbeard's time; this night was going to be like entering a movie set (think Johnny Depp and *Pirates of the Caribbean*) and this theme and the way we would produce it would make every other event they'd ever done (and oh, they had done many) be a distant memory. And so, the theme was accepted.

Guests were encouraged to dress as pirates, and they did. They could have been extras for the movie; they were so authentic. Everything about the evening was unconventional. No 72-inch rounds with pretty florals on this night! Nay, matey!

Okay, close your eyes (after you've read this, please) and imagine what a true pirate's lair might resemble. Eyes open again? Visualize 18-foot-long tables set for a pirate's banquet. Satin linen topped with brocade runners. Candles, tons of candles, and wrought iron and silver candelabras. Troughs and chests filled with jewels and pirate bounty, eye patches, beards, hand hooks, hoop earrings, faux knives and faux swords. Plenty to play with (and take home to the kids). Everything a pirate could want or a wench could covet (not to mention that this also fulfilled the sustainable mandate of no floral).

Pirates such as Bluebeard, Blackbeard and Redbeard, and their wenches, held court on vignettes set on risers throughout the room; joining guests, singing songs, playing dice, flirting, making raucous toasts and merriment.

Huge platters of food overflowing with hearty fare were delivered family-style to each table by costumed servers. This type of service was a total departure from years past as was the creation of interactive entertainment this daring, not to mention a challenge to the staff of Atlantis when first suggested. But as always, we challenged the chef to be playful, and a masterful menu emerged.

Then meeting with the wait staff, and "incentivizing" them to play along, we found some great new cast members that we didn't even have to hire, merely reward.

Atlantis told us we'd set a new standard, taught them something different, and, yes; they would be copying this for future events. Well, imitation is the sincerest form of flattery, isn't it?

During dinner, wenches tried to steal husbands; pirates wooed the ladies, told stories, sang ribald songs and in general regaled everyone with tales of treasures lost and found. They led sing-alongs of pirate ditties all night long, one table challenging another.

The stage was a focal point for it was a life-size stern of an authentic wooden pirate ship at dock complete with masts and a full set of sails. Oh yes, and a plank, for guests that dared to challenge the instructions of one of our pirates, most especially the dreaded Blackbeard.

Dinner over, the president, dressed as a gentleman-pirate, went "on deck" and told the audience that with treasure comes magic. That magic would be to time travel the guests from days of old to the modern world. As he said these words, the helm of the ship opened and the lighting in the entire room changed to contemporary rock and roll; the entire mood changed as a hot L.A. party/dance band was revealed. Blackbeard's Disco opened for the second portion of what was a fun, imaginative evening. In the words of the client, "This was the most amazing event we've ever done." And they had seemingly "done it all" in the past.

Yo ho, mateys and a hearty "aarghhhhhh."

Mechanics and Logistics

The cohesive program theme reflected the location of Atlantis as well as the current impact of the economic times on the client's company. Incorporating the history, culture and lore of the location into the overall program theme gave it more meaning to the guests. It also afforded a platform for the company executives to address the attendees about the current economic situation in an honest yet hopeful manner using the lost city of Atlantis as an allegory for the hope that many have to find something once lost and bring it back to full glory.

The mechanics of making an allegory come alive are not easy. They take creativity, inspiration and a little bit of live narration to tell the story. On the first night, we let the guests begin their journey in the present day at a local fish fry which featured the beauty of the site, the island's down-home cooking, the best of the local talent and simple yet authentic decor. The message? Sometimes you already have the treasure you seek.

Treasure continued as a theme during the General Session and Awards. In the General Session, the theme was about discovery and hope, capitalizing on the location and the story of Atlantis. In the morning, the event theme sent guests on a search for treasure, and that night, they found it as they were fully recognized for their accomplishments as well as given hope for the future. This was done through innovative use of décor, special effects, scripting and stage sets. Although the message was certainly serious, whimsy and comedic relief were inserted where appropriate to help keep spirits light and match the president's own message.

The final night, the Blow Out, was homage to the pirating and buccaneering that shaped so much of the islands' history. We turned the ballroom into a pirate's lair. The family-style meal, a replica of what it would have been in those times, encouraged true camaraderie where old and new friends sat together.

And, as it fits within the "story," the message of the pirate's evening reminded guests that life is about celebrating and playing as hard as one works.

Another objective was to work with multiple companies to create and execute a single vision. Logistically, we have learned a great deal working on this event for the past many years. One of our biggest lessons has been to forge strong relationships with other companies – our team – who worked on this job with us. We led the charge on the program theme and then worked with the others to ensure that their parts of the program met that theme and that our client's objectives were fulfilled.

Challenges and Solutions

Our biggest challenge, and the one that affected everything, was the location. Aside from the fact that we had to bring in just about everything, the island's sense of time was a huge stumbling block. What should have taken a few days to accomplish in pre-production took weeks. Moreover, when we chose to select local vendors or products to help keep the budget in line, we were limited in our options. However, we were committed to giving back to the local community and its economy.

Communication was another big challenge. During pre-production, the hotel assigned us a Convention Service Manager who didn't live on the island or operate the events at the hotel, which made communicating about the actual property a problem. Two weeks away from the event, we were assigned another CSM, this time one that was on property and operated the events. The two CSMs were supposed to communicate and transfer information, yet it didn't always happen. This meant the Banquet Event Orders weren't accurate until we actually started setting up for the event and sometimes not at all. To counteract this, we made sure that we checked and double-checked everything and that onsite we would begin setup hours earlier than we would in another location.

We are often accused of being overly meticulous in our paperwork ("Please sign every page of the 96-page production schedule to confirm that you've read it all.") In this case it paid off. We had paper trails of paper trails and onsite delivered a complex and detailed document to every provider of every service along with holding daily wrap-ups of the day before as well as the day to come with the entire team.

Another important challenge was our sensitivity to issues affecting the client's company. It was important to the client that we addressed the current economic times with honesty and hope while still recognizing and celebrating the good job that attendees had done. After all, that's why they were there. They had earned this program. Through decor and scripting we provided an environment that was meaningful and serious yet interspersed with humor and fun. For instance, the use of singing and living statues on the Awards

Night added a whimsical element, and guests loved the fact that they sang songs that matched the award category (i.e. Marvin Gaye's *How Sweet It Is to be Loved By You* during the spousal appreciation awards).

Food and beverage was an issue. This was the first time the hotel had ever served an event family style. New serving platters, bowls and utensils were purchased just for the job, and the wait staff needed a little extra training on how to approach this style. Additionally, the client had never done anything like this before, which of course begged the big question – would guests get it? Would they get that they would have to serve themselves? Turns out, it was no problem at all, and everyone loved the different serving style. The client was thrilled to watch guests happily offer to serve for one another amid bubbling conversations.

We also had to recreate the non-existent wheel. The hotel staff had little to no CAD drawings of the event spaces. And ones that we were told did exist were simple line drawings that were not to scale. We spent time measuring every inch of every possible event space (palm trees etc.) to build all our – their – CADs so that we would have accurate representations of the rooms. This was important as we were creating some very technical stage and room treatments.

There were no pre-set event locations. During the site inspections there were a couple of venue options per event, and each was contingent upon some outside force over which we had no control … like other holds on the space. Thus, during the second technical site inspection, we prepared for the worst-case scenario, planning events for both locations so we'd be ready regardless of where the event actually took place.

Finally, back-up plans for rain are always necessary in tropical climates. Luckily, only one event was slated to be outdoors this year. However, we still needed to have a back-up plan complete with floor plans and a schedule. We let the client know exactly what percentage of the event we could salvage (and how that translated visually) pending on the time of day she made the call. By thinking about this ahead of time, it enabled the client to know what she was up against and helped prevent the last-minute scrambling up of revised floor plans and production schedules.

Sustainability Practices

Because, as I mentioned before, our client was very "green" conscious, we used soft goods for stage sets and perimeter decor, which are by nature more environmentally friendly as they are less wasteful in the materials used to create them. They are easy to store and therefore kept and used again and again. (We used several pre-existing ones throughout this program, and they are easier to ship and can therefore save on fuel in the long run.)

In designing the events, we kept in mind the mantra "Re-use and Recycle" and so tried to think of themes that could incorporate decor we already owned as well as come up with ways to use existing decor elements in new and different ways to fit our needs. Additionally, when we created new concepts, we made sure that the props or fabrics (such as custom painted backdrops) would go into our designer's inventory and be re-used at a later time.

Lighting is becoming more and more sustainable and energy-efficient, and we tried to use the most up-to-date equipment wherever possible to minimize our energy footprint.

By minimizing our floral usage, we decreased the waste of flowers and plants. We also recycled floral wherever possible by using flowers that lasted more than one day.

Results against Objectives

The objective of this event was twofold – to reward these achievers for their accomplishments and to convey a message of hope for what was undoubtedly going to be a hard year to come. This is not an easy message for an incentive event – an event that traditionally focuses on fun, relaxation, awards and connecting.

We had a fine line to walk, and it would come down to the theme we chose whether or not we stayed on message. The location, although it had been selected several years earlier, actually turned out to be the key to the theme. We took the site – the Atlantis Resort in the Bahamas – and built on the sophisticated (and not always easy to convey) theme of finding what was once lost; adding hope, renewal and ultimately the rediscovery of the treasure that lies within us. We did this without ever being preachy or, worse, maudlin.

A month after the program, the evaluations came in, and the scores were higher than they'd ever been. The people got the message. They felt valued. They felt appreciated. Each event has been the best they've ever attended. Yes, they would work harder than they'd ever worked to achieve more than ever before, and they would do it in order to earn the next trip. The greater majority of attendees said that the program made them feel their efforts and contributions were valued and appreciated and that they wanted to participate in this same program in the future. An even greater majority said that this program motivated them to meet and exceed and stretch their goals. Almost everyone said that the awards night made them feel valuable and that they wanted to repeat the experience. Morale was high over the next several months as sales were tracked and the results of the program began to show with improved sales.

And even when the economy began to tank in late Spring, the letters poured in reflecting how much those in attendance "got" the message, supporting that morale, even in bad times, was still kept higher than it might have been otherwise.

The Lesson

So what does this all mean? These folks earned this trip. It was the carrot that was dangled for them to achieve. And achieve they did. So by not taking the easy road and cancelling the program during economic hard times, the client gave them their earned "bonus" and rewarded them for their hard work. The "return" on this was loyalty and a team of people actively willing to stand behind their leaders during economic troubles. In today's world, I hope you agree that means a lot.

During economic hard times, those who are loyal to you – whether in business or in friendship - should be protected, particularly when you have a dime left to your name. Reward loyalty with loyalty.

It's not always easy to be loyal, either. My ex-husband Mark was constantly testing my loyalty. Because he was my husband and I felt I owed it to him, I would watch horrendous behavior that I would stand behind or try to fix or smooth over because the act of loyalty was so important to me. I was his pooper scooper. Unfortunately, if I ever said anything to him in private about his behavior, I was immediately accused of being disloyal. And it made me think long and hard about what loyalty was, and is. It has definitely influenced my behavior ever since. Loyalty is not just a word. It's an action. And, the true test of loyalty is standing behind others even when it isn't easy.

31

Lo-gis-tics: The Art of Calculation – The Handling of Details

Vancouver 1995

I want to take you behind the scenes of the opening of GM Place in Vancouver, B.C. on September 17, 1995, for a snapshot of a typical day in preparation of four entirely separate events. The smallest was scaled for 7,500 guests, and the largest designed to entertain 100,000 or more – a three-and-a-half-hour spectacular finale show custom-choreographed and created for a "never-before-and-never-again" event. Now add to the mix three producers (Extraordinary Events, M. Van Keken and Associates and Opryland) from two countries, each with a different view of what and how things should be done. The cast of support staff included a creative team of 30; a paid production crew of 80, plus 150 volunteers and a brand new event staff at a newly-built venue.

An Immediate Challenge

Unfortunately, no one had exact venue specifications. No one knew how anything worked since everything was a first time. The typical question was, "How much weight can this bear?" The typical answer was, "I don't know."

"How many platforms will you have?"

"I don't know."

"How long will it take to make the ice?"

"I don't know. We've never done it here before."

"Where is the loading dock?" was a reasonable question that both our team and the Bryan Adams crew (for a show that would go on the day before ours) seemed eager to learn.

A surprisingly confident voice replied, "What loading dock ... There isn't one ... Just roll everything out of the trucks." A silent voice seemed to whisper, "...And roll it up into the trucks once we're done ..." A heavy sigh was heard in the Adams camp.

Day One

Open House Day, or Day One in our "Schedule of Events" production booklets, began at dawn. The Open House had been advertised in the newspapers and on radio and television. Expectations were high. We anticipated 60,000 to attend between 11:00 a.m. and 4:00 p.m. It was a Sunday, and it was raining. Surely this would "dampen" the attendance?

We had arranged parking in lots that had never before been used. All overflow parking in the area had been located and mapped out. The stadium adjacent to our venue was home to the city's football team, and on this day a "home" game had promised to draw even the mildly ardent fan. The cars would exceed the lots available. With arrangements made through the Mayor's office, we were able to meet with the City's Festival Committee, police, fire, St. John's Ambulance, public transit and the City Corps of Engineers. We talked through traffic flow with mass transit authorities; buses would be added and one line rerouted. The Vancouver Police Department would add extra officers. We had already met with the venue's security and coordinated with the police department to ensure a "high level of safety" for such potentially large attendance numbers. We had spent endless hours with venue staff and catering to talk through the first big reveal of the shops and merchandise, the food outlets and even the restroom facilities. We planned entertainment for the line-ups outside to alleviate "line anxiety." We had entertainment in the arena around the perimeter of the concourse, creating a "lots-to-do-and-see" atmosphere. Music and strolling characters provided non-stop fun. We'd planned strategies to move crowds quickly if needed. *Over 100,000 showed up.*

Details, Details

Meanwhile, back in the production office, the phones were ringing. Twenty-two separate performing groups, including two choirs (140 people), 80 bagpipers, 60 First Nations performers, two professional sports teams and dance teams ... Oh, my ... were either arriving or rehearsing. That meant our volunteers were shuttling to and from the airport, delivering band gear to over 30 different locations throughout the city, tending to VIP rooms, limos, tour buses and cabs (if needed) and juggling food requirements and meals. When was the last time you had to fulfill **one** artist's rider, much less over 20, and lived to tell about it?

Simultaneously, the production staff was working out the last-minute details for *Horizons*, the show. Details included: sound, lighting and the movement of 22 different sets of band gear on and off the stage seamlessly both for rehearsal and show; the rigging for one of the most complex aerial acts ever conceptualized and the last-minute writing of original musical arrangements to be performed by the Vancouver Symphony Orchestra, which at one time or another during the evening would be conducted by three different conductors, another logistical challenge!

Twenty-five rehearsal halls, seemingly endless airport pickups and delivery of people, packages and midnight pizza continued. What could possibly be added to complicate this scene? Of course, passports and Canadian work authorization permits for these entertainers and production personnel! The airport had been briefed thoroughly on who was coming in and why, but ... the best laid plans, as they say. Not *every* customs agent seemed to get it. Various entertainers were stopped and interrogated. We finally finessed the immigration officials with the help of the Canadian Ambassador in New York and posted our associate producer at the airport to meet all arrivals to help them clear Canada Customs, Immigration & Naturalization. Another all-nighter.

A Slight Modification

Simple so far, but ah, it gets better. As we three producers juggled all this, as well as everything from racing between the arena concourse to smiling at our clients, evaluating traffic flow and supervising, we met with our client CEO who happily informed us that BCTV had decided to grant a live broadcast of the first half of the show on September 21st (it's now the 17th).

"Isn't that just wonderful? ..."Break a leg!" he smiled cheerily as he seemed to skip down the hall.

A leg? How about broken contracts! We responded with a smile - a smile that hid all of the thoughts, concerns and logistical calculations that lay behind it. All of our contracts had been written for a live performance *without* broadcast rights, and that included artists and key production staff alike. It affected the director, the lighting designer, the musical director, the symphony (and the Musicians' Union) and scores of others governed by performing regulations. We had negotiated payment based on *live performances*. That meant that while everything else was going on, we had to contact all of our talent and production staff to secure approvals based on this *slight modification*. (Do you recall just how many different venues? This is a quiz, folks!) Needless to say, this change was not without some adjustment in fees and the government services tax (which applied to all Canadian talent and crew, but not to non-resident aliens or Canadians on exemption). This meant trying to track down over 30 agents and managers and drawing up amended documents for all to sign. Would you believe that the Musicians' Union was the most difficult? Of course you would.

Logistically, this provided a host of challenges; amongst them, how to be in over 30 places at once, since volunteers could hardly be called upon to negotiate such a feat. Yet another component required immediate creative attention; the show had not been designed for broadcast format. Lighting and sound had to be restructured and modified to fit into a whole new show. Timing had to be re-examined since the show's components now had to fit into a television special with commercial breaks. Timing was crucial. Every second of showtime would now be *critical air time*. Working with the BCTV staff now became a mounting production challenge added to a week that was already short on time.

Pre-planning could not have been more exacting, nor could it have been provided by more amazing professionals. (Just mention the name Patrick Stansfield, our production stage manager, to anyone in the entertainment industry, and they genuflect.) Yet, on three days' notice so many of these plans flew out the window when the television element was added. Had the staff not been so professional, organized or committed to making this the most memorable event ever produced, these demands would have been insurmountable obstacles rather than the challenging heights to which the team climbed. As one, the team soared with the belief that together we could make miracles, and indeed we did.

Another Little Twist

To spice things up *even* more, the General Manager of the venue added yet another little twist later that day. He decided to invite politicians and celebrities from all around the world. Enthusiastically, the word came, "By the way, we're going to need to add a VIP reception *before, during and after* the show on the 21st. For 600 or so. Upscale. Elegant. You don't mind, do you?" *Menu planning, décor, more limos. Find a space. Music. No problem!*

So, just think, this was still Day One.

Subsequent Days

On the days that followed, we produced, produced and produced some more. No one slept. Rehearsals in the arena itself began in earnest which meant that we took shifts around the clock. Lots of ginseng. Lots of tolerance. While the aerial ballet was overhead, the symphony was across the street. Crew feeds, up to 700 at one time, took place in the garage.

Our artists often presented us with mini-problems that added to our already full days. One, upon her arrival, needed to get to a "social engagement." Tired and annoyed, she hit us with "They," she sighed, and in a look conveyed all that her silence seemed to punctuate, "They" (the airline, Our airline, the one WE booked) "lost my luggage and all of my makeup." Within fifteen minutes we had a makeup artist in her waiting limousine, and together they rode off to the Bryan Adams concert.

Every day as one event was going on another was being planned. And honestly, as tiring as it was, it just kept getting more exciting as the final night gala concert loomed.

Last Day Adjustments

Last day to make adjustments. Last day to double check. Last day to .... add a press conference? "Just a few media," the client didn't seem worried; "You know, a few cameras and reporters." He finished with that ever-present phrase, "It's not a problem, is it?" The nation's leading newspaper with an equally officious reporter, six cameras and all of the local print media; a problem? What was a problem was when the client added, "Oh, by the way, you don't mind covering one of the conferences for us, do you?" Let's see, put on an event, plan a show for thousands and run a press conference for celebrities. No problem!

The Finale

Finally (and doesn't this word also mean "finale" which is very appropriate, the coup d' grâce) the three-and-a-half hour finale …700 performers, every trick in the book, almost no rehearsal time in the space and "firsts" (like the aerial bungee ballet 400 feet over an ice floor). Let me give you my reaction. I cried for almost the entire time. And at certain points, so did the audience. I've talked a lot about my dreams. This was one that came true, but not without its challenges. Another lesson in staying calm.

The show started with the three First Nations tribes consecrating the building. Did I mention that all three had never appeared together before and didn't want to do so? It took multiple visits to each reservation to cajole them into working together, and the result was magical, though "testy" right up to the end.

And then, the first notes of The Canadian National Anthem were sung by the Nylons, but you couldn't hear them. Over the radio I heard Patrick Stansfield say, "I'm nervous; I'm really nervous." Moments later the sound system kicked in as it should have, but it was a long few moments.

The first act finale was amazing. The Vancouver Symphony, the Canadian Boys Chorus, the Men's Choir, a Canadian Opera Singer, 16 rapellers and four aerial bungee artists plus aerial ballet people all performed to *Turandot,* and it brought down the house. There were cheers, and there were tears. Lots of them mine.

We had another act to go. This was just Act One. How were we going to top it in Act Two?

When originally planned, the concert was to feature David Foster and Friends, and the finale would be a reappearance of the aerial ballet, fireworks and lasers. But as the finale evolved, here's the end result. The finale song was *St. Elmos's Fire,* a David Foster composition called *Man in Motion* dedicated to Vancouver's Rick Hanson, a local hero. Hanson, a paraplegic athlete and activist for people with spinal cord injuries, was paralyzed at age 15 from the belly button down after being thrown from the back of a truck. He is most famous for his Man in Motion world tour and is a world class champion wheelchair marathoner and 1980 Gold Medal Summer Paralympics athlete. He has won 19 international wheelchair marathons, including three world championships. Rick was in the audience and acknowledged by thousands as the song played. And then, a reprise. As the lyrical notes to the grand finale rose from the orchestra to every corner of the balcony, every single performer joined together on stage. It was a completely spontaneous action. Completely unrehearsed. Completely heartfelt. Completely unexpected.

The planning had paid off. Everyone felt so much a part of the show and of the arena that they **wanted** to be a part of the finale. And, as the last notes echoed and faded into a standing ovation, the joy of the moment infectiously pervaded the cast and the audience. And so it was, the Inaugural Celebration that soared beyond the horizon and was forever memorialized.

A Funny Aside to the Finale

I always take humor away from my events. I just can't take everything so seriously. Remember, if someone doesn't die or get hurt, it isn't all that important. I always look back to see if anything about an issue was funny.

The entire second act of the finale show was David Foster and Friends. David is the best friend of the arena owner and a mega star, and he was performing with the Vancouver Symphony and all kinds of other entertainment. We scheduled rehearsal with the symphony (which cost a zillion dollars a second) on a night at David's convenience, and he mandated what technical we could use. As he came on stage for rehearsal, I excused myself to eat something at the end of my 72-hour work session. I was filling my tray in the cafeteria when my radio went off requesting me to get back to the stage immediately. As it turns out, David Foster had walked off stage saying he would not return until the sound was fixed. At this point, approximately 15 minutes had passed, costing the production about $75,000! I questioned Patrick Stanfield as to if he could fix it, and Patrick, who is very bombastic, said "no."

I learned that David had gone to the owner's suite and was not speaking to anyone. I found him having a drink with friends and his mother and said: "I've been here for three months and have missed my husband who is a musician, but I don't miss him anymore because you are here. He always wants the sound to be perfect or he won't perform. Now you are doing the exact same thing."

Then, I turned to his mother and said, "Madam, please make your son behave. You have brought up a boy with very bad manners." She laughed.

I then turned back to David and requested, "David, please don't cost your friend anymore money than you all ready have. We will fix whatever sound problems there are to your satisfaction if you will just go back and finish the scheduled rehearsal. You have all ready cost your friend $75,000." And, he went back.

Everyone wanted to know how I did it. It was simple. The entire thing struck me as funny from the first radio call on. I had lived for years with a musician who was a male diva and put up with it. Not this time. Would that I could have been so untouched when my ex-husband Mark flew into rages!

The Lesson

This particular event fulfilled a dream of mine. I had always dreamed of doing a "mega event" on the level of the Olympics or SuperBowl with great taste and inspiration. And, this was it. Just as big, just as visible with broadcast television and a re-broadcast as a holiday special and even more challenging because we didn't have the "mega event" budget. My hard work once again paid off.

It's odd how life and circumstances place almost insurmountable obstacles in the way of your dreams. It's like you have to prove that you are indeed worthy of them, but then, dreams are only realized when you work hard to achieve them. And, when you do, they often surpass your wildest expectations.

When you see others whom you view as successful, don't ever think for a minute that success just "fell into their laps." It's almost always about hard work, sacrifice and persistence.

I look at young people today who think they can get from A to Z without it. This is particularly true of an industry like mine that is viewed as something "fun" to do. Creativity is fun, yes, but just getting it put together is a massive undertaking.

Even over the 2008 holidays, while our office was closed for two weeks (with pay I might add), I was thinking about how we could increase sales. I was calling clients, reading trades, coming into the office to get ready so that I could be ahead of the game. I'm the only person who did that. Intermittently some did a few things, like check emails, but no one called to say, "I have an idea for what we can do."

This business has been successful because I don't wait to be asked. I don't wait to be told what to do. I invite clients and prospects to my home or invite them for an inexpensive hamburger or take them to Starbucks, always seeking an opportunity. Hard work is diligence; the people who succeed are those who never let up. So just keep at it.

32
Finding Inspiration

Tamara

I'm often asked where I find my inspiration. I seem to find it everywhere I go. One night many years ago, I attended a play called *Tamara*, which took place in an old building in Hollywood. It inspired me then as it does to this day.

The setting of the play was Fascist Italy, the era of Mussolini. *Tamara* enacted the true story of Gabriele d'Annunzio, a popular revolutionary poet under house arrest and Tamara, a Polish aristocrat and artist summoned to paint his portrait. The key to its creativity, however, was that it was an interactive play involving the audience.

Audience members entered the building and were interrogated by a costumed and dangerous-looking guard, who placed doubt as to whether entrance would be allowed. The ticket was a passport, and, of course, everyone was given entrance into a parlor with a 1920s motif. A waitress served champagne while a pianist entertained. With everyone gathered, the guard jumped up on top of a table and ordered us to follow "the rules." They were: Each of us must meet all the characters of the "house" in the parlor. If one of them left the room, each guest could follow throughout the house, unless the character slammed a door, at which point the guest could not follow. Whenever any character left a room, the guest could choose to stay (as other characters would be entering the room) or follow the one who left.

Soon all actors assembled in the parlor. After much interaction, some left running, others walking. All dispersed to various authentically decorated areas of the house. In each room, including the kitchen and bathroom, the play evolved. So, instead of viewing a single stage, the audience scattered into small groups that chased twelve characters from one room to the next, from one floor to the next, following them everywhere to co-create the stories that interested them the most.

During the night (and midway through the play), everyone gathered together in the kitchen, and a dinner of Italian fare was served. The cast re-entered afterward, and the play resumed as they again moved off into all other areas of the house. At the end of the evening, everyone somehow assembled in the parlor, and the play concluded.

Now the passport was not only a souvenir but also an invitation to return, which I did fourteen or fifteen times! And each time I saw a different version of the play as I always followed different characters to different places. And after five times, guests could attend free for a lifetime. With a dozen stages and storytellers, the number of story lines an audience could trace figured in the millions!

Now, why was this an inspiration? Shortly after my first visit, a large hotel in Detroit approached me to conceptualize an event for its best clients. When I asked hotel personnel to identify their challenges as well as their objectives, they shared that they wanted these guests to see the entire hotel and needed a creative way to move them around. That was my "aha" moment. Following is what I suggested, which they accepted, and I produced for them. It was the forerunner of the corporate mystery party.

Guests received a very formal invitation to attend a party in honor of Her Majesty, Queen Elizabeth II. When the 1,500 guests arrived, would it surprise you to know that they brought gifts of wine, food and flowers? *Why?* Seven hundred had been anticipated, but people thought the *real* Queen was attending! No matter; it was a wonderful turnout.

Guests were ushered into small areas that were privatized. (We actually turned the garage into meeting rooms.) Here they were entertained by a pre-recorded (but seemingly live) broadcast that told them that a theft had taken place. A jade Buddha that The Queen was taking to China had been stolen, and Her Majesty was asking the guests to help her find it. They would have to travel to different countries, and they would be issued a passport that would take them to various areas of the hotel which represented these different countries. We stationed a guest detective (various actors) in each area to create the atmosphere. Every area was decorated to represent its specific country. For instance, we had Magnum, P.I. in Hawaii, Inspector Clousseau in Paris, Sherlock Holmes in London and Charlie Chan in China. And those were only a few. The detectives gave guests clues and stamped their passports. When all the clues were assembled, guests had to solve the crime and figure out the location of the Buddha. True and false clues were distributed by an organ grinder's monkey, a juggler (look for the man with three balls), a magician doing card tricks (look for the man with 52 friends) and a variety of other entertainers. Some clues were even in fortune cookies.

Guests were then escorted to the pool deck where The Queen (a lookalike) was hosting a private concert and awarding prizes (raffle-style) to those who had discovered the Buddha's location.

The evening was a huge success. The press coverage was amazing. So, the objective was achieved in an innovative fashion that stemmed totally from *Tamara*.

The Lesson

Finding new approaches is always a challenge. It's also the greatest joy. Like a lawyer or a doctor, it's always important to stay abreast of new trends, new equipment and new ideas. You can easily find inspiration in everything around you from: movies; television; books; magazines; conversations; collaborations and competitors and history. Everything is a possibility. Bank your experiences in your mind and pull them out when you find a perfect fit. That's what I do.

I tell people to start by listing 100 ideas for every project they want to produce. The next day cross off 50 of those ideas. The next day cross off another 25, then 15, then 5, then take what remains and put them in order of preference. It can easily take 100 ideas to generate the one good one that will work, is appropriate and can be fully developed.

Next, sit down and write a letter to your best friend and describe that event as if you had attended it that very day. Start at the arrival and end with the departure and describe everything you've seen and experienced throughout the entire event. Put the letter away for a few days and then reread it. If it sounds dull, it probably will be. If you wish you had been there, it's time to start planning it for real.

The work is endless. The rewards are boundless. It's what shrinks call "immediate gratification."

33

Believe in Yourself

I was working in Atlanta in July of 2009 and was able to meet a long-time friend for coffee early one morning. She revealed something to me I wish I had learned a long time ago.

For many years I had worked with this friend supplying talent, theme events and a variety of services to the company for which she then worked.

When she changed companies, she introduced me to her new job and her new boss. He and I hit it off, and I was hired to supply talent for a two-week cruise around the Mediterranean. It was a fantastic experience. However, there were glitches because the cruise ship had promised a great sound system, good lighting and quality staff to run both. None of that happened, and the band was very unhappy. Considering the band had ten performances, this was not a good thing. To make matters worse, none of the technicians spoke English, yet another snafu.

Since we had great cabins, could eat in the dining hall with five-star cuisine being served and could avail ourselves of days in Dubrovnik, Malta, Corfu and Venice, how bad could it be? Fabulous, actually. "See you next year" were words I embraced as I disembarked and headed for home.

Next year I did ask for some concessions. "The boss" agreed

and told me to contact the ship to tell them what changes I needed from the prior year.

I checked with the ship's contact and told him what we needed in the way of equipment, and he promised to have it on board. I explained that I could not accept the same lighting tech because he was incompetent and was told that someone else would handle it. I asked if I could have English-speaking technicians and was assured this was possible.

This year was a Greek Island cruise. YAY! We landed in Athens and boarded the ship, greeting our old friend, the captain, loading on instruments and getting settled. The showroom on the ship was being used to store arriving baggage, so we couldn't do sound check until departure. I asked where the sound system was, and the attendant pointed to the stage, which had none. My contact with the ship was not on board, but "at the home office" nowhere near Athens. Then I saw "him"... last year's lighting tech. He proudly told me in broken English that THIS year he was doing sound. Hmmm ... incompetent with lighting and this year he was doing SOUND? So we had no audio equipment and, as far as I was concerned, no audio engineer.

I had ordered band gear from a local Athens company and put in a hurried call as we were leaving Athens in about an hour. I pleaded, and my contact was wonderful and got it all together and brought it down to the ship. Whoops! They wouldn't let it through customs. I enlisted the captain's help (begging and cajoling), and he finally managed to get it on board. I informed "the client" who thanked me for being pro-active and fixing the problem. A bit off-handedly but this was understandable. He had hundreds of arriving guests and that was his priority.

Fast forward to the first night. Feedback. Too loud. No wait, now it's not loud enough. No lighting. An engineer who couldn't figure out the equipment and would take breaks while the band was playing! When keyboards would take a solo, there was no amplification.

Horn solos were never heard because he wasn't quick enough to ascertain who was playing what and when. The band, in the meantime, was jumping around and pointing out who was playing so he could, but often I'd see him at the bar and not paying attention.

This went on for two long nights, and the band was beginning to really complain. I called my band gear and sound system hero and asked if he could fly to our next stop and sail with us to run the sound board for the rest of the trip. He could, and he did. He had never before been on a cruise ship, so I think he was tickled to step in. Again, I so informed the client who approved this having heard the squealing and feedback for two nights.

The rest of the trip was great, and the band was happy. Now the story really starts.

The ship had a house jazz band. The prior year my client had expressed to me that he wished that our band and the jazz band could have had some impromptu moments to play together so that the guests could have some fun with that experience. Knowing this, I pre-planned with the cooperation of both groups and the singers in each. We coordinated a great set using all the talent on board.

The evening opened with the house band, joined by our rock band playing together. The singers had rehearsed and now performed some fun standards and light rock. The audience loved it.

The ship's captain (the same captain who had saved our butts with customs) approached me and asked me if his girlfriend, a professional singer, could sit in for one song. What could I say? I agreed, hoping that she was a good performer. She was.

No sooner had she begun one of her showstoppers than my client, red in the face, came over to me and said, "Aren't we paying you enough that you felt you had to hire additional talent for the night?" I thought he was kidding.

He wasn't.

I asked him what I had done to upset him and explained that I couldn't really refuse the captain's request. (Could I?) I explained that the two bands had jammed because the prior year he had wanted them to do so but it couldn't be accomplished. He didn't let up. He was pissed and let me know in front of everyone. And he kept it up the entire rest of the night.

The next day we left the ship to go home, and I got a terse goodbye. And here I thought we were friends.

When I returned to the office, I sent off a bill for the sound equipment and my engineer who had flown in to save the day. For months it was ignored and my phone calls and emails were unreturned. I finally went to my client's boss, who had been on board, and succinctly explained my position. I was told that I had been paid enough and I should have known in advance that those problems would occur and it had been my responsibility to fix them. In frustration I walked away, knowing that a lawsuit wouldn't help. My only real witness, the guy who provided all the sound and did the engineering (with the client's approval), was in Greece.

This was years ago. All that time I wondered what I did to receive such a negative reaction. What did I do wrong? What else could I have done to prevent this? How did this friendship (with the client AND his wife) go awry?

It was only during my visit over coffee with my long-time friend that I learned that my client was an alcoholic and that this episode was not the only one of its kind. Oh how I wish I had known that the erratic and irrational behavior had nothing to do with me or what I had done. I would have saved myself years of grief. Today, after agonizing over what I perceived as an error on my part, I have peace with it, but it has taken a long time.

The Lesson

When you know in your heart you have done nothing wrong and you are victimized by someone else that doesn't know right from wrong (for whatever reason), don't waste any time internalizing someone else's problematic behavior. Just get on with it and put it behind you. Believe in yourself.

34

Travel Adventures

I couldn't resist sharing some of my travel adventures with you. I mean, if you travel as much as I do, you've got to have some good stories to tell, right?

Morocco

I went to Morocco with a FAM trip/conference as a guest speaker. One of the Moroccan host activities was camel riding in the desert. We were given some wonderful authentic outfits to wear and met our camels and handlers in the desert ... and I mean *desert*.

My camel was a nursing mother with an adorable baby. I didn't realize the implications of that until somewhat into the ride when I realized my camel wanted to kill anything and everything in sight ... and sometimes that included me. The baby got less cute by the minute.

Anyway, we were told that we would "race" each other with a great prize for the winner. Me, competitive? That was all they needed to say. I had my cell phone with me, and, remarkably, it worked in the deserts of Marrakesh! Go figure; it doesn't work at home part of the time, but here, it worked. As we raced through the desert, my cell phone rang, and, of course, being an obsessive personality, I answered it. It was a very good client of mine from Japan who wanted an immediate creative treatment and estimated budget for a huge awards show in Las Vegas.

So, for the next 40 minutes (yes, as we raced through the desert), I threw out ideas and approximated budgets. Everyone was so amused that they photographed me doing this ... and by the way, winning the race. As a matter of fact, one of the photos appeared in the local paper the next morning. And we were awarded the job in Las Vegas.

The Lesson

Never miss any opportunity to win, no matter the circumstances!

Laguna Niguel

I used to live in Acton, a solid hour from Los Angeles. Laguna Niguel is about 90 minutes away from Los Angeles. Got the picture? I was bidding on a job for SmithKline Pharmaceutical taking place in Laguna, and I was asked to drive down to the hotel for a 9:00 a.m. meeting to show them my capabilities. By the end of the day, I showed them much more. But more about that in a bit.

Do the math. I had to leave EARLY.

I made some coffee and headed out with a mug-to-go accompanying me. There was traffic. Three-and-a-half hours later (yes, I left very early so I was on time), I arrived and ran not for the meeting but for the ladies' room. Whew, what a relief!

I gathered up my portfolio and whisked myself through the entire hotel to the meeting room and greeted everyone. They smiled, I thought, indulgently. *Little did I know.*

I gave my capabilities presentation, respectful of my allotted time slot. When I ended and thanked everyone, my contact looked at me and said, "Andrea, do you realize that your skirt in back is tucked into the waistband of your panty hose?" And, folks, *all I* was wearing beneath my skirt was pantyhose. The folks in the hotel lobby got quite a show.

I replied, "Well, now you've seen my best side," and straightened out my skirt. They laughed, and the client said, "You've got the job. If you can handle this situation so calmly and with humor, you can handle anything."

The Lesson

Even when you embarrass yourself, don't let it rattle you. People will admire you for it.

Laguna Niguel Again

Years and years ago (I still lived in Acton), I was asked to drive to Laguna Niguel to meet the planners from Shearson-Lehman (through American Express) to play them some demo tapes of guitar players. Guitar players? The profit on booking a guitar player wouldn't even cover the gas to get to Laguna!

Moreover, it was another 9:00 a.m. meeting, but this time on a Saturday. However, I was happy that the hotel had referred me, and this was a courtesy. So with a few audio tapes in hand, I drove to Laguna and played the tapes for the client. They booked one of the guitarists for two days (three days apart) and said, "You will be there, won't you?" Naturally, I said, "Yes, of course."

Now it would be a loss, but it was a good contact. I drove down for both jobs (being paid in AMEX Travelers Checks ... a first).

A month passed, and my same contact at the hotel called and said the Shearson-Lehman planners were coming back and wanted to hear tapes of bands. Would I come down? Of course, so I made yet another trip to play them tapes. They chose one for two evenings, three days apart. I drove down for both jobs. Being a New York company, they weren't thrilled with the band because it was not "New York-style," but they were very pleased that I was there from set up to tear down.

Another month passed, and I got a call, this time directly from the client with whom I had now developed a relationship. They wanted to book Peter Allen (that'll tell you how long ago this was) who was a huge celebrity at the time. Now that was going to be truly profitable. They wanted to hold their gala evening event at the Mission San Juan Capistrano, which proved to not be possible because of sound restrictions.

Lo and behold, I asked if I could assist with helping them find a place, and that quickly led to constructing a massive tent on a bluff overlooking the ocean in Laguna, catering, rentals, lighting, audio, staging and, yes, Peter Allen and all of his needs. For two nights, three days apart, I was there for every wonderful, profitable minute of it.

Six months later, I won a repeat of this program, this time at The Greenbrier, where we did three nights of themed events, entertainment and Liza Minnelli.

The lesson

Don't ever assume that a job is too small to undertake or that personal service doesn't pay off. It's the key. There is always opportunity if you are willing to extend yourself.

The Trip from Hell

My best friend John Daly and I had just finished a conference in India and took a day to sightsee and visit friends in Dubai. (John's wish … I had been there before.) We were then planning on a three-day vacation to see more of India as during the conference we went from hotel to convention center and back other than a very short visit to the Taj Majal.

We left Dubai at 2:00 p.m. on a Saturday after a wonderful time. The Ritz in Dubai had been first rate. We even found baby clothes for my grandson and a Starbucks. I bought nothing, NOTHING, for myself as I was saving up for those few days in India.

After we landed at the Delhi Airport, I went through immigration without mishap and then noticed that John was not behind me. Shortening this story, they did not allow John into India because his visa said "single entry," and they had let him in before by mistake and were not going to do it this time. They wanted to send him back to Dubai where he could apply for another visa. We quickly figured out that this scenario wouldn't work, because by the time he got his visa (remember it was a weekend) our vacation would be long gone.

Nothing worked after multiple calls to sort this out with the conference planners. We had a very nice tour, driver and rooms booked in India, which I had to cancel. They wouldn't let John out of immigration. Since I had had to go out to make phone calls, they wouldn't let me back in with him. I finally negotiated that we could go home from Delhi, as long as John didn't "enter" the airport. Of course, our luggage was now at the Intercontinental Hotel in Delhi, far from the airport, especially in Delhi traffic. These negotiations for every decision went on for hours and hours with people who would listen (or pretend to) and then disappear, sometimes never to be seen again.

After a while, I sent a driver back to the hotel to get our luggage. And while John was still being guarded, I went outside of the airport (oh, if you think arriving is bad, you should see those huddled masses outside the domestic terminal late at night!) to look for the driver with our luggage. I had no clue who the driver was or what he looked like or how to find him. In the meantime, we had no tickets to get home three days early, and I couldn't find any of the people to whom I had previously spoken.

When I tried to get back inside the terminal, they didn't want to let me in since I had no ticket. I finally was met by someone from Air India who ushered me in and helped me meet the driver with the luggage. Then I had to try to find John with no tickets to anywhere while being told that flights not only had no business class available but were sold out. We were told that we could wait in the lounge all night and fly to London, New York and then Los Angeles ... economy.

At the last minute, we did get business class to New York. This was after ALL AFTERNOON and NIGHT in the lounge with no food. There's a poem that starts "let me count the ways." Paraphrased it was "let me count the days" as we had now been gone from Dubai more than 24 hours and had not either food or beverage of any kind since we left.

Here was our itinerary. Delhi to London to New York and then transfer to American to Los Angeles.

Our luggage did arrive in New York, and we got through customs and immigration and over to the American terminal. There we were told that the flight was a code share and, therefore, we needed to go to Qantas. So, we changed terminals and stood in another line. Alas, Qantas said "no" we could not go to Los Angeles unless we went to Australia first. So, back to Air India we went.

You can imagine how helpful they were. Not! Finally though, they accommodated us on an American flight that would get us home close to midnight, L.A. time. Unfortunately, no one knew where our luggage was, but we thought it MIGHT be on the Qantas flight. No business class was available. We took it. ANYTHING. I had a cold and a bladder infection. Actually, as I think about it, that was the best part of the trip.

In any case, we arrived back in Los Angeles around 12:30 a.m., and as we went to report our lost luggage, I looked around at the long line of people waiting to report their own lost bags. What a line! And then I spotted our luggage sitting on the floor in front of the "lost baggage" area. It had arrived on the Qantas flight an hour before we did. By the way, other than a pair of earrings I got at the Delhi airport, nothing to declare. That's a first!

John rented a car and drove me home. Finally I curled up in my own bed with my cats. Wired to the gills. Hungry. But ever so glad to be there. *Home.* Was anything ever more wonderful?

The Lesson

There's no place like home, Auntie Em.

My Travels in Argentina

The perils of Pauline had nothing on the adventures of Andrea when I was asked to be a guest of the Society of Incentive Travel Executives (SITE) and trek to Argentina to deliver a seminar on how to attract incentive buyers to Buenos Aires.

Let me begin with another Andrea airline story. Somewhere mid-flight we heard the captain announce, "Folks, we are going to make an emergency landing in Paraguay." With no further information, we started descending. Landing on a postage-stamp-size runway somewhere in the jungle, I was amazed that uniformed militia with uzzis had surrounded the plane. Great! Almost stabbed to death on one airplane, and now I'm going to get riddled with bullets on another one!

We found out a few hours later that there were severe winds in

Argentina and that the pilot didn't think we had enough fuel to make it, so we had to land to pick up more fuel. We finally did and took off again.

As part of the trip, the SITE Chapter had invited me and my husband (at that time) to spend a few days in Jjao Jjao, Baliroche, at a gorgeous resort high in the mountains. We arrived, and almost immediately I went to the tour desk to find out what we could see. You know how my curiosity overcomes me!

We were told of a stunning tour that took a bus to a boat that would take us to an emerald lake where condors flew freely, monkeys played and where lush waterfalls would leave us breathless. We signed up.

Next morning, we took the bus and then the boat. Then we walked miles and miles straight uphill on a rocky path. My husband Mark was ahead of me and called out, "Andrea, you should see THIS." At that exact moment, I put my weight on a wooden step and heard a loud crack as the step *and my ankle* cracked in two. I called out, "You're going to have to tell me about it!"

Of course, no one else on the tour spoke English, and a lady tried to tell me in Spanish to remove my shoe. I refused. I know what happens when you take off your shoe. Your foot swells up.

I knew my ankle was broken and somehow I had to get down that hill, but I couldn't step on it. I combined my Spanish with sign language and indicated what had happened and then hobbled down the hill on one foot, holding on to some young men who were on the tour. Where was my Mark during all this you might ask? Complaining, whining and being difficult. Where else!

Part way down, the ship's crew met me with a stretcher. I climbed on and immediately heard one young man say to the other, "She's really heavy." (Remember I lost 100 pounds *after this* not too long ago). This made me so mad (actually mortified) that I climbed off and hopped down the rest of the way.

Everyone seemed to have a camera or video recorder and somehow this *amused* the tourists. I thought the condors, monkeys and scenery would have meant more, but apparently I was now the star attraction.

On the boat, people were trying to feed me pain pills, but I had no clue what they were and declined. The boat took off, only to stop at a nice restaurant along the way. Still no pain, but I was feeling anxious about needing to see a doctor.

Finally we arrived back at the dock, and the crew had been nice enough to call ahead and have us met with a private car to take us to the one local clinic that was open. It seems that it was Columbus Day in Argentina, and clinics and hospitals were closed. *Did Columbus ever go to Argentina?* Hmmmm ...

So off to this clinic that was so dirty that it was frightening. After several attempts with an old X-ray machine, the doctor said, "You have broken your ankle." *No shit, Sherlock.*

Then, he put me in a cast, not a cast as we know it now, but a cast that weighed a ton. And he wrote me a prescription for crutches. All the pharmacies were closed, and, of course, that's where they carry crutches. My husband Mark and I returned to our five-star hotel, and I spent the rest of my time with my leg on the room's heater. It took three days for the cast to dry and set. Our meals were room service.

Okay, time to go to Buenos Aires to deliver my seminar. The crutches were not the new and snazzy aluminum ones but were hard wood with no cushion for the underarm. They hurt. All the floors were marble, so I slipped and skidded a lot, fearful all the time of breaking more bones.

When we arrived at the airport, a wheelchair took me up to the plane, but I couldn't get up the steps that were very narrow and not manageable with crutches. No jetways at that time in Baliroche. They finally got me on the plane ... *with a horse hoist.* My God, could it have been any more embarrassing?

Next stop Buenos Aires. We arrived in time to change and get to the dinner and meeting, which started at 9:00 p.m. I figured I would speak right away. By now I was on pain pills and a bit woozy.

Dinner began at 10:30 p.m., and I was the AFTER dinner speaker.

I managed and went to bed at 3:00 a.m.

The rest of my trip had been arranged so that I would look at the city's venues to talk to the Buenos Aires tourist commission on how to best sell the properties for incentive events. I was the expert. Unfortunately, none of the venues were ADA-compatible, and almost all had either tiny winding stairways leading down into them (tango clubs) or huge stairways leading up to them (mansions and museums). Consequently, a limo drove us around as our guide explained what was inside them. IF ONLY I had been able to see the insides.

It was just one of those trips when nothing goes right!

The Lesson

Sometimes nothing goes as planned, and you just have to go with the flow.

The Ultimate Travel Adventure - Rio

Rio de Janeiro ... glamorous, exotic, exciting. Little did I know HOW exciting. After a whirlwind trip to Sao Paolo for a Latin American trade show, a group of us was invited on a FAM trip to Rio. Now I had a client interested in a Latin American destination, so the timing was just perfect. And I had been dreaming of Rio since I was a little girl.

The flight was uneventful (for a change ... at least in my life); our luggage arrived and five of us plus our hostess/guide gathered together and found the van that would take us to this wondrous beachside resort city. We babbled happily about the sand and sea (and beautiful bodies in skimpy bikinis) and Sugar Loaf mountain, and we rhapsodized about The Copacabana Palace, a five-star legendary hotel.

We were off on our adventure. It was late at night. There was no traffic on the roads. I was seated behind the driver on the left of the van so I could see everything there was to see. I was excited. Five minutes from the airport as I gazed out the window, I could see a car racing toward us, and my immediate impression was that this car was going to run us off the road. It did.

As this was happening, I reached into my purse and took out my credit card case, my passport, my travel money (most of it except for a couple of hundred dollars which I kept separately) and my eyeglasses. I left everything else in my purse and then tucked my valuables under me. Why? Only instinct.

The driver swerved and stopped. In what seemed like a millisecond, two young men with glazed-over eyes boarded the bus waving guns and saying things like, "Give us everything, or we'll kill you!"

Now, like me, I'm sure you wonder what you'd do in a situation like this. I started mentally composing an email back to the office. Next to me my travel companion was calm. Not so the people behind us. One man started playing tug of war with one of our gun-waving friends. "You can't have my wallet," he was saying as he pulled his travel bag out of the thief's hands.

Another woman started wailing hysterically. One other passenger decided to be quite macho and threatening. The problem was that when they did this, the obviously high gunslingers started waving the guns in our faces. I took this opportunity to distract them and hand them my purse, saying, "Take it."

They left me alone. They left my seatmate alone as he handed over his wallet calmly.

Ultimately they took our purses and wallets, got off our van and took off, tires squealing. Understandably, our group was mostly hysterical. However, I was still composing my email, my adventure story. And I had all my possessions that mattered.

We arrived at the hotel, and since our driver had called the police from his cell phone, they were there to greet us and take our statements. Other than me, no one could provide a passport for check-in or a credit card for incidentals. A representative of the government arrived in short order and assured us that the city would take care of everything, including issuing new tickets for our departure a few days ahead.

Our hysterical lady retreated to bed for the rest of the trip. The macho men continued to rehash the story until I asked them to stop. Fortunately, our hostess was calm and collected and efficient throughout.

Not only did the government reimburse us any cash we had lost, its representatives brought us new tickets and personally walked everyone through customs and immigration both in Rio and later in Miami where we landed in our first U.S. stop. And I had a great story in my opinion.

The Lesson

During a business or personal crisis, keep your wits about you. Stay calm. Overreacting doesn't help the situation or you. And, there are decent, helpful people in this world.

More Travels with John Daly

Early in our careers, John and I traveled to Toronto to a Meeting Planners International conference and decided that afterward we'd take a mini-vacation to New York to see some theatre and get some creative juices going.

Our "story" begins in Toronto. Each of us was being challenged with some personal problems, and we took a long walk to talk and commiserate. We sat on a bench in a lovely park, and I turned to John and said, "Life can really be shitty, can't it?" Just as those words left my mouth, a pigeon flew overhead and literally *did* shit on us. That actually set the tone for the rest of the trip!

The trip from Toronto to New York City had some distinct challenges for both of us as we communicated with home, but we really looked forward to the theatre. The first night I bought tickets to *42nd Street*. As soon as we sat down in prime seats, John looked at me and said, "I'll be right back," and rushed away getting greener by the minute. That was the last I saw of him until I returned to the room we shared. Oh, well, we had tickets to *Cats* the next night. Unbelievably, as we sat down in some primo seats, the theatre started spinning around me. It was my turn to leave the theatre and return to our room.

One more night left. We were spending the last evening with a limo driver (and his wife) that John had met and befriended. We did sightseeing with them during the day and then returned to our room at a lovely five-star hotel to get some sleep and catch an early morning flight to face our problems back home. Unbelievably the door to our room wouldn't open, and all our belongings were inside. We called the management. They couldn't open the door. Much, much later the fire department showed up with axes to hack down the door and let us in. In the meantime, we called our new friends as we needed some moral support, and they suggested picking us up at the hotel. What the heck. By now we had mere hours before our flight. Would you believe that when we went to check out of the hotel that they tried to charge us for the room for that night? Just go figure. Arguing with the assistant night clerk proved fruitless, so we just left telling him that we wouldn't pay for a room we couldn't even unlock.

Our New York couple wanted to show us off at their local hangout which was a disco in Brooklyn or the Bronx. (Sorry, I'm from California, and I cannot tell the difference!)

Their friends were straight out of *Saturday Night Fever* and soooo impressed that we had actually met *movie stars*.

A few hours later we retired to the eleventh floor apartment of our friends, or at least we tried. Around floor nine, the elevator stopped with the four of us and an elderly lady and her Chihuahua in it. A half hour later it started up again. Once at the apartment, the couple insisted that John and I take their bed to catch a couple of hours of sleep, and then they'd take us in the limo to the airport. We tried to refuse but to no avail. So we retired. Fully-clothed and on top of the covers, John and I started laughing hysterically over how ridiculous our trip had been.

I had a camera, and we snapped some shots of ourselves attempting to sleep. Then, from the other room we heard, "Ya see, I told ya ...." Which made us laugh all the harder.

The Lesson

Sometimes you just have to laugh it off, no matter what anyone else thinks!

The Adventure of Learning to Give Permission

Often when I travel or meet new people, I think a lot about giving permission and how doing so affects relationships.

Now I am the ultimate wallflower. I barrel through meeting strangers (most of the time), but there's probably nothing that makes me more uncomfortable than walking into a room where I do not know anyone. Some people are great at this. I'm not. I am in terror of such situations and would much rather go home (or to my hotel room) and watch *Law and Order* reruns. But I don't. I strike out and shake hands, introduce myself and try to engage. It has brought me so many rewards that, by now, this should come more easily to me, but it doesn't.

I've come to the realization that there could be several reasons why that crowded room might not seem friendlier. Maybe the other people in the room feel the same way I do and thus wait for me to make the first move.

Or, maybe a different culture might consider it rude to make the first move. This came to light when I recently attended a conference in Goa, India. I arrived at the first welcome reception, and the one person I had previously met was not yet there. I felt the very familiar *oh, no, now what?* as I gazed around the room. Absolutely no one made any move to greet me, talk to me or approach me. For sure they knew I was the foreign guest speaker as I was the only person in the room who was not Indian.

So, I walked over to the closest person in the room, offered my hand and introduced myself. Immediately the group welcomed me; we exchanged cards and conversation was initiated as I started asking the group to help me with thoughts for my keynote the next day. I excused myself after a while and approached other groups with the same results. Over the next days at the conference, everyone was friendly, approachable and welcoming. Relationships continued to build, and by the time I left for home (not having watched a single *Law and Order* episode), I had 85 new friends. It was a fantastic experience.

I gave myself permission to make the first move; not even knowing if that was right or wrong.

I remembered back to the days when my business was in booking bands. Until the bandleader would say those magic words, "Please join us on the dance floor," or anything invitational, everyone just sat in their chairs and waited. They needed permission to get up and dance.

The Lesson

How often do we need to offer permission? *Please join me for dinner. May I sit next to you at the meeting? May I introduce you to some people here that I know?* These are invitations to a relationship … a hospitable extension that gives you permission to extend yourself and that gives someone else permission to join you.

Now I am still terrorized by a room of strangers, but when I think of the benefits of diving into the situation, they are infinite. Next time you're at a conference, meeting or social gathering, offer permission. I know I will.

An Unforgettable Torino Experience

Previous to the Winter Olympics in Torino, Italy, I traveled there on a FAM trip. It was winter and close to the Christmas holidays. I clearly remember the chilly air on my face as one of the group and I wandered down the main street, peering into shops and eating freshly-roasted chestnuts. Somewhere along the way I spotted a very small wooden church that looked really, really old. Once again my insatiable curiosity took hold of me. It was a weeknight; I figured we wouldn't be intruding, so I suggested we go inside.

We were in luck! It was a night with a wonderful Italian choir doing American gospel music in this gorgeous ancient church that must have seated 80 at the most. It was the most enchanting setting, and the music performances were riveting. Once again I was rewarded for opening a door others might pass.

When we returned to the group to regale everyone with this wondrous experience, they were all so jealous. Yes, they had done some shopping or hit a bar while we, on the other hand, had an unforgettable experience because we were inspired by curiosity.

The Lesson

Keep on opening all the doors that pique your curiosity! You will never regret it.

An Unexpected Travel Emergency

I was asked to pitch Extraordinary Events for a project for the National Fleet Management Association (NAFA) sponsored by all major U.S. car dealers at Opryland, where the event would be held. I took an early flight to Nashville, dressed, made up and ready to get off the plane and catch a cab with only about an hour to spare before my presentation.

On the flight, my ultimate nightmare played out and involved a kicking, screaming baby. As the flight attendant announced our descent, the mother of this lovely child considerately gave her baby a bottle to quiet her down. Kicking and screaming, the baby launched her bottle into the air and over my seat. As luck would have it, the bottle opened up over my head, and I was doused with formula from head to toe. Remember, an hour to spare?

Because I had planned to return that night, I unfortunately didn't have a suitcase with a change of clothes. As soon as I deplaned, I headed to the washroom and "rinsed off" as best I could, caught a cab and headed to Opryland. My first stop was a dress shop where I bought a new top for my suit. I couldn't find anything that matched, but at least it was dry. Then, I ran to the hair salon and said, "Wash and blow dry this mess, please." They did. I was a wreck but let them do their best as I kept saying, "Please hurry." When I turned around and faced the mirror, "Miss Nashville, circa 1950" stared back at me! This incredibly hysterical style featured huge hair ending in a flip and tight curly bangs. As much as I tried to push it down, I couldn't. So, with huge hair and a mismatched floral top, all I needed was a beauty queen sash!

Since I had no other choice, I waltzed into the meeting room and was met with slack jawed welcomes. *I was such a vision,* albeit not a good one. I said, "I thought I'd get into the spirit of the venue" and relayed what had happened. Then, I launched into my pitch.

I didn't win the business, but the clients did tell me that my poise astonished and impressed them.

The Lesson

You can't win them all, particularly when babies dump the contents of their bottles on you with no replacement clothing. Always try to plan ahead for emergency contingencies and try to come up with creative solutions when you don't. And, don't ever leave your sense of humor at home!

Roses from Rome

My inquisitive spirit convinced me to stay an extra day at the end of a BTC trade fair in Rome. So, I signed up for a cooking class displayed at the trade fair. The small classes (one to eight-people) took place out in the country.

That morning of that last day, Fabio (yes, really) picked me up and drove me into the country, 30 minutes outside of Rome through gorgeous countryside. We arrived at a Medieval town (from the 1200s or so), home to 80 residents, where I met an 84-year-old man who makes wine in his tiny cellar. He does only a few bottles at a time, which he shares with friends, as the "recipe" has been in his family for generations. It reminded me of making moonshine! He was a delightful old man, and the wine was wonderful.

Together, we then drove to various little stores - one for cheese, one for meat, one for eggs (in case the ducks and hens hadn't laid any), flour, butter, things like that, all with which to make lunch. All the vendors were lovely, warm, welcoming and *old*. And, Fabio knew everyone.

Then we were on to the cooking master's herb and vegetable garden where we picked fresh herbs for our lunch recipe. And, the ducks and hen had indeed done their jobs, so we gathered our eggs. We were then off to his ancient town and climbed up a zillion stone steps to his apartment, which was awesome. I immediately wanted to redecorate my entire house. It would take forever to describe it, but imagine perfection and innovation in tile and wood. And a kitchen for which I'd die. I have never remodeled my kitchen, because I never knew what I wanted. Now I do.

We quickly began cooking. Huge ravioli freshly made (a first for me) with ricotta and Roman spinach and herb filling. Not easy to make correctly. Deep fried stuffed olives (I asked for that one) - green olives stuffed with meat then rolled in bread crumbs and deep fried. Yummy. Involtini, a thin piece of meat stuffed with herbs, bread crumbs, bacon and cheese and then simmered in olive oil and wine. Absolutely delicious. This is an item for my next dinner party, and it's easy and wonderful. We finished the meal with some purchased hazelnut biscotti for dessert. Needless to say, I was in heaven during both the prep and the devouring of this authentic, delicious Italian meal!

After cleaning up, Fabio and I went to a winery for the Italian version of Beaujolais Nouveau that is only available for three months a year. Eh! Not impressed. Then, we drove to a hotel on two lakes where the manager was in sales mode for any business I could bring to him. It featured lots of horses, but the rooms were not so wonderful. However, the manager (another old person) was adorable.

Finally, we stopped at a village on a rock. From a distance it looked like a carved rock but is actually a fortress/village and a wonderful stop.

Nearby we passed the castle where Tom Cruise and Katie Holmes were married. No time to go. Next time. Oh, yes, there WILL be a next time.

We were running late, but I wanted to be back in Rome by 6:00 p.m. Fabio, whom I was really enjoying, was telling me that during another class he was held up behind a flock of sheep. Guess what …. Sheep. Lots of them, totally blocking the road! Then traffic.

I was in a rush, because Andrea Bocelli was giving a free concert in Piazza de Poppolo. This was something I really wanted to see. We drove in gridlock traffic for two hours, but we arrived, much to Fabio's relief, at 6:50 p.m. He left me a few blocks from the Piazza, so I could walk the rest of the way. The stage I had seen the day before was lighted and occupied by two full orchestras (Rome and Prague), as well as a 150-person choir. Bocelli and five female opera singers did a 90-minute concert for what were at least 100,000 people. It was a once-in-a-lifetime spectacle. He was funny and charming (I assumed from other people's responses, because it was all in Italian) and amazing. It was wall-to-wall in the Piazza. Behind it, the city walls and the backs of the statues were outlined. The sound was perfection.

The Lesson

Sometimes life gives you roses. I almost didn't stay the extra day, but I am so glad I did. Just think of the missed opportunities if I hadn't stayed. Take advantage of all your situations to discover what awaits you.

Unbelievable New Year's Eve Experiences

In Tokyo

Five or six years ago, a shopping center in Tokyo invited me to spend the holiday season analyzing why sales were down. They wished for me to propose creative solutions to bring in business. I decided to visit other malls to see how they were doing and therefore got to see much of the City. I was accompanied by one of my associate producers and two designers, and we were scheduled to stay through New Year's Eve to complete our business.

As it happens, an old high school girlfriend was working in Tokyo as the President of a Christian university. Oddly, while I was going to be in Tokyo, she would be in Los Angeles but told me to be sure and go to Zojoji Temple at Midnight on New Year's.

We didn't have a clue how the Japanese celebrated New Year's Eve. We soon discovered that everything was closed. Christmas was the time for all the stores and restaurants. Fortunately, we found a restaurant and then went to the temple. It was amazing. Hundreds of booths were filled with incredibly-prepared food, fortune tellers and crafts, all with zillions of people milling around them.

We were given an iridescent balloon and a little piece of parchment-style paper and told to put our wishes on them and tie them to the balloon. We carried them around until 10 minutes before midnight when a huge log was launched into an even larger metal gong calling everyone forth. Everyone around us began to sing and chant with the intermittent sounds of the huge gong. Then, at one minute before midnight, the countdown began and appeared on nearby Tokyo Tower. At Midnight, everyone released the thousands of balloons which simultaneously rose into the sky. It was not only a spectacular vision but a heart-pumping spiritual experience. I felt that my wish was going straight to heaven and was going to come true.

We were the only ones not Japanese, but you would not have known it as everyone embraced and wished each other a Happy New Year. It was an amazingly beautiful and soul-wrenching moment, and I experienced it because of my work.

Lesson

My work has brought me some of the most beautiful and moving moments of my life. It would be hard to separate the business from the personal in this and many cases, and I think a mistake to try.

New Year's Eve 2007

In Rio

I had a site inspection outside of San Paulo, Brazil, scheduled for the middle of January 2008. One of my mother's dearest friends, when she was a teen, lives in Rio, and I had previously visited him and his wife briefly. So I emailed him that since I was coming I'd like to stop and visit them. He had an even better idea – "Come to Rio for New Year's and spend a week with us before you go to San Paulo!"

They have a penthouse apartment with a gorgeous balcony overlooking Copacabana Beach where they hold their annual New Year's Eve party and watch the incredible celebration below. I arrived mid-afternoon, and Walter picked me up as his wife and daughter were about to do the annual New Year's ritual: They wade out into the ocean and jump the waves seven times. Then, they dedicate seven stalks of white flowers (or water candles and other gifts) to someone near and dear to them. They then cast them from the rocks as an offering to Lemanjá, the ocean goddess that, according to the Umbanda religion, is believed to be fishermen's and shipwrecks survivors' protector. This is their way of asking for a prosperous and happy new year.

At night, their house servants prepared a huge feast, and the entire beaches of Cocacabana and Ipanema were teeming with people, sectioned into groups, all dressed in white, all dancing. It looked like one big voodoo celebration. Each group had its own space and stayed within it with barbecue, drinks and entertainment. Millions watched in awe of the finale, the largest fireworks show since the Olympics. It was Times Square times 5000!

The Lesson

Do I need to say it? I experienced it because of my work. Is it not all the same?

My Most Tragic Adventure - September 11th

You probably know exactly where you were on September 11. I'll never forget it. My husband (at that time) and I had been visiting friends in Germany and attending the German Sieger Shau (German Shepherd Show, comparable in Germany to SuperBowl here in the States in size and attendance). We flew back from Frankfurt and were due to be one of the first planes into JFK. While we watched the seat video screen with the tiny plane showing us our location, we realized we were over Nova Scotia. At that exact moment, the pilot announced with his voice cracking, "We are going to be making an emergency landing in Halifax." Flight attendants immediately began scurrying down the aisles and, of course, everyone felt very unsettled as the announcements to take our seats started.

Minutes later, I was alarmed to see one of the attendants passing by in tears. Tense moments passed, and then the pilot announced that due to an act of terrorism the American border was closed and there would be no flights into the U.S. The plane was instantly filled with audible gasps and questions.

Our loaded 747 was the first plane to land in the tiny airport of Halifax, followed by over 60 more jumbo jets - some from Europe; others from Asia. We sat on the tarmac for a very long time. Even then I had the thought that if we were the first plane in, we would most likely be the last plane out.

Finally, customs came onto the plane and cleared us to enter the airport; however, we were not allowed to take any of our luggage. That stayed on the plane. Along with passengers from the other planes, we waited in the airport and watched the terminal televisions in absolute disbelief as the Twin Towers were destroyed over and over through the wonder of instant replay. I felt sick at heart, and my thoughts were filled with dread for my friends and associates in New

York. My mind raced with the possibility of further harm to those I loved.

Hours later we were picked up by school buses. Everyone from all the flights was being billeted either at school gymnasiums or local clubs, like the Rotary. All flight passengers were kept together. We were taken to a school where cots were brought into the gymnasium. Drug stores donated soap, toothpaste and toothbrushes. The locals cooked in the school cafeteria and brought their cell phones and chargers so we could try to call home. Try. There were few connections.

We all slept on the concrete floor or a cot, each with one blanket and no pillows. We shared the school showers. Everyone had one towel. This was a luxury to what it might have been.

Our school had a computer lab, and I headed to it immediately and soon discovered that I was the only person who knew my remote code in order to get connected. So even though I communicated with my son, my mother and my office, I spent the rest of the time as command central emailing for my plane mates.

The Lesson

Beyond the horror of this unbelievable tragedy, I took away something uniquely special: the people of Halifax. They literally took over in minutes and hours what anyone else would have struggled over for days. They organized quickly and got everyone as comfortable as possible immediately. My friends who had traveled with their dogs on another flight said their pets were housed immediately with local families. We had food prepared for us 24 hours a day, so much we couldn't eat it all. We had drivers who took us shopping to Wal-Mart. Everyone opened up their pocketbooks and their hearts with total generosity of spirit. One man shared with me that because of the terrible air crash years prior they were well rehearsed in disaster training.

Isn't it wonderful and terrible to know that such a crisis would unify people, cross cultural hurdles and bring out the best in everyone? I salute the people of Nova Scotia, and most especially Halifax, for they are heroes. Supported by the local Red Cross, I have never before or since experienced the warmth and hospitality that was shared with all of us during those tragic days.

Special Places I Have Been

I am incredibly fortunate to have a career that allows me the phenomenal experiences I've had. I have met amazing people and travelled to fabulous places. And all of it continues to bring great joy to my life.

I have ridden camels in Morocco and Jordan. I have tasted incredible cheeses and wines in Sardegna. I have seen wonders of the world ... Petra and the Taj Mahal. I spent two weeks in a fairytale Lake Como with one night spent on the lake during a local festival where rowboats were decorated beautifully and singers and musicians drifted by passing out the contents of picnic baskets to share the bounty of local sausages, cheeses and wines.

I've visited Moscow in the dead of winter and have been enthralled with the concept of standing in Red Square and The Kremlin and then taking a midnight train to St. Petersburg. I fantasized that I was living out *Dr. Zhivago*. My fantasy ended at breakfast over blinis and caviar with hot tea served from a golden samovar. In St. Petersburg, while covered by a fur robe, I took a troika around Catherine the Great's Palace, stopping for vodka and more blinis and caviar along the way.

Berlin was a revelation, and from there I visited Christmas markets all over Germany eating roasted chestnuts and drinking cider.

Cuba was another amazing experience for the joy of the entire population and the vibrancy of the music of the clubs ... even though the buildings looked like they'd fall over at any moment!

I traveled to the DMZ in Korea, had dinner on The Great Wall of China and was entertained in The Forbidden City. I've bargained and bartered in marketplaces from China to India to Korea. I have had a Turkish bath by a loin-clothed man with a gold tooth and a Korean massage (completely exfoliated by a woman clad in a red bra and panties who tossed me around for two hours as she scrubbed me clean). I experienced a tornado in Rome, happened upon impromptu opera concerts at The Pantheon and at La Scala, ice skated in Rimini and visited the site of the Olympics above Torino.

And those are only a few of my adventures. I have memories which are indelible; not only of the sights, but mostly of the friends I have made who will be friends forever. Not just people with whom I've traveled or worked, but locals that I've met unexpectedly. In Jordan, our tour guide and I explored our differences and our similarities, he Muslim and me Jewish. I have walked the trails of history and explored art and culture which now decorate my home. I try to bring home something from everywhere I've been. Haj, who only builds hotels and speaks nothing but Arabic, made me a beautiful hand-painted chest that is the centerpiece of my living room. Paintings by the very elderly Claude Idlas from the South of France are displayed throughout my home. All around me I have memories of places I've been, but mostly people I've met. And every time I look around, I realize how lucky I am to be doing what I'm doing ... working at what I love in an industry that invites me to continuously grow and experience new people and things.

The Lesson

Never stop growing, never stop learning. Use your sense of curiosity to explore new places and make new friends, no matter where you are. Never feel that you are limited to your immediate surroundings. Reach out. The world is waiting for you.

Traveling will show you how to exceed your limits. It did for me. I have a major and truly neurotic fear that literally can incapacitate me. It is the fear of getting lost. The idea of it will immobilize me; I can't think; I can't figure out what to do; I could just sit for hours and cry if I get lost. Can you imagine that for someone who travels as much as I do? I've had to cope with my fears as I have expanded my travels internationally.

And I am navigationally impaired. Don't give me a map and expect me to follow it. Tell me that I have to walk out of the building, turn right or left, go to a specific street and turn in whatever direction. I can't even go on the subway myself. I can't figure out the entrances and exits. I was once in Tokyo with Mark and Carol McKibben (the former publisher of *Special Events* magazine). We had been taking subways for days under Mark's direction when suddenly he turned to me in the train station and said, "It's your turn, Andrea. Take us back to the hotel." I absolutely refused.

I actually had to go to Yokohama on the subway by myself and was told it wouldn't be a problem because everything would be announced in English. Of course, it wasn't. So, I went to Starbucks and found a man who walked me to the train. Once on the car, I had to ask if anyone spoke English. One did and told me where to get off. Then, the station was huge, and I had no clue where to go to exit. When I finally did get out, I then had to get to a hotel. This pushed the limits for me. The next time I know I will be fearful, but perhaps I'll be a little braver.

I have a fear of helicopters but take them because they are often the best way to see the countryside.

My friend Audrey Gordon is terrified of the ocean, yet when we were in Australia together at the Great Barrier Reef, I convinced her to go into the water with me by telling her she would always remember it. She gathered the courage to do it.

Everything about travel, unless you are on a guided tour, is about growth and constant exploration. It enables you to exceed your self-inflicted limitations, even if ever so slightly.

35

Miscellaneous Short Stories

John Daly and Me

A very loooong time ago, the Dodgers were playing in the World Series in Los Angeles. As luck would have it, the game took place over the Jewish holidays, and John created two fantastic themes in a tent at Dodger Stadium. One was Arabian Nights, and the night of THIS theme fell on Yom Kippur, the holiest of the Jewish holidays!

The leader of our band (I was working at his entertainment company at the time) was Ron Rubin, who was Jewish as was half the band. You can only imagine the consternation this caused! Of course, the band was to be costumed in Arabic robes and headdresses. Prior to the game and at all band breaks, the boys took off to the parking lot, and there in their Arabic costumes, they prayed.

There is no lesson; you just had to be there to see it!

Another funny memory that John and I share happened at the Biltmore Hotel during McDonald's introduction of Chicken McNuggets. John and I turned one of the smaller meeting rooms into Old MacDonald's Farm complete with wooden fencing, a live animal farmyard, hay bales and the entire floor covered with hay. With a hillbilly band playing, and, of course, McNuggets being served, the party was well underway when the fire marshal showed up and said, "Close it down; you can't have hay on the floor."

Well, closing it down just wasn't an option. So John and I grabbed his crew, picked up the brooms, and as we sang along with the band, started sweeping up the hay as if it was part of the entertainment. We managed to do this before the fire marshal's eyes, and he approved how quickly we had reacted.

The guests never knew; the client never knew, and Chicken McNuggets was launched successfully.

The Lesson

Think on your feet. Solutions are almost always at hand.

My Birthday Snafu

It was December and my birthday. I was young. I was pretty. I was beginning to taste success in my chosen career. And I was in love. Knowing that it was my birthday, the hotel in which we were working comped my room and sent me a bottle of champagne. As I took a bath to get ready for the evening, I freely drank the bottle and luxuriated in my happiness. Afterwards, I dressed in my snazzy red velvet outfit, backless at that, and prepared to monitor my band in the ballroom.

When I walked in, people literally turned and stared. The band stopped playing. Though I knew I must look good, I was mystified. I didn't normally get such a reaction. And then …. as I saw that everyone's eyes were riveted to my chest … I realized I had put the top of my outfit on backwards. Instead of being backless, I was frontless (for the most part).

The next night I attended another event, and some of the same people were there who had attended my birthday debacle.

"Oh, I remember YOU!" some said.

The Lesson

How do you want to be remembered? I never forgot that lesson, and thirty years later I want to be remembered as professional, engaging, interesting and personable. I don't drink with clients or employees. If I am going to err on the side of anything, it should be dignity. If I drink champagne at all, I drink it at home nowadays.

My BMW

I had just purchased a snazzy new BMW Z3 red convertible. I had seen it in the Neiman Marcus catalog, and I coveted it.

Right after I bought the car, we were engaged to produce an event for BMW North America, and we secured a beautiful area at Warner Brothers to do so. I told my client about my wonderful car and offered to bring it to the event as a centerpiece for the party. The client loved the idea. So I brought my pride and joy and parked it in the center of the event space where everyone could ooh and ah over this vehicle that was hot off the assembly line and still didn't have license plates.

The party was fun, and everyone loved Warner Brothers and the atmosphere, the incredible food and the Southern California weather. I took a break for a few minutes to take care of some details for departure, and when I returned ... the hood of my car was open and surrounded by various BMW guests, each holding a piece of the engine and smiling for the photographer!

Now, at that time, I still lived in Acton about an hour away from the studio and off a dark country road with next to no traffic. Cell phones didn't work once I left L.A. proper. Would you believe that I was not happy?

I calmly (at least my outside demeanor anyway) went to my client and explained that I had not acted generously so that my car could be ripped apart by her guests; and why wasn't she on the watch for what they were doing? She was somewhat embarrassed and promised me that they could put it back together.

They did, but it was a very nervous drive home that night.

The Lesson

No matter WHAT you do, put in writing the rules and regulations, such as "No messing with my car." How many times have I said it? Worth repeating, don't you think?

Cash Bash

CASH BASH .... Do you even know what that is? I didn't when I was asked to provide entertainment and support services for a producer coordinating this very unusual event.

Basically top salespeople are given faux cash and the opportunity to spend it in a variety of ways. They can buy items such as televisions, jet skis, refrigerators and watches. You get the picture. Or they can gamble (the event was in Las Vegas) and attempt to increase their spending money. Or, in this case, they had the opportunity to open up safe deposit boxes which contained more faux cash. The money is given out at registration, and the preliminary amount is based upon their sales records. The more they sold the more faux money they got. Pretty cool idea, isn't it?

At this particular event, registration opened up about six hours before the actual event. Whoever would have guessed that this group of Type A personalities (well, after all, they ARE salespeople) would go to the nearest Kinko's and run off THOUSANDS of fake dollars on the color copiers? Merchandise sales that night were "over budget" by $400,000, and for a long time no one could figure out why until later one of the perpetrators blabbed.

The lesson

Think ahead and never underestimate your audience!

Mother Nature Challenges Andrea .... Again

I had not been in business even one year in 1989. I was in Italy working on the beautiful island of Sardegna at a resort called Cala d Volpe. Unfortunately, I didn't get to stay there. Instead, I was at the Italian version of the Bates Motel up the hill. It had been closed for the season and had no amenities (including a restaurant), so I did get to enjoy the guests' experience except for the sleeping arrangement. The event involved two weeks in Sardegna producing Neil Sedaka for two shows, a week apart.

From Sardegna, I was flying to San Francisco to produce a very unusual theme event for the same automotive client. This one was complicated, and I had spent almost a year auditioning about 100 entertainers, scripting them, rehearsing them and getting them ready for an amazing show. While sitting with my client in the resort's television room, we were all rather shocked to see visions of San Francisco and a treacherous earthquake which shut down the city, including our event which had already been loaded in. It was obviously not going to happen. The reality of a city in disaster quelled my disappointment over the cancelled show.

The same show was rescheduled for Reno the following year. We recast the talent, rehearsed them and went through our preparation again. Let me give you the vision. Guests watched a car reveal and then followed those cars up ramps which took them to another area of the convention center where they walked across a deck built high above the floor of the center. From there they looked down on a carpeted map of the entire United States. On that map, all of the client's automotive plants were emphasized with recreations of images of that part of the U.S., with our talent acting out various roles. For instance, in San Francisco, we created the Golden Gate Bridge with a sidewalk Italian café and roaming opera singers. In Memphis, we had Elvis impersonators as used car salesmen in an authentic drive-in diner. The entire event was really amazing.

After the event, the client donated the "carpet map of the U.S." to a Nevada non-profit/Section 8 group to carpet low-income units. We all still smile when we remember one recipient saying, "I may be poor, but my place is bigger than Kansas."

The Lesson

It's all about perspective, isn't it?

Small, Important Lessons

Neil Sedaka

When I began working internationally, I discovered a common thread: no matter how much I thought I knew I didn't know everything.

As I indicated in the previous story, right after I started

Extraordinary Events, I was invited to produce a show in Sardegna, Italy, a gorgeous island with phenomenal hotels. There was no ballroom at the Cala del Volpe, but a lovely oceanfront. After reviewing a lot of acts, the client chose Neil Sedaka for two shows, one week apart.

We built a stage right on the water and brought Neil over on a private jet. It all seemed very easy, and then the Italian version of the musicians union showed up, asking me for a list of Neil's songs so they could charge us accordingly. Or at least I think this is what they said. It was all in Italian. I replied in English that every song was written as well as performed by Neil Sedaka, so I couldn't understand why the union would want to charge me performance fees when they were to go directly to the artist I had hired. Makes sense to me; how about you? But, they insisted, so I had to gather all of Neil's songs and report them to the Union representative. I was charged for each song.

The Lesson

This was one more rule that I've since learned has to be observed in every country. Keep it in mind.

And one more lesson. Always ascertain in what hotel YOU AND YOUR STAFF will be staying. In this case, it wasn't the stunning Cala del Volpe. As I described earlier, it was the Bates Motel up the street. It was closed for the season with no staff, no kitchen, no air conditioning and no services of any kind. This meant no change of linens, no breakfast, nothing for two weeks!

My team finally begged to eat at the guests' hotel, and reluctantly our request was granted. Now I don't blame the client for not wanting to pay the rather pricey fare, but there was nothing else around. We had no choice.

A Very Grand Finale

To create a finale for Danny Gans in Las Vegas for a gala dinner for an automotive company, the client requested that we end our show by providing some kind of special effect that would wow the audience. Little did we know how much of a wow it would be!

We elected to use two well-placed confetti cannons to spew forth large bursts of confetti straight into the audience when Danny performed his finale. Unfortunately, one of the pieces disengaged from the main frame of the cannon and rocketed out into the audience, whizzing by the top executive's ear and missing his face by a scant quarter of an inch or so. It then barreled into the arm of one of the hotel's servers. Fortunately, we were well insured (although the confetti cannon vender wasn't), and there was no serious injury. However, there could have been. Accidents happen, and I frankly never anticipated one like this.

The Lesson

When your vendors don't carry insurance, don't hire them.

Staying Current

A few years ago in January during The Special Event, Extraordinary Events had the opportunity to present a proposal to a relatively long-standing client for whom we felt we had a true understanding. I flew with my team from The Special Event to the client's offices in Los Angeles to meet with its planner and representatives.

Having prepared a costly proposal that we felt perfectly suited the client's needs, we were ready. As we greeted our clients, the fatal question came, one I will never forget.

"How long has it been since you've visited our Web site?" the client asked.

Smugly I replied, "I took a look during the Christmas holidays."

"Well, then," she replied, "you're too late. If you haven't checked it out this week then you wouldn't know that we've changed everything about our direction, our directives, our mission statement and … the list continued. So unless your proposal addresses this new directive, then we're not interested."

I apologized, said she'd have what she needed within the week and went back to The Special Event, tail between my legs and lesson learned.

The Lesson

It is what's happening TODAY that matters. I will never again visit a client without knowing the latest in what's new in his or her corporate culture.

The Consummate Gentleman

Many years ago at an International Special Events Society (ISES) conference awards presentation, Extraordinary Events was nominated in conjunction with Martin Van Keken for the opening of GM Place in Vancouver. Though not a member of ISES, I was happy to attend, very sure that this magnificent event would surely win its category which was Best Corporate Event (or something much like that). Martin was also nominated in the same category for another event he had produced in Vancouver. We sat together, and when the award and Martin's name was announced, I jumped up and followed him onto the stage. Then it hit me ... the picture on screen was for the "other" event, and there I was ... on stage ... with Martin ... and very, very embarrassed.

I learned about grace in that moment when Martin took my hand and, as he gave his thank you speech, acknowledged that I had been a friend and an inspiration to him.

The Lesson

Martin taught me about generosity and graciousness. He was the consummate gentleman and made an embarrassing moment far less humiliating.

I also learned not to jump the gun so quickly and listen more carefully!

The Snake Pit

This is actually a story about managing people, always a challenge. In this one case, Extraordinary Events was hired to produce Don Henley (of The Eagles) for a private corporate event in Cannes, France. Because we were also providing technical support for the entire conference, we had a large team of people working on the event. I'd brought on an independent contractor as one of my staff to serve as the executive producer, as well as a logistics person and a technical director. We had a three-day setup, since we were in a marquee (tent) where one side of the structure was for our show and the other for a dinner. Every day there was a very elaborate crew lunch. In France, this translated to an enormous buffet of wonderful, tasty and beautifully presented foods, complete with a variety of wines. We ate well.

On the second day of our load-in, the executive producer told me he wasn't feeling well and needed to see a doctor. He was sure he had food poisoning. Since we all ate the exact same food, I found that unlikely but advised him to get to the hotel and contact a doctor. I thought he had the flu and didn't want him near me much less our entertainer. He did so and didn't show up again until our show started, so the rest of us took over all of his responsibilities and worked ungodly hours to make everything happen. At the show I suggested, "Since we covered all your work, please let us all get some rest and take over the load-out."

He looked at me askance and said, "I can't. A friend and I are taking an early morning train to Paris for a little vacation."

Though I tried pressing the issue, he was adamant. He was going to Paris.

So more late hours with no sleep, we loaded out sans our producer.

When we returned to the U.S., his invoice awaited charging me in full for every day. Now in our company we pay one rate for in-office work, another for local production days and more for working abroad. I told my independent contractor that I would pay him the in-office fee, but since he did not do any of the producing, I would not pay a production rate, much less the rate for abroad.

He cried. Then he argued that he couldn't accept other work at that time so he was offended that he was being punished. I replied that if he had been sick at home he couldn't have worked anyway. That made no difference to him, but I stuck to my guns and refused.

It didn't end there. Weeks later he submitted phone bills to me from the last year of working with EE. Every call made that had anything to do with our business, whether it was ten seconds or a long call, was marked with a Hi-Liter. He charged me for the cost of the calls as well as his time making them! Now I know you'll believe me when I tell you that it added up EXACTLY to the same amount as the difference between in-office work and on-site pay abroad!

The Lesson

Learn to deal with vendors and employees (and, yes, even clients) who operate with situational ethics. No matter how fairly you treat others, people can justify their actions by putting you in the wrong to achieve their own end. Treat them fairly but always stick to your own ethical boundaries. It's a small world; actions have a way of catching up with people.

To take this just one step further, I was quoted by Kenneth Kristoffersen (Experiential Events) in a *Special Events* magazine article and Debbie Meyers (Bravo! Entertainment) during a panel discussion with the same comment about staff retention. Both quotes boiled down to this: "My friend Andrea Michaels refers to this [producing events] as a lifestyle, not a career, and I learned a lot from her with that comment ... It's our role to make our potential employees [and vendors] understand what that means ..."

This goes back to both work and life. Our work is so much a part of our lives and how we treat other people. It really can't be separated. It simply must be a life of consistency, honesty, ethics and heart.

An Olympic Moment

I've been multi-tasking again. As I work, live and write this book, I've been glued to the television watching the Olympics. Like everyone else, I've been devoted to the swimming and to watching Michael Phelps' remarkable achievements. There's been a lot of talk about whether he's the greatest Olympian of all time, or the best athlete, but who cares? What endeared him to me forever started after his first pre-race qualifier, because when he won his heat, he looked up to find his mother. Through the days that followed he continuously and proudly looked, with love and devotion, for her in the stands. As he collected more and more of his medals, his need for his mother's approval became obvious to the world. During one awards ceremony with the camera directly on his face, he turned to another medalist and said, "I can't find her." The announcer immediately asked Mrs. Phelps to stand so that her son could see her face, which was promptly displayed on one of the jumbotrons. The delight in his eyes when he saw her needed no translation.

Well, I'm a mother and proud of the man my son has become, so I appreciate that this young man with the eyes of the world upon him didn't want to be "cool" or nonchalant. His real values screamed out, no matter how many endorsements were flying his way. He wanted his mom's approval, and, each time he was interviewed, he acknowledged her. After he won his eighth gold medal, his eyes again turned to the stands where his family was sitting. As he made his victory round with his team, he left them and climbed through the mob up into the stands to hug his mother. I think that meant more to me than any other moment in the Olympics. He was real. He was humble. He was a true role model for what each mother wants her son to be. Forget the world records. His greatest contribution was how he set a new standard for humanity.

The Lesson

We all have it in us to achieve remarkable things. Maybe it's a new technology that will wow an audience or tirelessly working for a humanitarian cause or just making people happy. But this Olympic moment showed me that we are not what we do; we are who we are, and that is not defined by our jobs but what lies inside our hearts. I hope I never forget that.

An Unusual Request

It rained every day from guest arrival to outdoor events on the first and second nights during a three-day event headquartered at La Costa in San Diego. Every event had to be reset indoors instead of in the balmy Southern California weather.

The final night was planned for the ballroom, and the client came up with a request unlike any I'd ever heard. She thought it would be "so much fun" to turn on the sprinklers in the ballroom during the event as guests would get "the gag." I thought she was joking. She wasn't.

I explained that the cost of replacing the carpet, the wallpaper, the brand new chairs and everything in the newly refurbished ballroom would be enormously expensive. She didn't care.

We didn't do it, but she was not a happy client because she could not understand why we wouldn't (not couldn't) make this happen for her.

The Lesson

This leads me to more of a question than a lesson. Is there such a thing as having TOO much money? When you know a request is just wrong, say no.

The Wedding at Casa Loma

One of my good clients presented me with a wonderful challenge. His company was merging with another, and there was tension between the two entities. He wanted his annual event to somehow create a bond between them.

The event would be strictly a hospitality affair and part of a national conference, this year held in Toronto. We met for a site inspection to find a venue for the event, and when we saw it, the solution came immediately to mind.

Casa Loma is a banquet facility that is host to many, many weddings. Wedding? Well, there's an idea. How about *marrying* the two companies? Sold!

The ideas developed in a zany way. I had seen *Tony and Tina's Wedding,* a satirical performance of a wedding in which the audience members are the wedding and reception guests. This spurred my creative juices as I developed a loose script for the event that included a ceremony that had a cast of characters representing both companies. Cast of characters? Where do I find them in Toronto?

Friends referred an excellent improv company. I interviewed and hired them and together we developed a zany, customized and complicated event.

Two weeks before the event, I called them to go through a last talk through. No answer. No answering machine. The next day the same thing, and the next and the next. I sent a telegram to the address I had. No response. Finally, three days before our show I sent a friend to the address. She reported back that the apartment looked abandoned.

HELP! I called another associate in Toronto and explained the situation. She immediately went to work, finding me a talented actress who then called in some friends. In three days we worked to develop a script . . . a somewhat new scenario, and I prayed.

I arrived late the night before the event and met the cast the day of. They looked great. We reviewed the program, and the event began.

One member of the cast was stationed on each arriving guest bus. We had the justice of the peace; the bride; the groom; the mother of the groom ("Oh my boy shouldn't be marrying that tramp; she's not good enough for him"); the maid of honor who was the groom's former girlfriend and wanted him back; the wedding planner and the groom. The best man and the bride's mobster uncle were at Casa Loma mingling with the guests as they arrived.

After a reception on the terrace, guests were ushered into the craziest wedding ceremony ever. Since the flower girl had locked herself in the bathroom, one of the guests had to take her place. Another was engaged to walk the bride down the aisle. Merriment ensued, and soon the entire audience was engaged.

The ceremony was followed by a receiving line and then a reception where the companies were purposely seated randomly with one another (half of each at individual tables) to enjoy the wacky wedding festivities.

The mission was accomplished; the companies were united. After the party, I told my client about my disappearing actors, and we had a good laugh.

The Lesson

Make friends wherever you go. It's comforting to know that you have friends away from home when you are in need.

Gone with the Water

The year after "The Wedding" the same wonderful client brought me to Atlanta to produce the next annual event. Encouraged I suggested another whimsical theme, *Gone With the Water … the Lost Pages of Margaret Mitchell.* The venue was the Atlanta Historical Museum.

Our premise was that Ms. Mitchell's book should have been called *Gone with the Water,* but the manuscript was lost and thus her second version, *Gone with the Wind,* was eventually published.

One of the lost pages was the invitation. Guests arrive and had cocktails outdoors in the lush Southern Gardens. Dinner was comprised of Southern delicacies such as Shrimp and Grits with desserts served off the skirts of our roaming Scarlett O'Haras.

And then all guests were invited into the Museum's theatre to re-film scenes from *GWTW.* However, this time the script was all about water. One scene had Scarlett crying to the heavens, "As God is my witness, I will never go thirsty again!" with Rhett's replying, "Frankly, Scarlett, I don't give a damn!"

Oh, in case you haven't guessed, our client manufactures water-related products.

The Lesson

Build humor into your events wherever appropriate. It's great to make people smile, and it will always lift your own spirits!

A Night with the Music of Andrew Lloyd Webber

Unplanned humor can, unfortunately, ruin an event. Our venue was The McCallum Theatre in Palm Springs. The client had used it on a former program, but at the time Palm Springs had few venues for incentive clients. So I suggested that we use the theatre in an unusual way. Instead of performances on the stage and guests in the theatre seats, we were reversing this and guests would dine on stage and performances would happen in the house.

When guests arrived, they had cocktails in the foyer of the theatre and were then ushered into the theatre itself. Seats were roped off, and, of course, there were some moments of confusion. *Where do we go?* A scrim with the client's projected logo hid the stage from sight.

Once all guests were in the aisles, we dimmed the projections on the scrim (to dramatic music) and revealed that behind it were stunning tables set with beautifully candlelit, elaborately dressed placesettings and the most elegant of appointments.

Then the music swelled and the scrim lifted. Guests were invited by handsome wait staff to take the stage and their seats at the tables. Dinner was served as a pianist on stage played Broadway show tunes on a gleaming Baby Grand piano.

After dessert, lights were once again dimmed, and the sounds of an Andrew Lloyd Webber musical overture floated through the air. No musicians were yet seen. Soon, from the hydraulic orchestra pit, the musicians emerged until they were at stage level and now part of the stage. As the overture ended, the centerpieces were lifted skyward off the tables ... the beauty of working on a stage with so many pipes and pulleys.

Immediately the show began with performers from various Lloyd Webber shows appearing from different places throughout the theatre. *The Phantom* roamed the stage. Rusty (from *Starlight Express*) roller bladed down the aisles and stunt jumped onto the stage. *Evita* sang from the upper balcony. Well, I'll stop there, because that's a story unto itself.

I had hired all but one of the singers based on past experiences with them. The new hire was a woman who would sing *Evita*, one song from *Jesus Christ Superstar* and another from *Starlight Express*. She had come highly recommended, and her demo tape was fabulous.

When she arrived in Palm Springs, she told me she had a slight cold so would not be singing full out during rehearsal. Dress rehearsal revealed that she was truly out of voice.

With only two hours to go until guests arrived, I had my hands full with other requirements of the night, and she assured me that with some rest and gargling she'd be fine. I was skeptical, but it was far too late to get someone else. If we eliminated her from the show, the entire performance would be affected since some of the cast would not be able to make their costume changes. I decided to let it go.

I made a mistake.

Her first song was from *Starlight Express*, a country ditty. It wasn't good, but it wasn't horrible. Country can hide a bunch of flaws. Then, she began to sing *I Don't Know How to Love Him*, and if you remember Mrs. Miller from the 1950s, you'll know what I mean. It was too horrible to be funny. It was just excruciatingly bad. I radioed the conductor and told him that when she did *Evita* to get the band to play as loudly as possible. It didn't help. *Don't Cry for Me, Argentina* took on a whole new meaning. The wonderful show was ruined. Even the other incredible performances could not salvage this debacle!

The Lesson

When you know it's going to be bad, don't let it go! I did, and it was a disaster!

The Barcelona Bats

Working in Barcelona has always been a fabulous experience. With its wealth of culture, talent and incredible venues, it is exciting and inspiring. For one program we planned an amazing event at Cavas Cordoniu, one of the most beautiful champagne wineries in Spain, if not the world.

It was an evening featuring lovely décor, decorative lighting, tours of the cavas (caves), choreographed waiters parading in the champagne, a meal prepared by a legendary chef of Spain and a performance by The Gipsy Kings.

We had ample time for set up (and how often does that happen?), so I was surprised when my producer called me and said sheepishly, "We have a problem."

Was it lack of power? The event was in the large vat room above the caves, so were the age-old caves collapsing? Did the venue decide they didn't want our event there?

"Nope," she said, "but I don't know what to do. The room is infested with bats who are dive bombing the tables."

Bats? Probably not a good thing when our 300 VIP guests arrived. I doubt that it would be considered appropriate dinner entertainment. Don't you agree? Well, fortunately I like bats (don't snicker … it's true), and I knew the solution.

"Get some rotten fruit," I told her, "and place it in the farthest corners of the cavas, and the bats will head right toward it and leave the tables alone. Just make sure you have a lot of fruit so it'll last for a few days."

She did. They did. And 300 guests never saw our Barcelona bats!

The Lesson

When you're producing events, it's always good to have a working knowledge of how to rid your event of pests – whether they are human or non-human!

Biz Bash

I was asked by my friend Richard Aaron to be part of a competitive panel at one of the first Biz Bash conferences in New York. The other panelists were from Las Vegas, New York, Miami and Chicago. Each of us was to represent our area (mine was Southern California) and tell why it was the best destination/venue for events. We were each asked to prepare a presentation and FedEx it to Richard, which I did. He signed personally for the delivery, so I felt secure that he had received it. Even so, I brought a back-up disk with me.

Arriving the night before the early morning session, I checked in with Richard and tried to confirm that he had my presentation. With a puzzled look, he said, "I never received it." So, I pulled out the FedEx slip with his signature, but he still persisted that he hadn't received my presentation. It was obvious that there was no point in us debating who was right or wrong. He didn't have my presentation, so I gave him the back-up. He declared that he was tucking it in his suit pocket and walking it right over to his AV person. Reluctantly, I let my only copy go feeling that guilt would insure that the back-up disk would be delivered.

The next morning I arrived early and ran into Richard. Chipper even with the three-hour time difference, I requested that I see my presentation on screen. Richard paled. He had left my disk in his suit pocket, and his suit was at home, not anywhere near the conference venue!

Meanwhile, the rest of the panel began arriving. I saw tests of their presentations. Cheryl Fish (then of Mirage Events) had a full blown musical spectacular. After all, it was Vegas. Others were equally snazzy. I had nothing. I looked at Richard and said, "All I ask is that I go last." After all, we were competing.

I let the others rhapsodize about their home cities and the remarkable capabilities each had for events.

Then, it was my turn. I took the stage and said:

"Please close your eyes. It's time to use your imaginations. It's January. You're in New York. *Garbage strike.* Sleet, muddy sleet. It's a Friday night; traffic is at a standstill, and it's impossible to get a cab. You're so *cold.* Or, you're in Chicago. There's so much snow that even the snowplows cannot get through. *Wind chill* factor is immeasurable. Or, you're in Miami. Hurricane season. *Humidity.* Bugs. Or, Vegas. Howling winds from the desert. Traffic that keeps the Strip *deadlocked.*

"BUT you *could be* in Los Angeles, at the beach. Can you hear the *soft lapping of waves* as your guests walk through the soft sand of Santa Monica or Laguna Beaches? Can you see the sun setting over the water as you remove your jackets because it's so balmy?

"Or, it could be August. New York. *Muggy.* You're sweating. Another garbage strike. Chicago. Humid. *Rainstorms* in the middle of the day with thunder to wake the dead. Miami. The *bugs* have grown. And talk about humidity. You're *sweating* the minute you leave the hotel lobby. Las Vegas is *128 degrees* in the shade. And there's no shade. The cement is so hot it'll melt the soles of your shoes.

"Los Angeles. Remember that beach? Well, we're back there. It's *78 degrees,* balmy and dry with the same beautiful sunset.

You can open your eyes now. You know where you want to be."

I won.

The Lesson

There is very little that life can throw at you that you can't find a way to conquer if you use your imagination, and, in this case, trust in the imagination of your audience. Sometimes it's all about simplicity and not just technology. The spoken word can be more powerful than high-powered audio-visual shows.

And always carry two back-up disks for any important presentation!

Note: When I told Richard Aaron that I would be using this story in my book, here's what he had to say: "That is the greatest story of lemons to lemonade ever. Only a pro like you could turn it up."

A Hoax

I was asked to create a "wow" for a small FAM trip coming to Orange County, California, at a beach destination hosted by the convention bureau and a beachside hotel. Instead of elaborate décor and a lot of entertainment, I took a leap of faith (after all, I was donating, so no one could complain about costs) and created a weekend no one would forget … including me. It was a big risk, but by now you know risks are tantalizing to me.

Guests were feted for three days and nights. Days were filled with activities from tennis to golf. Evenings featured intimate soirees, two nights of dine-arounds and then a final banquet.

I registered two terrific actor/singers as a couple supposedly part of the FAM. Ivan M. Ahox and Bea Ahox, his wife. Ivan was a gentle giant type of man, and Bea was a petite simpering sidekick to him. They were very, very popular as both were extremely personable and down-to-earth. Bea was the meeting planner with an insurance company, and Ivan was a trainee at Burger King. They had prominent name tags that they had to wear at all events.

Ivan won the golf tournament. Bea won the second night's dance contest. Ivan always talked about the burgers he was learning to make and the various compositions of oil for the fries. It was obvious they were in love. It was apparent that they were the most popular couple there.

At the final banquet, everyone wanted these two at their table.

When I arrived I could hear, "Ivan, join us over here." Or "Bea, are you saving a dance for me?"

After the lovely meal and great wine were served and before dessert, Ivan got up and announced that it was a very special day. It was their anniversary. To show his lovely wife how much he loved her, he wanted to sing her a special song that meant a lot to both of them. Ivan spoke to the piano player who had a microphone for him and then walked over to Bea and started singing. He was amazing. The audience was speechless, because he sounded like a Broadway star. But his body language was that of the Burger King trainee, humble and awkward. Bea got up and hugged him and shyly took the microphone and told the group that Ivan always was trying to get her to sing a duet, but she never would. But, if he was brave enough to sing in front of the group, she would, too. And … by now you've guessed … she was equally fabulous.

At this point the audience was beginning (and only just beginning) to suspect that Ivan and Bea were more than who they said they were.

Ivan took the microphone again and said, "Just in case you haven't guessed, we'd like to tell you who we really are. I.M. Ahox and my wife Bea Ahox (now pronounced like hoax) are not a meeting planner and a Burger King trainee!" And the place broke up with laughter and applause.

Ivan and Bea continued to entertain for about fifteen minutes to a wild reception. After their show, they were surrounded by their new friends to congratulate them on their three-day performance.

And think about THIS. This was years before any of the "faux" shows like The Three Waiters or any of the clones that followed.

The Lesson

Taking creative risks often yields big time returns. Don't be afraid to try something new and different.

Carrot Top

Warner Brothers …the allure of attending an event at a working

"Hollywood" studio is always a hit for guests. In this case, the guests were incentive winners of a Los Angeles-based Mortgage Company, and the meeting planner pulled out all the stops to create an unforgettable evening.

It began with a studio tour, and when guests assembled on Main Street, a parade ensued. Led by a local marching band, cheerleaders and baton twirlers, the parade was an amazing display of the gifts that guests could win during the evening. A luxury boat, a car, a big screen television … nothing shabby here … were all presented as floats. The guests then followed the parade onto a New York street scene and an amazing meal catered by the WB commissary. All along the street scene, the "gifts" were displayed with a larger variety of wares from jewelry to electronic items, to luggage to trips. At the end of the street, a local Rhythm & Blues band entertained while guests dined and used their faux spending money to buy the items they coveted. Then it was time for the featured entertainment of the evening, and therein lies the story.

The very young corporate meeting planner had specified one of two acts … Gallagher or Carrot Top. Gallagher was unavailable. I strongly advised against Carrot Top who might be great at a college fraternity party but, to me, was dangerous for a corporate event. The client insisted, rather outraged that I had given my opinion. So after having her sign disclaimers that the act was booked against my advice, Carrot Top was contracted.

As the show began and Carrot Top pulled out his bag of tricks (oh, you cannot even imagine), the mature gentleman standing next to me said in a quietly lethal tone, "Whose idea was it to book 'HIM'?"

I turned to him and introduced myself, and, of course, he was the company's CEO. I pulled out my disclaimer and said, "Your meetings department specifically requested Carrot Top, Sir."

He walked off, seething. But, to be fair, the very young audience laughed uproariously every second of the performance.

The Lesson

I have no idea if the meeting planner kept her job, but I know that

I did everything possible to make the client understand that it is important to please everyone, especially the boss, and not just go for personal taste.

The Disappearing Parking Lot – Checklist Example #1

Years ago my company was hired to produce the gala party for a very large trade show. We were told that it was to be in the parking lot of the Las Vegas Convention Center. Fortunately, we were very familiar with the exact space and had all the ground plans.

The event itself was fairly simple, but, of course, I felt it important to fly our production team to Las Vegas to review our plans. Can you imagine our surprise when, upon arrival, we discovered that the parking lot had been dug up and was not scheduled to be reinstated until well after our event date? Three weeks out, the city was sold out and no facilities that could hold 6,000 people were available.

We finally did secure space but had to completely revise our plans. One challenge was met. There were more ahead. On our lengthy checklist was a line item of great importance ... the power source and the fee for power charged by the facility. Budgets have been thrown out of sight when the cost of power was not considered. The Convention Center contact assured me that the trade show paid a flat fee for the facility and that fee included power charges. Smugly I asked if they would sign a paper to that effect. They did. What they didn't tell me was there was a $10,000 fee to hook up the power. Once they revived me, I added that new element to my checklist!

The Lesson

Developing a very detailed checklist is crucial. Any item missed or ignored can be costly or dangerous.

Too Many Decibels for the Laguna Bluff – Checklist Example #2

Remember the event in a tent overlooking the bluff in Laguna back in Chapter 33? In those days (when I was just getting started), I knew enough to file plans for my tent with the City. Certainly I had the fire marshal visit in the afternoon to check the lights, fabric and florals. But, little did I know that the police would visit my in-the-middle-of-nowhere tent at 8:30 p.m. The problem? Laguna Niguel had strict regulations on the decibel level of noise (in this case, music) legally acceptable, and we were exceeding it.

"Stop the show NOW," they said. It had just started and was costing my Fortune 500 client a very pretty penny.

The Lesson

Of monumental importance when planning events is a thorough knowledge of the laws and regulations in every city and on each and every individual property. Your checklist should be your bible on an event and should include every element that affects your event, even those for which you personally are not responsible. Anything that can disrupt your event is your responsibility and your obligation to oversee.

A Soggy Tale in Leu Gardens – Checklist Item #3

A number of years ago in October we planned an event in Orlando for a very prestigious company that did not want to have its elegant banquet either in a hotel or a theme park. We found the stately and romantic Leu Gardens overlooking a lovely lake. The romantic garden was perfect for cocktails with dinner in a clear tent on the lawn beneath magnificent trees. We could make noise all night long. There were even restroom facilities that we cleaned and filled with flowers. We even lit the paths with luminaries. We really planned this one carefully.

We spent the day before the event setting up the tent, spraying for bugs (after all, it was Florida), gelling the lights to make the trees amber, violet, turquoise, lime and tangerine, setting up the tables and pinspotting them. Even the linens were set on the tables. All that was needed were centerpieces, band gear and the food. Eleven p.m. and time to call it a night. Then the sprinklers went off and drenched everything in sight. The sprinklers were automatic, so no attendant was present to turn them off! Add one more item to the checklist!

"What did you do?" you might ask. Handled it. That's what a true professional does, like in any other profession. I emphasize that event planning is indeed a profession, because there are yellers and screamers in this industry. Fortunately, I have never found panic to be helpful. When it breaks, you fix it. We replaced what was wet and rolled back the sides of the tent so that the grass would dry overnight. And we made sure that the sprinklers wouldn't go off on the night of our gala event. However, that wasn't the worst of it.

As the day progressed, a chill descended. The air got increasingly colder. The evening turned into one of the coldest October days in Florida history. In mid-afternoon, knowing that it would be cold, cold and colder, we started calling rental companies to get heaters. Unfortunately, so did every other company holding an outdoor event that night. And Florida does not have a surplus of heaters available. We finally located one, but when it was turned on it was too hot, so we took turns turning it on and off so that minute blasts of hot air were continuously filtering into the party. The upside to this is that the grass was certainly dry by the time we left.

The Lesson

When you hire a professional, you hire the years of experience, the ability to cope and that pro's rolodex and resources.

Remote-Control Event Re-Configuration in a Matter of Hours

I was called in to produce the Meridien Hotel Corporation's annual General Managers meeting on a March 28th back in the 1990s. We had several planning meetings with the hotel staff. We issued a specific contract, and it was signed. I hired talent and decorators and put out a detailed production schedule. The event involved over 50 individual entertainers, four rooms filled with décor, staging, lighting and special effects. On March 22nd , I left to produce a job 1,000 miles away.

On March 24th, at exactly noon, I called my hotel contact to ask how many dressing rooms we would have available to us and received the answer. Then, she asked me, "When are you going to be here?"

"When?" I asked.

"Today," she responded.

"Why, today?" I inquired, "Do we have something going on today, too?"

"The general managers meeting," she said, beginning to sound quite hysterical.

"That's on the 28th," I said calmly.

"No, it's today," she screamed.

"What are you talking about?" I questioned. "Read the contract. It says March 28, and that's four days from now."

"No, it's tonight," she hollered.

Well, I slammed down the phone, threw my belongings into a suitcase, called my designer who was still sleeping from the 5 a.m. strike during the previous night, notified my office and gave them instructions and hailed a cab with those memorable words, "Step on it!"

While waiting for the next plane back to Southern California, I called the office. One of the elements we had planned was graffiti panels on the pool deck which was set as a Venice Beach scene. The painter hired a flat bed truck and was painting these panels on the freeway as they headed toward the hotel. We called all of the entertainers, and if we didn't reach them on the first try, we called someone else. We weren't quite sure who was going to turn up, and in some cases we were overloaded with talent. We had three piano players show up for one room's entertainment. We had ten bodybuilders instead of three.

The finale was scheduled to be a "Star Search" with the winning dance couple appearing out of a laser and light cone with trussing in the background filled with lights and effects. Well, my lighting designer/supplier was also out of town, and, when I finally reached him, he did not have any of the necessary equipment with him. He stopped at construction sites all along the freeway to pick up wood, fencing, chain link and scrap iron. From that and scaffolding, we created a funky, high-tech look.

The event went off without a hitch!

The Lesson

Having a team that is always willing to do whatever it takes to make the event happen successfully is critical. Creativity is the life's blood of an event planner. Finally, and worth saying repeatedly, never panic.

August in New Orleans

They said it rained mildly a couple of hours out of every day, usually stopping about mid-afternoon and drying out within an hour or so. We had 10,000 military exchange services personnel coming to Louis Armstrong Park for an event that was to take place throughout the 31-acre park in New Orleans.

My client graciously decided to put me up in the nicest suite at the Royal Sonesta Hotel overlooking Bourbon Street. The set-up for the event went so well that we had the luxury of extra time to spare. So, on the morning of the event I decided to sleep in. After all, my ultra professional crew could handle it without me, right? At 6:00 a.m. my phone rang. It was my client. It was pouring rain. He had called the National Weather Bureau which indicated it was going to rain all day. I was the producer, he said, so it was my decision. Should we call it off? Should we try to move it? Should we hope that it would stop raining and stick with our original plan? I considered the options.

Where do you move 10,000 people? How do you move 31-acres filled with props, decorations, food stands and multiple stages? I chose the last of my options, "hope."

All day long it poured. I watched the canals throughout the park flood it. By noon I was calf deep in puddles wherever I walked. The tents sagged. The ballrooms drowned. By late afternoon we had no power, and I had no "hope" and was trying to figure out how to catch the next plane out of town and disappear. Instead, the whole team brainstormed, and with all of us joking and trying to keep our spirits up, we came up with some solutions. First, we called the city and begged for help. They found a way to send up several substantial truckloads of gravel and wood chips which when poured absorbed some of the water. Many of our crew went in search of hand-held hair dryers.

The event was scheduled for 7:00 p.m. At 6:00 p.m., it was still raining hard. As entertainers and musicians arrived, we kept them beneath some tents and, at 6:55, sent every acoustic instrumentalist and actor to greet the busses. We still had no power.

At 7:00 p.m. when the first bus pulled up, the rain abruptly stopped. Coached in what to do, the entertainers sang and played *Singing in the Rain* and led all 10,000 people in a splash contest as they entered the park. Now it was time to put the hair dryers to work, which we did. We dried off the electrical equipment, and by 8:00 p.m. we had our power restored. The party was a huge success, and though there were a few lakes where none had ever existed before, no one was unduly disturbed. And all because we worked together to create solutions and not lose our focus.

The Lesson

Every professional has his or her "war" stories. How they are handled is what counts. I pride myself on not making a minor crisis into a holocaust, and this often acts to keep my client calm. No theme party will ever alter world history. If the headliner's plane is trapped on another coast due to inclement weather and can't show up, it is unlikely that anyone will remember it in 50 years. It's difficult to go according to plan under those circumstances, but everyone can still have a great time. A professional will not spend time dwelling on what went wrong; he or she will simply fix it in the best way possible.

Wild Horses on Aviation Boulevard

Back when I was married to Mark, I created a circus for the Hughes Easter Picnic. This was long before the Cirque shows, and I reveled in putting together the individual acts under the Big Top – the ringmaster, the elephants, the clowns, the horses – for the hundreds of children. It was my very own fun circus. I even managed to get an elephant pick me up in her trunk so I could experience the thrill.

Fortunately, Mark came to see me during the event, and thank God he did! Just as the horse act was preparing to enter for a vaulting exhibition, the horses spooked and took off out the entry and down Aviation Boulevard! Mark was next to me, and when it happened, he bolted to his truck and took off after them. In true wrangler fashion, he returned a short while later with all five horses in tow.

The Lesson

Even in my marriage a husband could often be put to good use!

Making Something Better

While at the Atlantis in the Bahamas again in 2009, one of my experiences triggered a very important thought. When you know you can make something better, never hesitate, do it.

I planned an outdoor event in a very lovely location. It was the final night, following two other evenings which were also outdoors. The weather was not balmy; as a matter of fact, it was chilly and quite windy. In addition, the hotel had booked events in adjoining spaces, and music carried over into our events and was distracting. Taking all of this into consideration, I asked if there were some alternative spaces, first thinking of a weather contingency, but finally just plain aggravated that our events could not be perfect due to elements out of our control. I was told that there was no space, until I pressed the issue and was shown a space that was absolutely perfect.

It meant scratching all plans on a day's notice and starting all over again. But I knew that the result would be much MUCH better and the client would be happier. The redesign changed the look, the menu, everything except the band. So I went ahead though it was more work for my team. Now I could have stuck with the original plan because it would have been "good enough," but I don't really believe in that. I could make it better, so I did.

That really applies to my life as well. For years, I was stuck in situations that made me unhappy because I was resistant to change. Things were not good, but they were "good enough." When I started thinking of my life in terms of how I could make it better, I acted and thus improved it. Now I do it all the time because I've learned that being stuck is not such a good thing. An example that comes to mind is having the gastric bypass surgery. I liked myself before, but I knew that I could look and feel better, so I made that monumental move. And lo and behold, everything in my life improved.

Jon's Lesson in Listening

My son taught me a personal lesson in communication in a very interesting fashion. One of my personal goals is to not only be a good mother but a good mother-in-law. Being both a mother and a boss is very rewarding but can be challenging as the cross-over of roles is confusing. So I decided that communication on both fronts, even though good, could be better. Therefore, I posed a risky question to Jon, "Do I do anything that really annoys you or Danielle? If I do, I want to stop doing it."

The answer surprised me but changed my life. He replied, "Sometimes I just want to vent. I don't want you to solve everything for me. I just want to be able to talk to you without your opinion on anything and everything."

Wow. What a revelation. He was right. So now when Jon says, "I need to (or I want to) talk to you," my first question is, "Do you want to vent or do you want my opinion?" And whatever he answers is the way I respond.

It has dramatically improved our relationship and taught me a valuable lesson in communication, listening and the value of just being there for my family, friends, clients and staff.

Sharron and Louis – A Tragic Ending

Sharron and Louis continuously encouraged my creativity as I was growing up. With no children of their own, Louis, in particular, treated me like the daughter he never had and truly loved me.

When I was in my 40s, Louis got cancer. The day before he died, while I was visiting him in the hospital, he made me promise to take care of Sharron. He said that when Sharron passed he wanted me to have their estate, which included palace-like houses in the Hollywood Hills and Pacific Palisades. When he died the next day, I made all the arrangements.

I began the routine afterward of taking Sharron grocery shopping and running errands for her because she didn't drive.

In her 70s, she became quite neglectful. She became toothless and was filthy, because she never bathed or washed her hair. Her house became a garbage pit with no hot water. She had collected furniture, and it was just piled around throughout an unclean house with 15 cats that were unkempt and left feces to stink this beautiful house in the Palisades. One day when I was over trying to help her, she started talking about someone named Eric and was very coy about him. Over the next few months I questioned her about him. She said he was a young man she met while he was jogging down the hill in his Speedo! Not much longer after that, she told me Eric had moved in with her.

I had always had her over for Thanksgiving when I lived in Acton, and she asked me to invite Eric one particular holiday. So, they showed up, and she was her usual mess. But he was quite a piece of work. He was in his 20s wearing white pants, a white cashmere sweater, turquoise blue eyes created by contacts, bronze makeup and cowboy boots. His hair was completely white, and he was completely gay. The two acted like lovebirds. He was totally rude to Mark and me, and all the while Sharron was just so atwitter over him. I looked at Mark and said, "How long do you think it will be before he kills her?"

Not long after, Eric called me and said, "Hello, An-de," which is what Sharron called me. "I have some terrible news!"

My immediate response was, "How did you do it?"

He was having her cremated. Because I have Louis' ashes, he wanted me to have hers.

I immediately went to the house, and, of course, she was gone. The phone rang while I was there, and it was her bank. I explained that Sharron had just died, and the banker exclaimed, "Oh, no! The day before yesterday she wanted to have the joint account with Eric put back into her own name only." Eric had possession of all her CDs and everything.

Her house was infested with raccoons and was practically being held up with a tow jack. Then, I discovered Eric had built this gorgeous place about which Sharron knew nothing. He had everything of hers.

To make matters worse, I discovered that Eric had moved in with Sharron's older sister (Sharron was 85)! She then had a series of accidents, and I contacted the police. Later I discovered that Sharron's nephew, who hadn't left his house since 1958, had made Eric his beneficiary too. Everyone, of course, died mysteriously. We couldn't get him on murder but did get him on forgery (on the will). To top it off, his twin brother was working with him! They are both now in jail.

Poor Sharron. She was so totally taken in by Eric. She couldn't see that he was gay and didn't love her on her own. I was devastated that the single most creative influences of my life had such tragic endings. I wish I could have prevented what happened. They loved me and taught me that there were no boundaries, and I will always carry them in my heart.

Learn From My Mistakes

Each of these stories provides a valuable lesson. Always view mistakes as an opportunity to learn. I wanted to share my personal mistakes throughout the book so that you would see that I was always settling because I felt I was undeserving of better. I accommodated men in everything they wanted because I was so grateful for the attention. I was willing to buy love, attention or approval. I didn't always do it with money but rather by overdoing or over-giving, thinking I would be loved if I did everything for that person. Now, I understand that my biggest mistake was that I did not believe in myself.

Because of that realization, my approach to business changed over the years. So many businesspeople feel they have to give their clients everything for which they ask, even if they have no right to do so. Often what is being asked is unreasonable or wrong, and I've learned to say no while very much empowering the other parties.

For example, a client will tell me that my fee is too much; that my competitors are charging ten percent and I am charging 15 percent. I'm asked to cut mine to ten percent. My response is always, "I really wish I could do that. Let me explain what is included in our fee, because once you see the city tax, workers comp and overhead, you will understand that the ten percent our competitors charge isn't realistic. Hard costs are more than ten percent; however, what I can do to add more value to your job is ..." and then I'll come up with a few suggestions. I then end it with, "Tell me if that feels better to you." Rarely does the client say it doesn't.

The lesson is simple. In business, don't give away everything, particularly when promised to receive more next year; it never happens. In personal, it is the same. A relationship where one party gives it all doesn't work.

36
Friendships

Generosity

I have learned much about true generosity from the people I have met in this industry. My small family's celebrations have been supported by my friends. When my son Jon was bar mitzvahed in a very simple ceremony in my girlfriend's backyard, my friend John Daly decorated the entire event beautifully and simply, a fitting look for a 13-year-old boy. Musician friends of mine supplied the perfect music for him.

Years later when Jon married, my ever-growing group of industry friends was all present. My friend Joann Roth-Oseary catered a meal no one could ever forget. Lori Stroh custom made linens and the chuppah out of chiffon and flowers. Greg Christy's Brite Ideas added amazing lighting. Patti Coons supervised all the décor, and Lily Nagy made the most beautiful arrangements. Audrey Gordon took charge as the wedding planner and made the event totally seamless. Randy Kort was our Emcee/DJ. Regal Rents (now Classic) provided all the rentals for this off-site desert wedding. Jean Jacques Pochet memorialized the entire wedding in beautiful photographs. There was so much support, so much heart and genuine love that it was awesome. Truly awesome.

The Lesson

The friendships I've made with my associates in this industry are priceless. I am so fortunate to be a part of a warm and loving industry that truly understands how to celebrate relationships. It's amazing how you treat others comes back to you a thousand fold.

Peter my stepfather gave me a lot of great values. A very flawed human, he was still humble, caring, loyal, devoted and very sincere. Peter lived a terrifying young life, and as a result, he was a very frightened man. His father sent him out of Eastern Germany so he wouldn't be there when the Nazis took over. He traveled through Russia and spent seven years in the Shanghai ghetto hiding from them. It took him years to overcome those experiences. After he died, I found letters my mother wrote to him about how mean he had been to me when they were first married. I had forgotten that he would scream at me for everything and that he and my mother would have perpetual, horrible fights. The letters brought back memories of my being constantly terrified during those first few years of their very volatile relationship.

Even after all that, Peter had a heart of gold. When he told you something, you could count on it. Later, after I grew to adulthood, he became the man I remember most. The caring and loyal father into which he finally evolved is forever imprinted upon me and became a model for me to follow throughout all my friendships.

Competitors as Friends

One of my close friends is also my greatest competitor in the Los Angeles market. Janet Elkins, president of EventWorks, is a trusted, honest and loyal friend. There is nothing we cannot talk about openly. We share ideas, resources, management issues and even our private lives without reservation. We often bid on the same project and always wish each other well. I truly marvel at how lovely it is to share what is a major part of my life with someone who understands everything I feel completely and supportively.

From my great friend Joann Roth-Oseary of Someone's in the Kitchen, I have learned what real generosity of spirit is. Joann is there 24/7 - the ghastliest of expressions, nevertheless, descriptive -

for anyone who needs her. Joann is a loving member of the events community forever reaching out to give money, time and product with a true spirit that can only emerge from a soulful person. Joann has involved me in projects for the homeless, U.S. veterans and our local temple. With an open wallet and an even more open heart, she has been a role model for me in doing good for good's sake. It's been a remarkable awakening.

Within my office I have friends as well as colleagues. Ruth Moyte, long with EE, is a loving friend, and I value her loyal and fierce protection of me personally and professionally. I know I have her devotion and appreciation, and my mentoring of her career is greatly valued. Others in my work life are important to me as well. I met them through business (like our wonderful head of production Evan Grey who was my client when I met her) but now know them as close friends as well.

The Lesson

Sharing your success with others reveals your true humanity. Don't ever be afraid to open your heart to that practice. It has made all the world of difference to me.

Generosity without expectation best describes the people I have befriended in this industry. So many people are generous with a catch. But the people I admire the most and want to emulate are the truly generous. People like Joann, and friends like Sharron and Louis, who were so generous and gave me time, advice and guidance. This has made me want to be generous and give my time, advice and guidance without expecting anything in return. If someone needs my ear at three in the morning, they've got it.

Why is it important to give so much? In the past in certain instances, it was to get love in return. In general, it is just part of my psyche, and it makes me feel good.

If I have a piece of advice, it is – be the first to give. Don't wait to receive.

Relationships

As for friendship, next to my immediate family, it is the most important thing to me. It's rare to have friends like I've got. If I had as great a taste in husbands as I have in friends, what an even better life I would have had! My friendships are with real people who are sincere, to the point and don't care about small talk!

So many of my clients are friends, and truly I would rather lose their business than their friendship.

Most of our lives involve relationships; yet few of us realize how having a true relationship impacts our business lives. This was really brought home when I talked to my staff about new business opportunities. We were questioning why we had lost some significant pieces of business, and I commented that if we didn't have relationships with our clients we would never win the business. One of my team commented that she had a relationship with all of her clients. I asked her if she had ever spoken to a specific client in person, and she replied that she had had a couple of phone conversations with him. I then asked if he was married, and she didn't know. I asked if he had children, and she didn't know. Then I asked what type of restaurant he liked best. She didn't know. So then my question became, "What in your opinion constitutes a relationship?" What did it mean? Did it mean trying to sell him on our company's capabilities? Was that a relationship? Not in my opinion.

In my opinion, a relationship involves a give and take communication, a real curiosity on who the other person is. I sincerely want to know. I want to do business with people about whom I know something. My home is open for what I pretentiously call "soirees" or dinner parties where I put together some interesting combinations of people and get to know all about them, as much as I can.

Isn't it more fun to work with people you understand and with whom you share common ground? I get ribbed all the time that I send out birthday cards for my clients, their kids, their spouses and have a folder in my email where I keep pictures of all of their kids. And they well know my grandchildren, because I send them my favorite pictures.

Relationships are precious. I am very glad that my business gives me the opportunity to meet new people, get to know them, get to appreciate them and make them my friends.

This book is dedicated to friendship, and now you understand why.

37

The Final Lesson

I've had a lot of surgery. And I've been back on my game almost immediately. After the gastric bypass on July 3, I went back to work on July 5 or so. I flew to Toronto two weeks later to win the MPI Global Paragon award … didn't want to miss THAT. Then, two weeks after that I went white water rafting in Costa Rica with a few "ouches" when we bounced off rocks. And then after two more weeks, and still on a liquid diet, I flew to Australia to do an ISES presentation.

A few years later I was diagnosed with thyroid cancer, had my thyroid removed and missed around two days of work. The reaction from friends was "you recover so quickly." Actually, I don't recover faster than anyone else. I just decided a while back that "it" was not going to get me down. "It" wasn't going to get me at all … ever. I was going to get "it," meaning that in spite of surgery, in spite of cancer, I was going to resume my normal life immediately. And continue having adventures.

I have now had five cancer surgeries in the past two years, and I've missed a total of six or so days of work. I resumed all normal activities immediately after each (albeit with some prominent bandages) whether they were work-related or travel-related or just plain personal time with my family. I've lost the use of one vocal chord which has been a major challenge (I sound like Rod Stewart on a bad day), but I've continued delivering all presentations and public speaking engagements anyway.

At this point all my private and very personal travails have been revealed, so you know I've experienced obstacles and negativity and many times let them defeat me. But I made a conscious decision of "no more." So my greatest lesson for you is that, whether it is emotional or physical, we all control our minds and bodies and can make that one decision that says defeat or success. I choose success and hope you will, too.

38
Conclusion

So, what is the true conclusion to the stories that I've shared with you? Simply that everything in life, whether business or personal, is the same road. I'm not able to cut myself in half. I'm one human with one set of experiences on one road traveling to whatever destination I select. My entire life is one package. Every experience I've had has influenced every decision I've made. Every business experience has affected my life. The same is true of you. Anyone who looks at it differently is not getting what he or she needs in life.

One perspective might see me as a terrible mother. For years, I carried so much guilt, because I was always dragging my son to events or leaving him with babysitters (history is destined to repeat itself). Why did I do this? Because my chosen career demanded that I do so. But, in hindsight, what did I give him? I was able to provide him with experiences that other children don't have. He was able to see me at work, become a part of it, and, as a result, he now works with me. The experiences we have had together are irreplaceable. We are closer because of it. I'm not guilty any longer because I can see first hand the outcome.

The bottom line is that personal and business don't have to be exclusive from each other. The personal experiences I've had with my family and the men in my life have molded me into the driving force that I needed to be in business. I am a successful wallflower on the inside and a strong, accomplished woman on the outside, ready to face all the next challenges that life and business have to offer me.

I know that when I finally retire at the age of 96, my wrinkled face will break into a big grin. I'll tell you proudly about what a great time I had living a life that was always challenging and never boring. And, if I add up all my hours, I probably even made $1.45 an hour doing it. I would have done it for less!

THE END